14th Fighter Group

The 14th Fighter Group in World War II

John W. Lambert

Schiffer Military History
Atglen, PA

Dedication

To the late Colonel Harry Crim, Jr., without whose effort this history would never have come to fruition, and to all the officers and enlisted men who served with the 14th Fighter Group during World War II. They did not ask "Why me?," nor challenge the call to arms, but went forth to serve at the cost of their youth, and for many at the cost of their lives. They saw it as their duty, and that is what qualified them as the greatest generation. Bless 'em all.

Book Design by Ian Robertson.

Library of Congress Control Number: 2007939555

Printed in China.
ISBN: 978-0-7643-2921-0

We are interested in hearing from authors with book ideas on related topics.

Published by Schiffer Publishing Ltd.
4880 Lower Valley Road
Atglen, PA 19310
Phone: (610) 593-1777
FAX: (610) 593-2002
E-mail: Info@schifferbooks.com.
Visit our web site at: www.schifferbooks.com
Please write for a free catalog.
This book may be purchased from the publisher.
Please include $3.95 postage.
Try your bookstore first.

In Europe, Schiffer books are distributed by:
Bushwood Books
6 Marksbury Avenue
Kew Gardens
Surrey TW9 4JF, England
Phone: 44 (0) 20 8392-8585
FAX: 44 (0) 20 8392-9876
E-mail: Info@bushwoodbooks.co.uk.
Visit our website at: www.bushwoodbooks.co.uk
Free postage in the UK. Europe: air mail at cost.
Try your bookstore first.

Contents

Foreword

In the early 90s, while I was in the business of turning out aviation history (Phalanx Publishing), Harry Crim was assembling the pieces of archival fragments that represented the documentary history of the 14th Fighter Group. I agreed to see the matter to completion if he could find someone to write the text. Bill Hess, a noted aviation historian, volunteered to be the author. With the encouragement of Jeff Ethell, another aviation historian (and son of Erv Ethell, a 48th Squadron veteran), Harry Crim went at the chore like a badger on the hunt.

Harry made numerous trips to the Air Force Historical Research Center at Maxwell AFB, Alabama, and to the National Archives in Washington, D.C., to research and copy whatever records had survived the war, and a score of base moves, and still managed to get back to the official repositories. The informational gaps were substantial, but Harry was undaunted. He began a letter writing campaign to 14th veterans, interviewed many, and attended numerous squadron reunions while gathering scraps of history. His effort eventually filled three filing cabinets of papers and three of photos. Some of the photos came from USAF archives, and many from personal collections. If all the photos are not of top quality, please consider the often harsh conditions and the ravages of nearly 60 years.

Private collection photos were contributed by the following: Walter Brower, James Stitt, Robert Walker, Charles Mauss, Arnold Dickenson, Harry Crim, Don Luttrell, Norman Jackson, Charles Crocker, Ervin Ethell, James Hollingsworth, Lester Fields, and Robert Keel. Two black and white aircraft drawings are courtesy of Earl W. Steininger III.

In the late 1990s, Col. Harry Crim flew his final mission; Jeff Ethell was killed in a tragic crash of a classic P-38; and Bill Hess (also a World War II vet of the MTO) became ill, and was unable to undertake the writing of this history.

Harry Crim had sent me the photo collection shortly before his death, and Bill Hess shipped the documentary material to me in 2005. I can only hope that this history is worthy of the devoted effort of Harry, and will be found to be a fitting record of the achievements of the 14th Fighter Group.

In the narrative, where describing the results of air battles, I have chosen to show the victory claims of pilots for destroyed, probably destroyed, and damaged enemy aircraft by the simple device of numbers. For example: 2/1/1 would indicate two kills, one probable, and one damaged.

Jack Lambert

Introduction

This is the history of a World War II fighter Group of the U.S. Army Air Force. The 14th Fighter Group served in the Mediterranean Theatre of Operations (MTO), flying the Lockheed P-38 Lightning from North Africa to the heart of Europe. It was an aircraft designed for a high altitude air supremacy role. But in the contingencies of war, the 14th was employed wherever it was needed, often at treetop level. The pilots of the 14th fought as knights of old in duels with other aircraft, and often with enemy tanks.

At a squadron reunion several years ago, one of the pilots, Don Luttrell, eloquently discussed the unique nature of the combat. It was, he said:

"...the epitome of aerial warfare. We participated personally in this, and never again will we see the clouds of aircraft that we witnessed in World War II: the bomber streams that were 150 miles long; the swarms of fighters around them; the man-to-man combat that we saw. And all of us remember how we individually participated. Whatever your duty was—communications, armament, whether you were flying or in maintenance.... This experience has now passed, and it will never be repeated again. Much like the cavalry of the Civil War were darlings of the force, but technology outdated them, so it has with us, and never again will the world witness the great air battles that occurred over Europe in 1943-1945."

So here is the war as witnessed by the men of the 14th Fighter Group in pictures, and in their own vivid recollections.

1

Preparation for War

Sobered by the experience of World War I, and plagued by a recession in the 1930s, the people of the United States of America were disinterested in global conflicts that had begun flaring up around the world. More than disinterested, substantial segments of society were actively opposed to foreign entanglements. And the reach of global military technology was then incapable of bridging our great ocean barriers, permitting a degree of comfort in the perceived distance from wars on other continents.

Emboldened by America's seeming lack of resolve, Germany, Italy, and Japan had all embarked on paths of conquest. By 1940 Great Britain stood alone as the last bulwark of democracy against Axis aggression. Russia had played a duplicitous game of political alliance with Germany, dividing Poland, and its future intentions were unknown.

America was isolated from a world in turmoil, and both the active and passive isolationists constituted a majority that prevented a serious military buildup, and assured the United States of being a second rate military force. President Franklin Roosevelt and the military planners in Washington subtly worked to support England, while at the same time preparing America for an inevitable war. With funding from Congress severely limited, the expansion of both military technology and strength was sluggish.

One of the few additions to the U.S. Army Air Force was the 14th Fighter Group, activated in January 1941. Formed at Hamilton Field, California, it consisted of the 48th, 49th, and 50th Fighter Squadrons. Maj. Thayer S. Olds commanded the fledgling 14th Fighter Group. A 1928 graduate of the U.S. Military Academy, he had taken his flight training at Kelly Field, TX.

The unit was initially equipped with an assortment of trainers and a mish-mash of other aircraft: Republic P-43s, obsolete when they came off the production line; Vultee P-66s built for Sweden, embargoed by the U.S., and diverted to China, with a few remaining in USAAF inventory; and a handful of newer Curtiss P-40 aircraft, which were inferior in some respects to many modern Axis fighters.

Thus woefully equipped, the 14th was training when Pearl Harbor was attacked on 7 December 1941. With their motley collection of aircraft they began patrolling the West Coast, where it was anticipated that Japanese carrier task forces would soon strike.

Sgt. Arthur H. Wilcox, an armorer with the 37th Fighter Squadron (later part of the 14th Fighter Group), was stationed at Portland, OR, in December 1941. In his autobiography *Gun Plumber*, he irreverently describes the typical state of preparedness as the U.S. was thrust into the World War II conflict:

"The P-43 carried two caliber .50 machine guns mounted on the fuselage and, as usual, with backplates and charging handles in the cockpit. These were synchronized to fire through the propeller blades. One caliber .30 gun was mounted in each wing, as with the P-40A, when the plane was fully armed.

The two-gun Vultee P-66, one of the outmoded fighters supplied to the fledgling 14th Fighter Group. (Ray Wagner via American Aviation Historical Society)

Wade Walles in March 1941 on a 48th Squadron P-40. (Dickenson)

The Battle of Britain had just been fought and won with Spitfires and Hurricanes mounting eight guns in the wings. U.S. designers, and perhaps specification writers, still had ours firing between prop blades just as for Gary Cooper and Richard Arlen in the 1927 silent thriller, 'Wings.' For reasons unknown, it had been determined best for the American pilots to have a fighting chance of shooting off his prop blades at the same time he was being asphyxiated with the gun smoke and gas. 'What the hell? Let's give the guy a little challenge.'

Six of our P-43s sat on the ramp half armed, as they had been for weeks. At the moment we had no ammunition, but later in the day everything on base was divided between units, broken up and put in aircraft cans. It amounted to 50 rounds per gun, about five seconds firing, and that's all there was to go to war with."

While flying defensive patrols over California the 14th Fighter Group had gained experience, as P-40s replaced the more obsolete aircraft. But by February they began to receive the aircraft that they would take into combat, the Lockheed P-38 Lightning. Despite the prior limitations on defense expenditures, American aircraft manufacturers had been experimenting with new designs. The P-38 was the most revolutionary of the lot.

A twin-engine, twin-boomed fighter with tricycle landing gear—nothing like it had ever been seen before. Powered by a pair of Allison V-1710 engines that turned counter-rotating props, it had the potential for great operating range. The P-38 had a gondola fuselage housing one 20mm cannon and four .50 caliber machine guns, eliminating the dual problems of prop synchronization and/or convergence from wing guns that plagued other fighter aircraft.

However, the big 13,000-pound aircraft was regarded with some skepticism by single-engine fighter jocks. It was a lot of airplane, and several pilots immediately requested transfer to different units. The loss of an engine on takeoff could cause a spin

37th Squadron pilots pose before an obsolete P-43 in the summer of 1941 at Olympia, Washington (L. to R.): Wendell Kelley, Charles Heitz, Fenton Butler, and Jack Jenkins. (37th Archives)

37th Squadron hangar at Olympia, Washington. (37th Archives)

if the Lightning was not immediately trimmed. She also had some nasty dive characteristics with the then unknown phenomenon of compressibility. If the P-38 reached the speed of sound, the resulting shock wave rendered it uncontrollable, a condition corrected by the installation of dive brakes in later models.

The pilots and mechanics of the 14th Fighter Group were still trying to master their P-38Ds when the group was alerted for overseas movement. The air echelon departed east for Bradley Field, Connecticut, and the ground echelon entrained for Fort Dix, New Jersey, two weeks later. At Bradley, the unit's D models were replaced with the brand new P-38F.

At end of July, the air echelon began a series of leapfrogging flights that would bring them to England. With four-engine B-17s as navigational escorts, the P-38s followed a route to Presque Isle, Maine, to Goose Bay, Labrador, to Bluie West-1, Greenland, and thence to Iceland. This was the same route over Godforsaken portions of the sub-Arctic Atlantic that the 1st Fighter Group had flown just a month before. Pilots of the 14th were sobered by the knowledge that one six-plane flight of the 1st Fighter Group, along with its two B-17 escorts, had all ended up on Greenland's great central ice cap. The 1st had encountered severe weather going east toward Iceland. Returning to Greenland, it was discovered that the weather had closed in around all airfields. The only clear weather was that over the desolate central glacier. So, low on fuel, the eight aircraft bellied down together, and the crews trekked out to the coast. No one was lost, but the pilots of the 14th had no desire to repeat the adventure. As it turned out, the 14th Fighter Group completed the six-hour leg to Iceland with just one loss, the P-38 of Lt. Herbert Goodrich, which was last seen entering a cumulus cloud near Iceland.

The tiny island in the center of the North Atlantic was on the convoy route to Great Britain, and was the focal point for Allied anti-submarine operations. That made it a magnet for long-range German reconnaissance aircraft. In 1941 the AAF had dispatched the 33rd Fighter Squadron with its Bell P-39s to Iceland as part of a small defense garrison. The 33rd and the visiting 1st Fighter Group

The gun bay in the gondola nose of a P-38 displays its four .50 cal. machineguns and one 20mm cannon. The trays of ammo held 1,800 rounds of .50 and 120 rounds of 20mm. (Stitt) The instrument panel of a P-38 as viewed over the steering column. (Crocker)

49th Squadron pilots at Hamilton Field, California, in June 1942 (L. to R.): Standing: Richard I. Bong (To Pacific. Became America's leading ace.), Robert P. Kirschke (KIA), Robert F. Elliott (KIA), Jerome Adler, William Working, Livie F. Mullinax, Jr. (POW, EV), George C. Hand, Jr., Robert J. Moffatt, Russell F. Gustke, Lyle Williams (KPC), Emil A. Kielbasa, Wyborne T. Traut, Lewis H. Gregory, John O'Neil, and Robert H. Woodward (KIA). Kneeling: Lyndon VanHook, Albert C. Wolfmueller, James E. Ribb, Oscar G. Blueher, Harold E. Lewis (KIA), Charles L. Earnhart (POW), Paulette Spivey, Virgil Lusk, Kenneth S. Wade, Thomas J. Morris, Jr. (KIA), Ralph J. Knapp, William P. Moore, Jack Hutter, Frank E. Butler, and Robert N. Carlton. (Ethell)

The USS *West Point* was on its maiden voyage when employed as a troopship to carry American units, including most of the 14th Fighter Group, to Liverpool, England, in August 1942. (National Archives)

had a few rare encounters with the long-legged German snoopers, downing three, then the 1st moved on to England.

When elements of the 14th Fighter Group arrived at Reykjavik, someone in higher authority deemed it more important to beef up Iceland's air defense than to get the 14th Fighter Group into the war in Europe. Hence, the 50th Fighter Squadron was permanently detached and assigned to Iceland. During dismal months there they had rare encounters, but made the most of their chances, downing two. The victories over a Junkers 88 and a Focke-Wulf 200 were shared by: Lieutenants James M. McNulty, Jr., Harry R. Stengle, William Bethea, and Richard M. Holly.

Ultimately, the P-38 pilots of the 50th moved on to England, and became part of a reconnaissance unit in the Eighth Air Force.

In the meantime, the 14th Fighter Group's air echelon, shorn of one-third its strength, flew on to Prestwick, Scotland, finally arriving at Atcham Field, Shrewsbury, England.

C-47 transport aircraft traveled the overwater route, with the P-38s carrying a minimum number of essential aircraft mechanics and technicians. On 22 August 1942 one of these transports crashed in Wales, killing ten enlisted men from the 48th and 49th Squadrons.

The ground echelon departed from New Jersey aboard the transport *USS West Point*. A luxury liner designed to carry 2,500 passengers in peacetime, she had been modified as a troop ship, and was jammed with the 14th's ground personnel and other members of the military for a total complement of 8,000. The official unit history gives a brief glimpse of the sardine-like existence on the good ship *West Point*:

"Mess lines filled the corridors below deck nearly all the daylight hours. The odor of cooking, sweat, disinfectant, and tobacco hung heavily throughout the vessel.

On the promenade deck (that's the one where you can walk around the outside of the ship and look at the stars) after dark, men slept in a double row, their feet toward the center of the aisle. The space left for walking was a matter of inches. To negotiate this obstacle course in the dark, when the ship was rolling a bit, without stepping on the feet of more than a couple of men endeavoring to get a little sleep was considered somewhat of an accomplishment. If you were a bit 'off your feed' (and rest assured, you would not be without sympathizers) this deck was of no benefit to you.

Below decks men slept in shifts. Blowers forced ventilation into compartments where the men slept in hammocks. The bunks were in tiers of three, sometimes four, and besides the soldier, held all of his comforts of home."

On 17 August the convoy entered the Irish Sea, and the next day the *West Point* docked in Liverpool, where the 14th's personnel were transported by rail to Shrewsbury.

The group got its first sight of the Germans when a recon aircraft flew over Atcham airfield on 6 September. Lt. Robert Carlton, 49th Squadron, was airborne at the time, and attempted to intercept the high-flying Jerry. Climbing through a high overcast, his P-38 picked up ice and went into a dive from which Carlton was unable to recover. As his air speed indicator hit 500mph, he managed to parachute safely. There were other attempts at pursuit of German reconnaissance aircraft, but the "customers" always got away before any encounter.

The days in England were filled with indoctrination classes, followed by day and night flying. The pilots flew formation, practiced intercepts against Eighth Air Force bombers, and had mock dogfights with accommodating RAF fighter pilots. All of this led up to some English Channel sweeps with the first views of enemy territory.

Flying from Tangmere on 15 October 1942, the 14th had its first offensive mission escorting RAF Bostons to Le Havre, France. Colonel Olds led, but the Germans failed to display any opposition. The 14th provided escort to Eighth Air Force heavy bombers once more on the 21st, but again saw no action. A fighter sweep over France with Spitfires of the 4th Fighter Group on 26 October was the last operational test for the 14th from England, and it likewise provoked no German response.

The following day, while the squadrons were still near the coast at Tangmere and Ford, they experienced their first air raid. A single German Junker 88 sortied over both fields, dropping bombs and spraying machine gun fire. There were no injuries and no damage, but it was a new and helpless experience.

During the first days of November 1942 typhoid and tetanus shots were administered, instructions were received in tropical medical care, and personal gear was ordered packed. If there were any lingering questions about the meaning of these activities, the pilots' recognition classes for Italian aircraft made it certain that the 14th Fighter Group was destined for the Mediterranean Theatre of Operations (MTO).

2

Operation TORCH

TORCH was the Allied code name for the invasion of North Africa at its northwest corner. Simultaneous landings took place from Casablanca to Algiers on 8 November 1942. After invading the Vichy French colonies, the strategic plan was to push east toward Tunisia, while the British 8th Army (famed as the Desert Rats) drove the Germans and Italians west from Egypt, enclosing Axis forces on the mainland of Africa in a giant pincer, and simultaneously freeing the Mediterranean Sea routes. U.S. Army Air Force units arriving with the invasion were part of the newly formed Twelfth Air Force under Maj. Gen. Jimmy Doolittle.

On 14 November 1942 the 14th Fighter Group's 48th Squadron took off from Portreath, England, bound for North Africa. The 49th followed on the 18th, while most ground crews were at sea with the invasion fleet. The P-38s flew across the Bay of Biscay, skirting the coast of Spain and Portugal, and landing at Gibraltar. They flew on to Oran's La Senia airport the following day, merging with ground crews that had come to the same destination by air (C-47 transports) and by ship. It would be a month before all of the various contingents of the 14th assembled together in one place.

Vichy French forces in Algeria had put up sporadic resistance until honor had been satisfied, then stepped aside or joined the Allies. Their airdromes and landing grounds were taken over by arriving allied squadrons. Despite this token French resistance, confusion reigned supreme. With all of the complex organization of the invasion and the hundreds of ships available, the planners had neglected to expedite ground transport. After landing his P-38 on Le Senia's cratered runway, 1st Lt. Bill Schottelkorb, a pilot with the 48th Squadron, described the situation in his diary:

A 14th Fighter Group P-38 staging through Gibraltar enroute to Oran, Algeria. (Ethell)

The French air base at Tafaroui, Algeria, first stop for the 14th. (Ethell)

"As soon as we landed we were greeted by officers of the squadron who had come by ship: John Dees, communications; Capt. George Worten, intelligence; and Benson, intelligence. They were all completely fagged, as they had walked the 14 miles from the harbor the night before. Dees had huge blisters on his feet.

The buildings around the airport were largely destroyed as a result of shelling. French pursuit planes were lying about the field wrecked or damaged. One BT-14 was still in good shape, and a French A-20 was nearly so. We sat out in front of the administration building, marveling at developments. Arabs and ragged urchins passed by, picking up what scraps they could gather from the spoils of war. Soldiers who had seized cars were trying to make them run. A full colonel had seized a black deluxe sedan, and was using it for his official car. Other old cars and trucks were being pressed into service hauling supplies for our army. Another full colonel was speaking French with some natives, evidently trying to get the water supply turned on. Finally, a truck came from town loaded with supplies, and we managed to get some food: a piece of bread and a few apples.

Soon, however, we learned that we had landed at the wrong airport, and we were to go to Tafaraoui, a French naval airfield a few miles to the south. So we started up our planes and, dodging the bomb pits, taxied out, took off, joined up, and hopped over to the new field....

Tafaraoui had two runways, one concrete and one gravel, about 3,000 feet. When we landed there was a group of Spits flown

Col. Thayer S. Olds, CO of the 14th Fighter Group. (Ethell)

Junkers 88s like this one were among the aerial victories scored by the 14th shortly after its arrival in North Africa. The Germans used the versatile twin-engined bomber to raid Allied airfields in Algeria. (National Archives)

During a November 1942 mission, a pair of P-38s were forced down in Tunisia. Lts. Arthur Cole, 48th Squadron (left), and Robert Elliott, 49th Squadron, got directions from a native. Just a few days later Cole was downed and made a POW, and Elliott was KIA. (National Archives)

German bombing caused slit trenches to be dug into the hard rock of Youks les Bains, Algeria. Seen here is a member of the 49th Squadron. (Dickenson)

by American pilots [the 31st Fighter Group]. We dispersed out in the dirt and started to look for a place to live among the old French buildings....

As far as eating was concerned, we cooked our rations in the back yard after several of us gathered some stones and made a fireplace. The canned rations consisted mostly of stew, beef, coffee, and tea.

Water was the biggest problem. We had to stand in line to use a hand pump. Then we used water purification tablets."

Nor was this the end of the confusion. A few days later the 48th Squadron's P-38s moved to join the rest of the 14th Fighter Group, landing at Algiers airport, Maison Blanche. The ground echelon was air lifted by C-47 troop carriers, the only military transport that seemed to have arrived in sufficient numbers.

The one saving grace in those first days of the invasion was that the Germans were slow to react. That soon changed. On the night of 18 November 1942, bombing and strafing Ju. 88s hit Maison Blanche with a punishing two-hour attack. Eight Lightnings were damaged, along with hangars, but there were no casualties among 14th Fighter Group personnel.

On 20 November the 48th was ordered on a far-ranging strafing mission into Tunisia. Staging through Tebessa, the pilots found the landing ground ill defined and rough. One aircraft overshot and lost its nose gear in a ditch. Then the P-38s had to be refueled from 5-gallon Jerry cans brought in by C-47s. Finally taking off on their assigned mission late in the day, six pilots encountered weather and found little to shoot at, but experienced their first anti-aircraft fire. Lt. Virgil Smith's plane was hit by ground fire, lost an engine, and he and his escort, 2nd Lt. Leo Yates, fell behind. As darkness descended, the remaining four became lost, and elected to belly land at Negrine, an Arab village 60 miles west of Gafsa. Smith and Yates were also forced down, but all six pilots were well treated and returned.

Higher headquarters, realizing that Tafaraoui was too far from the front and Tebessa too small, again shifted the 14th's forward operations to Youks les Bains airport, south of Constantine. With the help of a troop carrier group, part of the 14th Fighter Group was shuttled to Youks. The majority of its personnel followed by train on the French railroad's vintage 40 and 8 cars, so designated as suitable for 40 men and 8 horses. Herb Barthel, an armorer with the 49th Squadron, recounts the experience:

"Locked in five narrow-gauge boxcars with a decrepit engine wheezing us slowly nowhere still equates with a night in hell. In each car half of us stood, while the other half sat and hugged their knees. There was scarcely room for breath, and normal body functions—no respecter of circumstance—thickened the already foul air.

Day was no improvement over this seemingly endless night. The sight of comrades in wretchedness was no encouragement. If

German bombs dug holes just about the size of a man made foxhole. (Dickenson)

A machine gun dug in for aerial defense at Youks. (Ethell)

there was a positive aspect, it was the wealth of inventive gallows humor and picturesque profanity that our unenviable condition provoked. Numbness, muscular cramps, and fatigue so clouded our consciousness that we drifted on through increasing unreality.

The jolting, clattering, creaking stops and asthmatic wheezing of the leaky little steam engine was no longer significant. It had stopped a hundred or a thousand times before—and would again. Time had become magnified, alien and endless. The shuffle of feet, the calling, the muffled and indefinable orders, were as before. It was then that bolts were thrown and the side door shoved open….

'C'mon guys, hop out,' ordered a smiling comrade.

'Hop hell! If anyone can still crawl, kill the happy sonovabitch' came the gargoyle croak from some tormented but still game soul."

It was not until 21 November that the group saw some aerial action. During an escort mission to Tunis with B-17s, the 48th Squadron encountered their first *Luftwaffe* fighters. 2nd Lt. Paul Ziegler had a Me 109 in his sights when, in his excitement, he pressed the microphone button instead of the gun button, and the German got a reprieve. However, 2nd Lt. Carl Williams, Jr., nailed his 109 for the group's first aerial victory.

The following day the 48th had an additional encounter in the area of Youks les Bains. 1st Lt. Mark K. Shipman downed a twin-engine Italian aircraft, and 1st Lt. Wallace A. Sorrenson shot down a Ju. 88 bomber. The diary of Bill Schottelkorb provides a view of the Boy Scout life at the new airfield:

"Our first living quarters at Youks were in the holes that the paratroopers had dug upon their arrival. Weather was good, and we were fairly comfortable, because we had the extra blankets left by the boys who were still missing in the desert. Smith and Yates came home the next day, but not so with the other four.

We worked hard, gassed and oiled planes, lugged ammunition, and helped in every way we could in order to continue operations.

Captain Wade Walles, CO, appointed a cook, so we all ate with the enlisted men. Three times a day we ate stew, crackers, and tea for several weeks straight. It got to be pretty tiresome, and it seemed that we were always hungry. In between meals we would get out our rations and cook them over a gasoline fire."

German forces in Tunisia began to get active, and moved to confront the Allied armies advancing from Algeria. This caused the Twelfth Air Force to throw the P-38s of the 14th Fighter Group into ground attack missions, although the P-38 was primarily designed as an escort fighter, and there were plenty of P-39s and P-40s for the tactical jobs. However, hunting and strafing columns of armored vehicles became routine for the 14th. On one such low-level mission, flying down the streets of Sbeitla, Tunisia, between the palms at 300 mph, Bill Schottelkorb saw an Arab throwing rocks at him. His P-38 was undamaged. "I don't think he had the right deflection," Bill noted.

On 24 November the 14th finally got a big score. The 48th was flying near Kairouan, a walled Arab city with minarets and spires that resembled a movie set, when Bill Schottelkorb and Jim Tollen spotted a German motorized column. They shot up the vehicles, and as they turned south, noticed an aircraft about 3,000 feet above them coming in their direction. It turned out to be a Ju. 88 bomber. Bill's diary recounts the ensuing chase:

"We did a steep climbing turn to the right and poured on the coal. I pulled 3,000 rpm and about 42 inches of mercury for about

The 14th caught and downed a number of Junkers 52 transports like this one in late November. The Ju 52 and the tri-engined Italian Savoia Marchettis were key to supplying Axis forces in North Africa. (National Archives)

five minutes, gaining height and airspeed of about 320 straight and level. The 88 was throwing out clouds of black smoke in an effort to escape.

At about 500 yards the rear gunner fired tracers at me, and they seemed to fall below me. At 300 yards I started firing, and held everything down in a steady burst. The pilot skidded the plane violently as my tracers ate into him. At 100 yards I was bouncing around in the prop wash, and I waited until I thought I was going to run into him, and then pulled straight up and back. Jim then put a steady burst into the left motor and side of the fuselage.

By then the right motor was on fire and smoking badly. The pilot started down, but then pulled up the flaming aircraft to give the tail gunner a chance to bail out. The gunner's chute opened OK at about 500 feet, but the bomber was losing altitude.

I banked back and forth over the plane as it skimmed the earth just before setting down in a landing attitude. The right main gear was hanging down, and I could see the top hatch off and two crewmen huddling there, looking up at me. It was terrible.

It plowed a path over fairly level ground and skidded to a halt at a road crossing. The right motor was torn completely loose, and was lying some yards distant. I didn't see anybody near, but noticed some Arabs approaching. Jim and I returned victorious."

That same day a flight from the 49th Squadron patrolling between Gabes and Sfax encountered another Ju. 88, and a gaggle of Italian Savoia-Marchetti SM 81 three-engine transports. Lt. Tom Morris downed the German bomber, while James Butler and Virgil Lusk bagged nine transports between them.

It was the rainy season in North Africa, and Youks les Bains turned into a sea of mud. Except for a couple of large French tents that were used as mess hall and hospital, officers and enlisted men lived in tents—more accurately, pieces of tarpaulin over scrap lumber. Several people edged up the hill adjacent to the strip and worked on dugouts covered by an array of scrap lumber, Jerry cans, and tarps. It was grandly dubbed "Beverly Hills." Still, there was no way of keeping entirely dry, and eventually beds, clothing, and everything else got damp. Rube Goldberg stoves fashioned out of 5-gallon cans and fueled with a volatile mixture of 100-octane and crank case oil provided some heat in the shacks. It sufficed for a little warmth and some modest laundry, but bathing was an unknown luxury.

The aircraft were also bogged down in the mud. While waiting for the late November rain to letup, the group watched their P-38s sink deeper into the mire. Captain Walles eyed a nearby 1,700-foot slope of a mountain—where some of the dugouts were being made—as an alternative to the existing runway. It seemed reasonably clear and solid; it was a steep rise, but drained well, and was without mud. Lt. Ervin Ethell said that he would give it a try with his P-38G "Tangerine," but found the wheels so mired that he couldn't budge it with 75 inches of manifold pressure on both engines. After the dispersal area had dried somewhat, and with his crew chief bouncing the nose wheel, Ethell got loose,

A P-38 of the 48th Squadron downed over enemy territory. This may have been the aircraft of Lt. James Tollen, KIA near Tunis on 11 December 1942. (Crow)

took off, circled the slope, and landed going downhill. From that time on, whenever rain threatened to make the lower portion of the field inoperable, the P-38s were moved to the slope, and all landings were made uphill and takeoffs downhill, regardless of wind direction.

Periodic air raids added to the general misery of the 14th Fighter Group. The official unit history described the situation:

"There were several raids by enemy bombers on nearby Tebessa, usually at night. Our field was slightly higher than Tebessa, and we would stand on the crest of the hill watching the 'sticks' of bombs burst with green and white flashes.

Jerry looked for us every other night. He would fly over and back across our field, and we would listen from our trenches. Pilots claimed that the field couldn't be seen from the air. One afternoon of a bright, sunny day a German plane came straight over the field at between twenty and twenty-five thousand feet. The ack-ack opened fire on him, but every shot they fired was a hundred yards in back of the bomber, though bursting at about the right altitude. It may be coincidental that a few days later several Ju. 88s came over just before dark, and proceeded to give us a fair idea of what a bombing was like. The anti-aircraft had opened fire and given away our location, which was all the bombers needed. One bomb struck a gasoline dump containing a few thousand gallons of precious fuel, but fortunately this was after most of the bombs had been dropped, since by the light of the fire their accuracy would have been deadly in its effect.

The ammunition dump at Youks les Bains was also struck, and for nearly two hours at intervals of about three seconds, high explosive bombs exploded....

Many men took bedding and left the field for the hills. By the light of the burning fires they could be seen going to the high ground. Many tents had been slashed by bomb fragments."

As Allied forces on the northwest coast of Tunisia drove to within less than 50 miles of Tunis, German resistance stiffened. Encounters between the Allied air forces and the *Luftwaffe* and *Regia Aeronautica* became daily affairs.

On 28 November 1942, during a reconnaissance near Gabes, a pair of Ju. 88s were intercepted and downed by Lts. Virgil Lusk and Robert Eubank of the 48th. Further north, near Lake Bizerta, a combined flight of the 48th and 49th Squadrons found some Junkers 52 transports. "It was like flushing a covey of quail," Erv Ethell said. "They tried to scatter, but we were on top of them." They dispatched five, with Ethell claiming four, and Redmond Evans one. However, escorting Me 109s attacked the P-38s, downing Lts. Skinner of the 48th and Butler of the 49th. Both were killed. Escaping the angry 109s, Ethell shot at one German fighter, then dove for the deck. He got a vector to the British base at Bone and landed to refuel, then went on to Youks les Bain, landing several hours behind the rest. He found that his buddies had already divided his tent and some of his belongings.

On 29 November 1942, the 14th flew a joint mission to the Gabes area with the 94th Squadron of the 1st Fighter Group, now sharing the mud and misery at Youks. Capt. James Watson of the 48th Squadron downed a Messerschmitt 110.

On 30 November 1942, the 48th Squadron flew a twelve-ship fighter sweep over the heart of Axis strength, near Tunis and Bizerta. Bill Schottelkorb's diary recounts the details:

"The boys called these the T & B milk run. We heard that the famous Abbeville boys from France had come down, and it was evidently wipe them out or wipe us out. [German fighter strength had been increased, but not the Abbeville unit.]

I was on Watson's wing, and Virgil Smith and Cole were the second element. Walles and Bing were leading other flights. The sky was covered with fair weather cumulus clouds at about 8,000 feet over the target area.

We saw a 109 above the clouds waiting to come down on us. He darted down a couple of times, and each time we sent him back with volumes of firepower. Soon we spotted other 109s, and a furious fight developed. We used our full rated power—47 inches of mercury and 3,000 rpm. We climbed practically straight up, with the indicator reading 4,000 feet per minute, made a circle around a cloud, and I noticed that all of us were in formation in Watson's flight. Then, Watson got a direct shot at a 109, and I had to duck, because another one was shooting 90 degrees deflection at me. Then one came in between Watson and I, firing at him. My tracers fell all around the German, but he went into a cloud.

Back on Watson's wing, we indicated 325 mph all the way out until we hooked up with Bing's flight. Virgil Smith and Cole had dived to the deck after a 109 on the very outskirts of Tunis. Smith got the Jerry, but we never saw Cole again."

The engagement that cost the loss of Cole had not been one-sided. Watson claimed an Me. 109 probable and another damaged. Capt. Walles, squadron CO, also claimed a probable, and Virgil Smith was credited with a victory. The German fighters were likely from JG 51.

3

The Struggle for Tunisia

In 1940, and again in 1941, the Axis *Afrikakorps* had been on the verge of overrunning the British Eighth Army and seizing the Suez Canal. By December 1942 the weight of Allied power, and the illogical demands that Hitler had imposed on the German military with his campaign in Russia, had sapped German strength. General Erwin Rommel and his *Afrikakorps* had been driven from the border of Egypt at the Battle of El Alamein. With the Allied Army at his back, advancing from northwest Africa, Rommel, known to the British as the Desert Fox, had no choice but to shorten his supply lines and draw into a defensive position in Tunisia. He did so in a fighting retreat, with General Bernard Montgomery's Eighth Army driving him west beyond Tripoli—the Desert Rats pursuing the Desert Fox.

In Tunisia, the Germans and Italians formed a defensive perimeter at a point in time that was the worst winter on record since the Punic wars. "General Mud" imposed limitations and hardships on both sides, but it favored the static defense. For the Germans, their bomber units largely operated from Sicily, while fighter and dive-bomber squadrons flew from Tunisian airdromes, just minutes from the front lines. German air-ground liaison had been highly refined, an art not yet perfected by Allied ground forces.

Many of the Allied advanced airfields on the border of Tunisia were crude bases that seemed suitable in dry weather, but disintegrated in the winter rains. They were also far removed from supply points in Oran and Algiers, having to rely on an already

Bore sighting the guns of a 48th Squadron P-38F at an airbase in Algeria. (Ethell)

Lt. Bill Hoelle, 49th Squadron, next to his P-38F "Maximum Goose." (Ethell)

stressed air transport capability. Thus, the ground war went into a stalemate of sorts for several months, as the Germans dug in and the Allies endured the winter, unable to advance. The war for air supremacy, however, continued.

The 14th Fighter Group conducted almost daily sweeps of the Tunis-Bizerta area, and invariably made contact with the *Luftwaffe*:

1 December: Lt. John Singleton downed a Messerschmitt 109 near Al Aouina Airdrome.

2 December: In the Djedeida area, a flight from the 49th Squadron ran into air traffic. Lt. Bill Hoelle shot down a Ju. 88, and probably destroyed a Me. 109. Lt. Tom Morris damaged another twin-engine aircraft, and Lt. William Working damaged a 109.

3 December: In a morning encounter with 109s near Tunis, Virgil Smith of the 48th shot down one, and three others were damaged. Later that day, a sweep near Tunis was met by many German fighters, and two P-38s were shot down. Lts. Jerry Tollen and Robert Eubank survived and managed to return.

4 December: The 48th Squadron found a pair of twin-engined German fighters near Faid and downed both. Sharing in the destruction were Andrew Bing, Wade Walles, John Goebel, and Wallace Sorrenson.

5 December: Escorting medium bombers to Sidi Ahmed airdrome, six P-38s of the 49th Squadron ran into a superior force of German fighters (likely from JG 53) that may have numbered as many as fifty or sixty:

Messerschmitt 109s of JG 53, one of the veteran *Luftwaffe* units that fought in the Mediterranean. (National Archives)

Bill Hoelle's P-38 shows the results of a low-level encounter with a telephone pole. (Dickenson)

Lt. Paul Ziegler (second from the left) and his 48th Squadron ground crew pose near their sun and sand bleached P-38. (Ethell)

These 14th Group ground personnel reflect a mole-like existence at Youks les Bains (L. to R.): Pappy Hagan, Joe Beirschmitt, Lloyd Bergquist, and Frank Resweber. (Dickenson)

"We were all split up," said Robert Carlton. "It was every man for himself. The fight actually lasted around ten or fifteen minutes, but seemed like hours."

Lts. Carlton and Russell Gustke claimed Me. 109 kills. Lt. Charles Earnhart, although surrounded by 109s, scored two probables and two damaged before his P-38 was finally disabled. He crash landed, and he was taken prisoner. Capt. Harold Lewis and Lts. Robert Elliott and John Steif failed to return from this action—all killed.

6 December: Capt. Ralph Knapp, 49th Squadron, downed a Ju 88 and damaged a Messerschmitt 110 near Faid. In the same area, Lt. Bill Moore shot down a pair of Me. 110s and damaged a third. Later that day Capt. Wade Walles shot down a Junkers 52 transport near the port of Sousse.

7 December: Patrolling near the port of Sfax, the 48th Squadron encountered a pair of Ju. 52s that were promptly downed by Capt. Ralph Watson and Lt. Virgil Smith.

12 December: Virgil Smith (48th) and Virgil Lusk (49th) had individual encounters with German fighters. Smith damaged his

After claiming his second kill on 15 January 1943, Lt. John Singleton (center) is surrounded by his 48th Squadron ground crew at Youks. (Ethell)

adversary, and Lusk shot down a Focke-Wulf 190 near Gabes, making him the first ace of the 14th Fighter Group, and the first P-38 ace in the MTO

Having had little effect with night raids on Youks les Bains, the Germans determined to hit it in daylight. On 21 December Lt. Robert Woodward, standing alert on the field, scrambled and caught an incoming Ju. 88, which he eventually downed 85 miles northeast of the base. Another small flight of 88s was encountered near Tebessa, where Lts. Lewis Gregory and Robert Moffatt teamed to down one and damage another.

28 December: The 14th Fighter group had scattered engagements with German fighters near Youks. Virgil Smith was scrambled to intercept a Me. 109 as it approached the air base. He downed it near Salines. In separate actions Lts. Robert Eubank and Livie Mullinax shot down other 109s, while Lts. Jim Ribb and Robert Woodward each damaged one. Later that day, on a long-range recon mission toward Tripoli, Lt. Mullinax P-38 went down and was taken prisoner.

Major General Jimmy Doolittle paid a visit to the units at Youks, and the Germans paid their respects with an air raid. The general was unhurt, but some of his crew and base personnel were killed and injured by bombs.

On 30 December the group suffered several casualties during two missions. While escorting A-20s of the 15th Bomb Squadron to an attack on Gabes, the P-38s were jumped by 109s of JG 53. Capt. Wade Walles claimed one German fighter, but Lts. Clark Smith and Richard Carroll were both shot down. In the dogfight that occurred, Virgil Smith became separated and was heard to call on the radio, but he never returned to Youks. His P-38 had been damaged, and he attempted a wheels-down landing inside Allied lines near Gafsa. However, he hit an obstruction and was killed when the plane flipped over.

During a later reconnaissance near the coast of Libya, an AA battery shot down the 48th's CO, Capt. Tommy Morris. Witnessing the incident, Lt. Bill Hoelle dove down to strafe the German guns and, at over 300 mph, hit a telephone pole, cleaving a gash one-third of the way into the right wing. The P-38 tried to flip over, but Hoelle kept it upright and returned to base on one engine at about 150 mph. He had blisters on his hands from the brute effort needed on the controls.

The bridge at Constantine, Algeria, spanned a deep gorge in the Atlas Mountains. Fighter pilots seemed compelled to fly under the bridge. (Mauss)

"We had a beautiful little service for Virgil Smith on New Year's day. Six of us carried his body to the waiting transport plane. He was buried near Constantine." (From the diary of Bill Schottelkorb.)

As 1943 dawned, Rommel's *Afrikakorps* left Libya and Montgomery's 8th Army in their wake. Entering Tunisia, German ground forces gathered in the narrow neck of mountains that almost reached the Mediterranean coast to form the defensive Mareth Line. From Mareth in the south to near Bizerta in the north the Germans dug in on the high ground to await the attack of the Americans and British from Algeria, and the Eighth Army from Libya in the east.

While the *Luftwaffe* had been reinforced in Tunisia with new units from Europe, and the arrival of other squadrons from Libya, its allied Italian units had mostly been transferred back to Sicily or Italy. The Germans now faced the combined Northwest African Air Forces, as well as Gen. Bernard Montgomery's Western Desert Air Force. A third P-38 unit, the 82nd Fighter Group, had recently arrived to share long-range duties with the 1st and 14th Fighter Groups.

On the morning of 2 January the Germans attempted, yet again, to sneak a single bomber in to hit Youks les Bains. Lts. Wallace Sorrenson and Robert Kirschke (49th Squadron) scrambled to intercept the raider, gave chase, and downed the Junkers 88 with their combined fire.

The next day, the 48th Squadron was dispatched on a ground support mission to assist French forces in the Pichon area being threatened by heavy Panzer units. Bill Schottelkorb's diary details the action:

"We made a 12-ship gunnery pattern. They were huge 30-ton tanks, and really tough. I could see my .50 caliber tracers shooting straight up in the air after they hit, but I think the 20mm were doing a lot of good.

Capt. Spivey, who was on Capt. Walles' wing, got hit by return fire on the second pass. His left engine out, his canopy off, and his forehead cut, Sorrenson and Goebel escorted him home.

We stuck around too long, and as we started for home two 109s hit us from above. We broke, and one got a lucky shot into Capt. Bing's left engine. It burst into flame; Bing cut the power and set it down on the belly in a short field between two ridges. He got out and ran about 150 feet when a gas tank exploded.

From one ridge he could see four Germans running toward him and firing their guns. Two other soldiers were coming from the other direction, and they proved to be French."

On 8 January eight P-38s of the 49th Squadron conducted a reconnaissance sweep toward Gabes and the south of Tunisia. Me.109s of JG 77 that had a height advantage attacked them, and in the ensuing battle three P-38s were shot down and two others damaged. Lts. Robert Woodward and Robert Kirschke were both killed, and Lt. Albert Wolfmueller was wounded in the arm, but survived. Lt. Bill Hoelle was also shot down, but not before he got one of the Germans:

"We were attacked from above by sixteen German fighters. The first I knew about the attack was when the fellow on my left was shot down. Immediately I pulled the ship up into an Immelman, which brought me out above the fighters tailing me and headed in the opposite direction.

It was useless for the enemy to follow, because the radius of their turn in a loop or Immelman would have brought them out well below me. When I rolled the plane over and out of the Immelman, I found myself amidst another enemy flight. There was a Messerschmitt in my sights, and I shot it down with one quick burst, but immediately I discovered three 109s on my tail.

I put the maneuvering flaps down in an effort to get away, only to have a cannon shell hit the flaps and make them jam in that position. When this happened, the best speed I could get was not sufficient to enable me to outdistance them, and by this time I was separated from my flight.

Finally they succeeded in hitting the left engine, and it burst into flames. At this point I was only 50 feet above the ground. I pulled up into a stall because I knew I had to get out. To crash land at this particular point over this terrain would have been fatal. As the ship stalled at about 500 feet, I jumped out through the booms and elevators just as the plane fell into a spin."

Bill Hoelle was rescued by Arab and French citizens, who returned him to Youks. Lieutenant Colonel Troy Keith, a charter member of the 14th and its executive officer, was one of the three survivors of the battle, and was credited with destroying one German fighter and damaging another.

With little regret, the 14th Fighter Group bid goodbye to its rustic camp at Youks les Bains on 9 January 1943. The ground crews boarded C-47 transports and flew to Berteaux, south of Constantine. Pilots in sixteen P-38s—all that was left of the group's aircraft—gave Youks a buzz job and followed. The new field, shared by a B-25 group, had been built and engineered with an adequate runway, dispersal areas, and drainage. It also had American rations, and the vagabonds camped like refugees. "We ate at the expense of the B-25 outfit," Bill Schottelkorb related, "and it was our first taste of American food in a long time. Boy the food was good, especially the coffee and fruit."

A few of the boys got to go to Constantine—a beautiful port town—where they bathed and relaxed. Bill Schottelkorb's diary tells of the simple pleasures for men long in the field:

"What a luxury; that warm water came down over my dusty, hot face and felt wonderful. We paid six francs for the shower, and five to some little kids to take care of our equipment, and to show us a barbershop. Then a nice shave for six francs, a shoeshine for five more, and we were all set. Sat on a veranda and watched the people go by.

Tunisian War Booty

German half-track and Sgt. Chas Bradbury. (Mauss)

A many-wheeled desert motorcycle. (Dickenson)

Italian Scout car used for 20mm target practice. (Crocker)

German tank destroyed on the road to Tunis. (Crocker)

A harvest of German and Italian weapons. (Dickenson)

German prisoners no longer needed helmets. (Dickenson)

Mark [Shipman] and I took a walk and got a good look over the cliff. It was a scene out of a fairy tale book: green hills, winding roads, and blue sky. Oh me!"

Some new pilots and a few new P-38s arrived, and hopes soared among the veterans that the combat tour of the originals was nearing an end. However, bomber escort missions were on the docket.

On 11 January the 14th flew two low-level escort missions with medium bombers. North of Bizerta, eight P-38s discovered a flight of transports bound for Tunisia. Colonel Olds, leading the formation, splashed one, and Lt. William Workman downed another. Lt. William Moore attacked and shot down a third transport, a six-engine monster that may have been a Messerschmitt 323.

Separate squadron escort missions were flown on 15 January. The 48th Squadron and its B-25s were over the Mediterranean when they spotted a flight of transports. Several P-38 pilots scrambled to attack a six-engine Me 323 and got hits, but the aircraft was credited to Mark Shipman. Lts. John Singleton, Wallace Sorrenson, and Elmer Warren each downed a Junkers 52 before the rest of the enemy flight found refuge in rain clouds. It was a long mission that elicited a comment from Bill Schottelkorb:

"Again we sweated out bad weather over the hills on return. Total time four hours. It is simply too long to sit in a cockpit tightly strapped under combat conditions. A pilot isn't alert enough after two hours if he is bounced."

That same afternoon a six-plane flight from the 49th Squadron encountered another flock of enemy transports with escort in the same area. However, the escorting 109s were not immediately detected. Lts. Oscar Blueher and Robert Carlton each downed a Junkers 52, and Lt. Soren Anton damaged a 52 and six-engine 323 before the unseen Messerschmitts attacked. Capt. Herbert Johnson damaged a Messerschmitt 110, but the Germans extracted considerable revenge. Capt. William Fulmer of group headquarters was seen to crash in the sea, and Lt Lawrence Driver did not return. Carlton made it home on a single engine, and Blueher crash landed at Bone on one engine.

Once again a handful of new pilots arrived, most with no more than 50 hours in the Lightning. Bill Schottelkorb tells how they tried to indoctrinate the newcomers:

"Singleton and I gave them the history of the squadron, regulations, combat theory, cockpit check, and oxygen, all on the ground. After that they all got in two or three hours in the air. The last flight of the day was carried out just like an operational mission. We lined up the flight, gave a takeoff time, channel for radio, briefing, etc. They did pretty well with it."

Colonel Thayer Olds had been ordered back to the States, and Keith, recently promoted to lieutenant colonel, took command of the 14th Fighter Group. Patrolling near Agadi Island on 18 January, Lt. Col. Keith and Capt. Paul Spivey of 14th Headquarters intercepted and downed a pair of Ju. 88 bombers. That same day a formation of the group escorted Martin B-26 bombers on a shipping hunt. Near Enfidaville, in the Gulf of Hammamet, they found a ship that the mediums bombed. As the fighters jettisoned their disposable tanks, Lt. Elmer Warren dropped out of sight and was not seen again. Somehow he had become separated, and was set upon by German fighters. A pilot from JG 2 claimed that he had shot down a P-38 in this vicinity. Later on it was learned that Warren was a prisoner.

The next day, 23 January 1943, sixteen 48th Squadron P-38s were sent far south to hunt enemy traffic on the road leading from Gabes to Medenine. While strafing and setting fire to some 25 vehicles, the low-flying P-38s were jumped from above by numerous Me109s of JG 51. As the 48th fought their way back west, Capt. Ralph Watson shot down a 109, and Lt. Alphonso Seagraves damaged another. But JG 51 had all the advantages in the running battle. Lts. Schottelkorb (the diarist), Shipman, Stuteville, Harley, Soliday, and Yates were all shot down. Some were recent arrivals. Only Mark Shipman, who crash-landed near Kebili, survived. Robbed of all but his pants by Arabs, and left to die on the edge of the Sahara, he walked some 100 miles to freedom.

Three months of grinding attrition had reduced the 14th Fighter Group from the 54 pilots who had arrived from England to just 38. (Shipman, bringing up the rear, would be one more.) Group strength had been reduced to only a dozen worn P-38s. Now a mere shadow of an AAF fighter group, the 14th was relieved of combat duty. Its handful of old Lightnings and the new replacement pilots were turned over to other P-38 units. Those surviving veteran pilots of the 14th who had completed their combat tours were airlifted home. The staff officers and enlisted men were sent to Medouina airport, near Casablanca, to rest and recuperate, and await the rebuilding of the redoubtable 14th Fighter Group under Lt. Col. Troy Keith.

4

Sicily and Beyond

The *Afrikakorps* battled hammer and tong to hang on to its bridgehead in North Africa. Confined to Tunisia from 1 February 1943, with their backs to the Mediterranean, they occasionally lashed out at American and British ground forces, and sent them reeling back in various set piece battles. However, as they were steadily pushed to the northeastern tip of Tunisia, and with their supply line across the Mediterranean continuously interdicted at sea and in the air, the outcome of the struggle in North Africa was not in doubt. On 6 May *Luftwaffe* units still in Tunisia were ordered to flee with their few operational aircraft. The next day Allied ground forces entered Tunis. Remaining German and Italian ground forces, narrowed into a perimeter near Cape Bon, surrendered on 13 May 1943. Almost 250,000 prisoners were taken.

The 14th Fighter Group had been away from the front for over three months, but their contribution in downing some 62 enemy aircraft and conducting flawless bomber escorts had been a considerable factor in the early campaign. They would be in on the kill for the last week of May 1943.

While rebuilding at Medouina, in Morocco, Lt. Col. Keith began to get a trickle of replacement men and new P-38G aircraft. The biggest boost in strength came from the arrival in Oran of the 37th Fighter Squadron from the U.S. The 37th's background and training had been similar to that of the 48th and 49th Squadrons. It was activated in January 1941 in California, and shuttled about the West Coast. Equipped initially with P-43s, its pilot ranks had been fleshed out by twenty-one second lieutenants from the flying school class of 41G. Not until February 1942 did the 37th gain its

Lt. Col. Troy Keith took charge of the rebuilding of the 14th Fighter Group. (Ethell)

The 37th Fighter Squadron at Camp Kilmer, New Jersey, gets ready to join the war. (Crocker)

first P-38s. Its training was hindered by the transfer of experienced men to new assignments and the usual accidents. But by January 1943 the 37th was finally organized, and heading overseas from New Jersey aboard the *USS H. F. Alexander*. James M. Stitt, 37th Engineering Officer, recalls the crossing to Algiers:

"Every now and then the old prop on the back end would come clear out of the water and she'd flog, and spray would fly, and more spray would come over the bow. Now, with something like that going on you can pretty well understand that the crew would get used to it. But for all of us pilgrims on board, that was something brand new, and there was a lot of seasickness. The poor little Red Cross girls and nurses aboard were just about sick from the time they got on until they got off. Some of them had hammocks strung up on deck so they could get some fresh air and keep an eye on the horizon, but it didn't do a whole lot of good. I think other than the ship's crew, I was probably one of the very few personnel on board that made all the meals. But by golly, I've got to tell you that down there in that dining room, with the rolling and yawing and pitching, when they brought out some of those steaming foods it put you to the test.

On arrival we rolled up our field packs, packed our musette bags, and we were issued a can of Eagle brand milk, a can of sardines, and an orange. I looked at that and thought to myself, what in the thunder am I going to do with those sardines. I don't eat them. And a funny thing happened. Within twenty-four hours those sardines were gone, and I've got to tell you that they were the most delicious things I ever ate in my life that I can remember to that time.

The USS *H.F. Alexander* plowing across the Atlantic in convoy to North Africa. She carried the 37th Squadron, among other units. (Crocker)

Veterans of the 1st Fighter Group who were selected to help reconstitute the 14th Fighter Group (L. to R): Standing: Rethman, Stemen, Owens, a visiting fireman, Capt. Eddie Rickenbacker, Bernie Muldoon, John Wolford, and Joe Smith. Kneeling: Bill Newman, Robert McCord, and Robert Riley (See Appendix C). (Rethman via Mullins)

Ground personnel of the 48th Squadron enroute from Casablanca, Morocco, to Telergma, Algeria, courtesy of the Algerian railroad and its 40 & 8 cars. (L. to R.) Top row: Unk., Unk., and Forrest Boots. 2nd row: Joe Beirschmitt, Lloyd Bergquist, and James Walker. 3rd row: Emmett Wilson, Paul Arney, George Swanz, Robert Calhoun, and ? Marton. 4th row: Joe Vallelunga, Preston Bingham, William Schwartz, Frank Resweber, and Ole Olson. (Dickenson)

We made our way down to a thing called a 40 and 8 train. It was a French narrow-gauge railroad; we loaded on board, and that thing took us as far as the track ran in the direction we wanted to go. We formed up, got organized, and began a pretty long march. There is a lot of argument to the day about how long the march was. I figured it was about twice as long as it actually was. Crim and some of the boys have me convinced, however, that it was about five miles. In view of the overall poor physical condition we were in from better than three weeks on that ship, the seasickness, and the food that we had, it's a miracle that we made it out to Mud Hill at all.

We marched into the camp area that evening, and we were assigned to a squadron bivouac. I drew a pyramidal tent with five other guys, and when I looked into the tent flap I saw that there was straw on the ground and six blankets. It doesn't take a mental giant to figure out that if six guys are going to sleep on the ground in February, lying on straw, with a few blankets thrown on top, it's going to get cold. And those poor boobs on the outside edge were the ones that would get the coldest. Well, the guys out there on the outside stayed as long as they could take it, and they would crawl over the top, drop on down, and wedge themselves in. And that is how that first night went.

Troops of the 37th Squadron enroute from the end of the track to camp at Mud Hill. (Stitt)

Mud Hill encampment in Algeria, January 1943. (Crocker)

That was a rough first night, because when we got there all we were issued to eat was some British rations—bully beef and hardtack. I looked at that and said to myself, if that is what I've got to look forward to in this old war, it's going to be a long one. Well, we made it through that first night, and when morning came we found that during the night another outfit had moved in next to us, about fifty yards away, and an interesting development had occurred. The first sergeant of that outfit had gotten his throat slit during the night. I mean, somebody just didn't think too kindly about him, and they got rid of him."

Brand new P-38s, some bound for the 14th Fighter Group, had also just made the Atlantic crossing as deck loads on various ships. Jim Stitt describes how they were almost all broken even before flight operations began:

"Crocker, Crim, and Wightman, while nosing around the harbor discovered some ships that had P-38s on them. It's a good thing for us and the war effort that they did, because the French and the Arabs charged with unloading didn't know beans about the planes. They had proceeded to throw a couple of cables around the booms of one airplane, and another around the gun compartment,

Maj. John "Gil" Bright, CO of the 37th Fighter Squadron. (Ethell)

Horseplay at Telergma: Pilots (L. to R.) Richard Campbell, Robert Gardner, and James Toth (KIA). (Crocker)

A 48th Squadron P-38 skids home for a landing, still smoking after consuming the contents of several fire extinguishers. (Stitt)

and started lifting the heavy airplane off the ship to set it on the dock and, of course, the whole thing got away from them, and they dropped the airplane in the bay. [Richard] Campbell heard about that, and immediately took control of the situation. I think Dick had to get their attention and make sure they were listening to him by showing them the muzzle of his .45. He pretty much put a stop to that.

We got organized, and proceeded to supervise the unloading of the airplanes. Our own men would rig the cables at the proper hoist points, so we could get the planes safely on the dock. From there we pulled them with Cletracs through the town and out to the airport, and into our roofless hangar. There we began to get ready to assemble them. French and Arab workers helped out at this point by cleaning off the protective gunk that covered the planes for deck shipment.

A P-38 makes a low pass over the tent area at the 14th's airfield at St. Marie du Zit. (USAF)

Lt. Robert Thayer, 37th Squadron, was lost in the Straits of Sicily. (USAF)

In our hangar we set up a production line to assemble and service the airplanes. It was a dandy. We made up some rolling wing racks so we could position the wing panels properly in relationship to the wing root. We then pumped up hydraulic pressure and moved the flap extension rods out as far as they would go. The actuating rod on the wing then was projecting out, ready to be joined to the flap extension rod. When connected, by retracting the flaps we were able to move and guide the wing up to the wing root, and to line up the main wing boltholes. Then we could slip in the heavy wing connector bolts, tighten them up, and replace the fairing. We checked the rigging of the flaps, rudders, ailerons, and elevators, and made sure the cable tension was right. We checked to make sure that the droop and control surface movement was right. Then we moved the plane to a new position on the assembly line where we serviced it, checking the coolant system, engine oil, and ethylene glycol.

At the next station on the assembly line we hung the big three bladed Curtiss-Electric propellers, and checked them out for operation. With a final check of strut pressure and tire pressure the airplanes were rolled out for preflight inspection and a test hop. When we got the assembly line running we were turning out three airplanes a day."

Commanding the 37th Fighter Squadron was Major John Gilpin Bright, a pilot of vast experience. Known as "Gil," he learned to fly with the U.S. Navy, graduating from Pensacola in 1940. He had served on the aircraft carrier *Ranger* as a pilot with VF-4 before resigning his commission to join the American Volunteer Group, General Claire Chennault's Chinese Air Force outfit, later known as the "Flying Tigers." During some six months of duty with that unit he flew at least 50 combat missions, and was credited with three aerial kills. When the AVG disbanded in July 1942 he was one of the few pilots who accepted commissions in the Army Air Force, and served with the successor unit, the 23rd Fighter Group, claiming another victory before returning to the U.S.

In March 1943 additional experienced pilots joined, or were shanghaied as it were, into the 14th Fighter Group from among

Lt. Henry Blood and unknown armorer inspect 20mm rounds going into a 48th Squadron P-38 at Telergma. (Ethell)

Lt. Jim Hollingsworth (white T-shirt) and his 37th ground crew. (Hollingsworth)

Capt. Lloyd DeMoss, 49th Squadron, and his P-38 "Bad Penny." (Ethell)

veterans of the North African campaign. Maj. Joel Owens recalls the event, first told in John Mullins' history of the 1st Fighter Group, *An Escort of P-38s*:

"I was relieved from assignment to the 27th [Fighter Squadron] at the end of March. I was a Major who had flown seventy-four missions, scored seven aerial victories (5 destroyed, 1 probable, 1 damaged), had been recommended for the Silver Star, and the DFC with four oak leaves, plus a bunch of Air Medals. The squadron had done pretty well in combat. The record stood at sixteen losses versus 64 victories (35-7-22); all but three were single engine fighters. I was really looking forward to stateside duty.

I hadn't attached much significance to my orders that directed me to report to the Northwest African Air Force Headquarters. I arrived at Casablanca, checked in to transient quarters, headed for the Officer's Club, and ran into several pilots from the 1st Fighter Group. We were having a rather boisterous time celebrating our escape when Major Joe Ruble came along. Joe had been a member of the 1st Fighter Group staff in England. After an exchange of pleasantries he said, 'Don't drink too much tonight. General Cannon wants to see all of you in his office tomorrow morning.' Nobody had any idea what lay ahead. We all agreed that he would probably hand out some medals, tell us what good boys we had been, and wish us well.

The next morning some of us were a bit bleary eyed as the general arrived. He was almost fatherly as he congratulated us on our records. Then he asked: 'What, in your opinion, is the one thing most needed in this theater of operations?' We all agreed that what was needed most was MORE FIGHTERS!! The general reacted with, 'I was hoping you'd say that. Now, here is what we're going to do. We are going to resurrect the 14th Fighter Group, and you men are going to be its leaders.' I don't remember that any of us thanked the General for this splendid opportunity.

Lt. Harry Crim, 37th Squadron, suited up for a mission. (Crocker)

The German 88mm artillery piece, shown here with the *Afrikakorps*, was one of the best AA weapons of World War II. (National Archives)

The next day we reported to Lieutenant Colonel Troy Keith, the only rated officer from the original 14th Group. He spoke briefly with the dozen or so pilots who had been ordered to Mediouna, a small village southeast of Casablanca. Colonel Keith told us that the 14th Group finally consisted of three squadrons: the 48th and 49th, with ground crews and officers, but no pilots or aircraft; and the 37th, which had a complete complement of personnel but no aircraft. The 37th was commanded by Major John Bright, an ex-Navy pilot and Flying Tiger ace. No one seemed to know how they came to be in North Africa, since the rest of the 37th's former 55th Fighter Group remained in England. Captain Carl Rudder, ex-94th Squadron and victim of the Greenland ice cap escapade, was a member of the 37th Squadron, as was Marcus Linn, who had joined the 27th Squadron in England from the RAF.

I was appointed the new group Executive Officer, while Muldoon and Newman were appointed as Squadron Commanders of the 48th and 49th squadrons. The rest of the 71st pilots joined the 48th, and the 27th men went to the 49th. They were assigned as flight leaders, operations officers, and such. We began the task of bringing the group to operational readiness. The 14th had a high priority on the acquisition of both aircraft and pilots. The 78th Fighter Group in England was converting from the P-38 to P-47s, and started ferrying P-38s to Casablanca. The first group of them delivered their planes, and immediately hopped a C-54 back to England. A quick call to Major Ruble resulted in the reassignment of the pilots on subsequent flights. Some of them were unhappy about being Shanghied, but we explained to them that 'War is HELL.' The group was at full strength in about ten days. After training in formation flying and maneuvers, the 14th moved to a forward base southeast of Telergma on 5 May, and flew its first mission on May 6, 1943. This, to my knowledge, is the only instance of a new group entering combat with leaders who had combat experience. It was a pretty good combination. The Old Heads had the knowledge of how to avert disaster, and the new guys were fearless and full of vinegar, or whatever it takes to make a fighter."

Also joining the group rebuilding project as operations officer was Maj. Clarence L. Tinker, Jr. His father, Maj. Gen. Clarence Tinker, had commanded the Seventh Air Force in Hawaii, and was lost on a June 1942 bombing mission to Wake Island.

Finally together as a unit, the 48th, 49th, and 37th Squadrons trained intensively in Morocco for six weeks. In late April 1943 the ground echelon boarded trucks for movement to Telergma, Algeria, just south of the ancient port of Constantine. The air echelon followed, with eighty-eight P-38s landing on 5 May.

Lt. Marcus Linn, a 1st Group veteran, scored against Italian fighters on 18 May 1943. (Crocker)

An Italian Air Force Macchi 202 of the 4th *Stormo*, abandoned in North Africa. (Crow)

Johannes Steinhoff commanded all German fighter units during the Sicily campaign, and frequently tangled with the 14th Fighter Group. He was credited with 176 aerial victories on various fronts, and survived the war. (Lambert)

As the 14th Fighter Group returned to combat operations, the squadron leaders were as follows: Maj. Gil Bright, 37th; Capt. Bernard Muldoon, 48th; and Capt. William Newman, 49th.

The initial combat mission involved escort for B-25s of the 321st Bomb Group hunting shipping in the Straits of Sicily. The final surrender of Axis ground forces was at hand, and ships of all types were being used to extract German and Italian troops from the Cape Bon peninsula. It was a "Dunkirk" of sorts for the Axis. No enemy aircraft were encountered, and a ship was bombed and left sinking. However, two pilots failed to return from the low-level operation: Lts. Thayer of the 37th and Moore of the 49th.

The anti-shipping missions continued for two more days without interruption from the *Luftwaffe*, which had fled Tunisia, and was licking its wounds in Sicily and Italy. And that is where the 14th turned its attention. For the first time the 14th was assigned to the Strategic Air Forces of the Northwest African Air Forces (NAAF). This joint British American unit was composed of all four of the heavy, four-engined AAF units in the MTO, three groups of medium bombers, and a wing of RAF Wellingtons. All three of the P-38 units of the Twelfth Air Force (the 1st, 14th, and 82nd) were assigned to escort of the bomber units. It was the long-range work for which the P-38 had been designed.

On 9 May twenty P-38s escorted B-17s to bomb Palermo, Sicily, on a five hour round trip. A mixed flight of German and Italian fighters put in a halfhearted appearance, and two were downed for their trouble. Capt. Herbert Ross of the 48th shot down a Macchi 202, and 1st Lt. Lloyd DeMoss of the 49th was credited with a Messerschmitt 109. The 37th Squadron spotted a passing SM 79 transport, and Maj. Bright claimed it.

Sicily was visited again on the 10th, with B-17s bombing the Bo Rizzo A/D near Palermo. Maj. Joel Owens, flying group lead, shot down a pair of intruding Me 109s. Lt. Dewey F. Varndell of the 37th was missing on return to base.

German tanks would duel attacking aircraft. This *Afrikakorps* crew bested an Allied aircraft, and displayed a victory symbol on the Panzer's main gun. (National Archives)

Sicily's Marsala A/D was next to be bombed by B-17s on 11 May, and Lt. William G. Newman (49th Squadron) shot down a pair of Macchi 202s. Lt. Wayne M. Chaves (49th Squadron) failed to return.

Further escort missions were flown on 13 and 14 May, but sightings of enemy aircraft were rare and distant. Lt. Mark Hageny (49th) ran across a Ju. 88 and downed it over Sicily, and Maj. Bud Tinker had an inconclusive engagement with a single-engined aircraft. However, a pilot was lost each day: Lt. John Burton and Lt. Edward Terwilliger.

The Axis air forces had avoided battle over Sicily, possibly repairing and refitting from the Tunisian defeat. That absence ended on 18 May 1943, when the 14th Fighter Group escorted B-17s to Messina, on Sicily's eastern shore. Harry Crim describes the seemingly endless mission, where the bombers got lost and bombed a target on the other end of Sicily:

"We took off with a full load of ammunition and two 165-gallon belly tanks, and rendezvoused with the bombers as they crossed the coast of Africa. The briefed flight path was northeast and then east, passing about 50 miles north of Sicily, then due south to Messina to the bomb release point, and then a 180 degree turn and follow our route in reverse direction to home base. The round trip distance was about 1,200 miles.

About twenty miles off the African coast a cloud deck built up below us. We stayed on our planned route without being able to see anything below, and at the scheduled time, the bombers cruise-climbed to 22,000 feet, and we went up to 25,000. As the B-17s turned south for Messina, the fighter formation was jumped by about 30 Me 109s in a very aggressive manner. Turns in formation were made into the attackers, but after fifteen minutes our formations became broken, and a free for all ensued.

Jim Hollingsworth was on my wing, and after we had fired at four or five 109s we noticed a P-38 going down in a shallow dive streaming glycol. We pulled out of the fight and covered the P-38 as it went down, fending off attacks by Germans. The aircraft we were protecting went into clouds at about 10,000 feet, and we followed. We broke out about 7,000 feet, and the crippled P-38

Crim's St. Marie du Zit Motorcycle Club (L. to R.): Len Conkle, Ken Waldron, Robert Carey, and George Wightman (KIA). Capt. McCarthy, Intelligence Officer, looks on disapprovingly. (Stitt)

was still in the same dive ahead of us. We tried to contact him on the radio but had no luck. Then we saw a 109 come out of the cloud deck, streaming black smoke, and continuing in a vertical dive to hit the water. Soon another 109 came out of the clouds in erratic flight. The pilot bailed out, and as he came down in his chute we saw four 109s circling him. Our crippled P-38 stayed in a 30-degree dive, hit the water, and sank immediately. The pilot didn't get out.

Jim and I went on down to the deck. During the fight I felt that we had drifted east. And because of the length of the flight, and the prolonged combat, we wouldn't have enough fuel to get back to base. So I called Jim and told him we were heading for Malta, as it was the closest friendly territory. Our plan was to fly south across Sicily and, when we hit water on the other side, to follow the coast on our right until it turned west, and then turn south for Malta. We had no maps, but I had a page from a dictionary that showed where Malta was with respect to Sicily.

As we leveled out on the water and cut back on throttles, rpm, and mixture to give us maximum range, two Me 109s tried to sneak up behind us. I turned into them and couldn't bring my guns to bear, so I tried to force one of them into the water with my wing tip. He saw what I was up to and dodged. Both Germans broke to the east, and Jim and I both shot at them, but couldn't afford the fuel for more fight. Then we settled down to find a place to land.

We flew into a harbor where the ships started shooting at us, so we took evasive action, crossed a peninsula, and hit water again, following the coast on our right. We flew and flew, but the coast didn't end like it should have. [It turned out they were following the coast of Africa, not Sicily.]

Finally Jim called and said that he was getting low on fuel, so I told him that we would buzz the town ahead and land on the beach if it looked friendly; if not, we would land in the water about 200 yards offshore. As we picked up speed to buzz the town I saw a line of P-40s with British markings [from the Desert Air Force], so I told Jim to go ahead and land. I was right behind him, and as we were taxiing he ran out of fuel.

Two lorries full of men met us, and were amazed at the sight of our P-38s, as they had never seen one. We told them who we were, that we needed to notify our group, and that we needed fuel and something to eat. We had been in the air 7 1/2 hours. Both our ships had bullet holes in them, and our guns were out of ammunition.

The Brits promised to take care of things, and took us to a mess tent and cooked us a much better breakfast than we were used to: eggs, ham, fried potatoes, and bread and jam, as well as coffee. While eating, we realized that there were four men stationed around our tent with Tommy guns. It seems they hadn't believed

Maj. Carl Rudder, 37th CO (left), and Lt. Lloyd Hendrix display their victory symbols. Hendrix was killed in action on 4 May '43. (Ethell)

Lt. Richard Campbell's P-38 "Earthquake McGoon" was named for a comic strip character. It shows both mission symbols and kills. Sgt. Bryan Ingalls poses with the aircraft. (Mauss)

George Wightman wears fur-lined boots for cold, high-altitude missions. Temperatures on the ground in Tunisia got up 120 degrees. (Crim)

a thing we said. They thought we were Germans, and with good reason. We weren't flying with dog tags, for some reason, and had no means of personal identification. Also, there was our scruffy appearance. Because of a water shortage at our base we didn't shave except under our chins, so that the oxygen mask would not leak. This, coupled with the fact that neither of us had had a bath or washed our clothes in two or three weeks, didn't fit their idea about what an American fighter pilot looked like. They also couldn't believe that a fighter could stay airborne for 7 1/2 hours, as their Kittyhawks and Spitfires had less than two hours of fuel.

Finally they got confirmation that we were really Americans, filled our fuel tanks, and sent us off. Still, we had no maps and no aids to navigation, so we elected to follow the coast, past Tunis and Bizerta, and landed at Bone. Some of our other planes were there, so we spent the night and flew to Telergma the next day.

The rest of the story is that the bombers didn't bomb Messina, but hit Trapani, on the west end of Sicily. We didn't have radio contact with the B-17s, so they couldn't tell us that they had changed the target. When we flew south after the fight we flew into the harbor of Tunis, and those had been Allied ships shooting at us. The lesson learned from this was, 'Don't expect to get to your planned destination if you don't know where you are when you start out.'"

In the air battle that day, the 14th had claimed six enemy aircraft destroyed (two each by Richard Campbell and Robert McCord, and one each by Marcus Linn and Verl Schoenfeldt), one probable, and five damaged.

However, the action had been costly. Maj. Tinker, Lt. James Goff, Lt. Robert Benton, and Lt. James Toth were all missing. Two P-38s had landed at Bizerta, each with an engine shot out. Crim and Hollingsworth found refuge near Gabes, and others at Bone.

Many months later it was learned that Jim Goff, 37th Squadron, had survived. Here is his tale of unwanted adventure:

"I was leading the second element of white flight with Lt. Ken Waldron as a wing man when the formation became broken. I had

The 14th frequently escorted these Boeing B-17 Flying Fortresses of the 97th Bomb Group. (USAF)

a mid-air collision with another 38. He was stalling out on the top of a 45-degree loop. My plane was also in a slightly stalled condition. It seemed that the planes would hit gondola on gondola, so I kicked as much left rudder and aileron as possible.

The ship just started to respond when I heard two clicks, and felt the rough air of the other planes' prop wash. My tailskid right boom had hit both of his rudders. I looked back and saw his plane was in a slight dive, but seemed in good control. There was nothing wrong with the controls of my ship. I checked them and decided to get in closer formation.

Then I heard on the radio, 'Last ship in three-ship flight, look out!' It took me a few seconds to realize that I was that ship. A couple of 20mm hit my left reserve tank, and at the same time the guy on the radio said, 'Oh my God! Oh my God!' I rocked it up in a tight turn, and the attacking plane went on by. He had shot out the radiators of both motors, so I put the nose in a slight dive for a cloud formation below. Cosmoline began to smoke, and it soon filled the cockpit with smoke. I rolled down both windows.

The quick descent had fogged my windows, so that visibility was nil. If the enemy had followed me down, I had made a terrible mistake, because I flew straight through the cloud. In any event, I let him fly up very close to me. His burst hit my left wing at the junction of the flap and the aileron. I made another mistake by flying through his field of fire. With my left motor dead the plane started to spin. I booted it to the right, and flew into his line of fire again.

At some point, I threw my glasses out the right window, my vision being impaired by blood, but glimpsed my attacker being pursued by a P-38. The plane hit the water with me in it. I just barely had time to take some of the shock with my arms. My head hit the gun sight, and I was in the water.

I had to think hard to remember that I had not pulled the emergency release. I found the CO_2 string on the left side of my Mae West with a great deal of trouble, got out of my parachute, and started sinking. After discarding my gloves I was able to withdraw the CO_2 bottle of the dingy, opened the valve, and was greatly relieved to see it take shape. As I crawled in the dingy a sea turtle swam by.

I cut the silk off the parachute, thinking it would keep me warm, but it absorbed water, and only kept the dingy about three inches deep in water all night. I damn near shivered to death.

About 1630 an enemy flight went over, and I was afraid they might strafe me, but they went by. A few hours later I was awakened by a violent bump on the bottom of the dingy. I sat erect in the dingy, and saw a swirl and a bit of foam about ten yards from the boat, and what looked like a big black stick approaching me. I looked over the right side and saw the white belly and open mouth of a shark.

While I was getting my hunting knife out he made another attack. I plunged the knife straight down, and it went in right behind the mouth. His momentum carried him forward, and the knife came out near the tail. I simply gutted him. I was a hell of a lot more scared of the fish than getting strafed."

The following day Jim Goff was rescued from the Mediterranean by a Swedish ship, and put off in Messina. The Italians hospitalized him, cared for his wounds, and then sent him to a prisoner of war camp, where he met Clark Smith (48th Squadron), who had been his classmate in flying school. Both survived the war.

Among other lessons learned was that seven hours flying could test both the P-38 and the pilots beyond reasonable limits. Harry Crim comments on the routine involved in long-range escort missions:

"Generals Spaatz and Doolittle kept stretching our range from the published figures of 250 mile radius, to 350 mile radius, to 450 mile radius, to 600 miles. It seemed that every time we went out [with B-17s] we went a little further. Finally, one day none of the fighters got home—that night that is [18 May 1943]. That must have shaken up the powers."

Lt. Col. Keith led a dozen P-38s back to Trapani on a bomber escort mission on 19 May. This time the B-17s hit Milo A/D. Fewer enemy fighters were observed, and 49th pilots had inconclusive results, probably destroying three 109s. Lts. Frank Hawk and John Wolford were missing on return. Wolford, one of those 1st Fighter group vets who had stayed on to give the rejuvenated 14th some experienced leadership, was escorting a pair of damaged P-38s out of the fight when 109s went after the trio. He turned into the enemy fighters to cover the retreat of the cripples and was not seen again.

Another B-17 escort mission was flown on 21 May, as the Twelfth Air Force continued its campaign to cripple German and Italian air defenses. This time the target was Castelvetrano A/D, Sicily, and again enemy interceptors exhibited a lack of aggression. Only a handful of fighters were sighted, and just three pilots scored enough hits to claim damage: Bernard Muldoon, Herb Ross, and Wallace Bland. But once more, a pair of P-38 pilots succumbed to the rigors of the long missions; Lts. Albert Little and Burton Snyder of the 49th failed to return.

The group flew one more mission to Sicily on 22 May, escorting bombers to Bo Rizzo A/D. The 37th Squadron's Lt. Charlie Crocker bagged a Messerschmitt 109, and Lt. George Wightman probably destroyed another. Lt. John C. Henry failed to return.

A bombing mission to a zinc and lead plant in Sardinia on 24 May brought some variation to the escort assignments. Enemy aircraft were encountered, and Bill Hanes, Don Leighton, and Jack Homan of the 48th Squadron each shot down a SM 79 transport.

May 1943 ended with four missions to a variety of targets in Sardinia and Sicily. There was little sign of enemy air defense units. Jim Hollingsworth claimed a Dornier 217 bomber that wandered into the path of the 37th Squadron on 26 May, and Lt. Walter Hoke (49th Squadron) was credited with bagging a lone Cant. Z506 seaplane the following day. It was not until 28 May that the *Luftwaffe* put up a contest, when many Me 109s tangled with the 14th. Victories were credited to Capt. Bob McCord and Lt. Sidney Weatherford of the 48th. Charley Crocker, Richard Campbell, Sam Palmer, and Daniel Africa all damaged or probably destroyed 109s.

Three pilots failed to return from these late May missions. Lt. William Collins of the 37th Squadron was hit by AA, and was seen to bail out successfully. Lt. Fred Sanders and Lt. Harry Simmons of the 48th Squadron were missing when their flights returned.

Claims and losses for the 14th seemed frequently to be in balance—no better than a tie. At this point in the war, the *Luftwaffe* pilots and their Messerschmitt 109s were worthy adversaries, and the numbers in a dogfight frequently favored the Germans. But apart from this, there were technical factors that limited victory claims. Harry Crim discusses the issue:

"In Africa the whole 37th Squadron started with just four gun cameras. The ground temperature was so high that film melted, so from these four cameras I saw only about ten feet of developed footage. To claim a victory, you had to knock off a major piece of a plane (like a wing or the whole tail), set it on fire, or see it crash. You also had to have a confirming witness. With no gun camera film, the only witness was a member of your flight.

Our major enemy was the 109, which couldn't be set on fire above 16,000 feet. It was a very strong airplane, and didn't shed parts very easily.

One other victory sign was a bail out. The German pilots at altitude didn't have any incentive to parachute above 10,000 feet, so you didn't expect it. The other criteria for a victory was to see the plane crash. Consider the problem from, say, 25,000 feet. A 109 in a vertical dive at 400 mph would require about a minute before it hit the ground. And in the skies over Africa, Sicily, or Italy, one minute taken out of a fight to watch a plane hit the ground would plant you right alongside him. Those boys weren't there to play.

This was part of the unresolved problem of aerial combat at that time. I didn't claim a single aerial victory in the 50 missions that I flew in the Mediterranean. As a rough estimate, I guess that I shot at a hundred aircraft, hit probably 40, and guess that maybe ten of those didn't get home. Later in the Pacific I flew P-51s and got six confirmed, five with gun camera confirmation. There are those who say that the P-38 was not combat effective. My point is that the P-38 *was effective*, but its effectiveness was not observable."

The Allied grand strategy had focused on the conquest of Sicily long before the campaign in North Africa had ended. Joint British-American staffs labeled the invasion as operation HUSKY. But first the high command deemed it necessary to capture the small (42 1/2 square miles) island of Pantelleria. Lying in the Straits of Sicily, almost midway between Tunisia and Sicily, it was thought that Pantelleria offered some obstacle to HUSKY. It is hard to understand why. The combined air forces of the Allies had been hammering Pantelleria intermittently for weeks, and after the surrender of Tunisia it had become a virtual bombing range for air units now just fifty miles distant. However, it was a rocky outcropping with only one beach suitable for amphibious operations, so the socalled "reduction of Pantelleria" prior to its invasion began in earnest in mid-May 1943. Coupled with a blockade by sea, the might of Allied air power rained bombs on the tiny island for more than three weeks before D-Day, 11 June 1943. As the Allied invasion armada disembarked, the island's Italian commander ran up the white flag. Pantelleria fell without another shot being fired. It was the first instance in history wherein air power alone had caused the capitulation of a fortress.

The 14th Fighter Group had many sorties to Pantelleria prior to the invasion with no losses, and again turned their attention to Sicily with almost daily missions. The defenders showed little interest in aerial combat. However, U.S. casualties continued from a variety of causes.

On 4 June 1943, 49th Squadron pilots Lts. John Green and William Bergersen collided over western Sicily while attempting to avoid flak. Both aircraft fell to the sea.

German flak was highly accurate and had great range. German heavy batteries fired 88mm shells set to explode at a predetermined altitude. Often controlled by range finders, radar, and/or listening devices, they could fire their box barrages as high as any aircraft could fly. Harry Crim claimed "The German 88 could knock the whiskers off a gnat. They were totally effective, and we did our utmost to avoid them."

In an accident unrelated to combat, the 37th Fighter Squadron had several officers injured when their vehicle rolled over near camp on 11 June. Capt. Barker, flight surgeon, and Lts Crim (pilot), Haddock (pilot), Kearns, and Anderson were injured. Anderson (communications officer) was killed as a result of the mishap, and Kearns (pilot) died of his injuries the following day.

On 15 June a dozen P-38s of 14th encountered a single Italian Macchi 202 near Milo A/D, Trapani, and Richard Campbell

Capt. Sid Weatherford (48th) in late August 1943 after claiming his fifth kill. (Dickenson)

brought it down. But once again, the 14th was savaged by a mid-air collision between two 48th Squadron pilots: Donald Anderson and Fred Browne. Both were assumed killed.

Yet another mid-air collision claimed two P-38s on 18 June 1943. Trying to avoid a flak barrage off the northeast coast of Sicily, Lts. Bruce Campbell and George Church were lost. Campbell survived to become a prisoner.

On 20 June the 14th escorted bombers back to Bo Rizzo A/D, and this time they were intercepted by a large mixed force of Me 109s and Fw 190s. The 49th Squadron engaged the enemy, scoring three claimed by Lts. Anthony Evans, Beryl Boatman, and Wayne Manlove, and two probables (Lts. Wallace Bland and William Gregory). The only loss was the P-38 of Capt. Richard Decker, damaged by a 109. Decker was forced to ditch offshore. He was circled by some of his squadron mates who radioed a "Mayday."

Decker managed to get in his dingy, and spent a cold, wet miserable night in the Mediterranean. Early the next morning he was again visited by a flight of 49th P-38s. They dropped him some food and cigarettes, and circled him while awaiting a rescue aircraft. Eventually an RAF Walrus flying boat landed and took him aboard.

With the invasion of Sicily now just weeks away, the assembled weight of Allied air power hammered the island's defenses, with particular attention to airdromes. The *Luftwaffe* had elements of three veteran fighter groups on Sicily: JG 51, 55, and 77. The air attacks came from North Africa, Pantelleria—where airfields were quickly repaired and put in Allied service—and Malta. The air offensive against Sicily went on day and night, with RAF Wellingtons doing the night bombing

In his excellent autobiography *Messerschmitts Over Sicily*, *Luftwaffe* ace Johannes Steinhoff recounts the destruction wrought on both men and machines by the constant attacks. German radar could not give sufficient advance notice of the medium bombers that approached Sicily from low-level, and the massed formations of high-altitude B-17s—the Germans referred to them as Boeings—were usually escorted by P-38s, and were able to take considerable punishment. The 109s were relatively short-range aircraft, and by the time they had scrambled and climbed above 20,000 feet, and groped about in the high pressure haze to find the target, they only had time for one pass at the bomber formations, and limited fuel for high speed maneuvering with escorting P-38s. With aircraft being depleted in aerial encounters, and the survivors being ravaged by repeated airdrome bombings, the attrition rate was high among the defending fighter units.

In order to limit reinforcement from Sardinia, the Allies sent periodic missions to its airfields. One such mission on 24 June inflicted heavy damage near Alghero A/D. Five German Me 109s were destroyed in aerial combat by P-38s of the 37th Fighter Squadron. Victors were: George Wightman, Jim Hollingsworth, and John Garbett with one each, and Carl Rudder with two. Probables were credited to Robert Wilson and Ken Waldron, and damaged 109s were credited to Rudder, Wilson, and John Joyce. Lt Harold Alexander was missing in action.

Retuning to Sardinia on 28 June, along with B-26 bombers and P-38s of the 82nd Fighter Group, the 14th Fighter Group encountered Me 109s over Milis A/D. Joe Miller bagged two, and his 48th Squadron mate Jerry Stidham downed one. Wallace Kennedy was credited with one damaged. 49th Squadron pilots who scored were: Lloyd DeMoss with two kills, and John Harris with a probable and a damaged 109. The 14th Group had no losses.

On 30 June the 14th went to Sardinia once again, this time escorting B-17 heavy bombers. Their appearance was not contested, and they suffered no losses.

The 14th had yet another station change. Between 1-2 June 1943 they began moving from Telergma, Algeria, to a new base at El Bathan, less than 20 miles from Tunis. In this location, near the northeast tip of Tunisia, the P-38s were closer to Sicily by one hour flying time.

When the group began flying missions once more, the invasion fleet for Sicily was gathering, and the incessant air attacks on that island had just about destroyed its air defenses. Sorties over Sicily in the first week of July netted only one Me 109, credited to Lt. Marlow J. Leikness of the 49th Squadron. On the following day it was better hunting, as the beleaguered *Luftwaffe* lost many fighters to the swarming air legions. Richard Campbell and Richard Atkinson of the 37th contributed a kill and a probable to the day's bag.

On the night of 9 and 10 July a great Allied armada approached Sicily. A fleet of C-47 transports preceded it, air-dropping the first troops of operation HUSKY. British and American amphibious forces, supported by an intense naval bombardment, came ashore at dawn between Syracuse, on the east coast, and Licata, on the southwest. Lt. Gen. Bernard Montgomery commanded overall, but was with the British in the east. Maj. Gen George S. Patton led the American Seventh Army in the west. With first light, the skies over Sicily were patrolled by hundreds of prowling Allied fighters: Spitfires, P-40s, and P-38s.

During the first days of the invasion, hundreds of Allied aircraft threw an aerial blanket over the island of Sicily that prevented enemy aircraft from contesting the invasion and the columns moving inland. Airfields already cratered and littered with wreckage were bombed again until Axis squadrons began to use unnamed landing grounds that inflicted further damage to their aircraft. Nearly continuous patrols, resembling foxhunts, sought the last of the German-Italian fighters. Between 9 and 11 July AAF fighters downed 51 enemy fighters, mostly Me 109s. The 14th Fighter Group shared in the destruction:

1st Lt. Richard Campbell, 37th Sq	1/0/0
2nd Lt. Richard Atkinson, 37th Sq	0/1/0
1st Lt. Marlow Leikness, 49th Sq	3/0/0
2nd Lt. Harold Harper, 49th Sq	1/0/0
2nd Lt. Wayne Manlove, 49th Sq	3/0/0
2nd Lt. Lothrop Ellis, 49th Sq	1/0/0
1st Lt. William Hanes, 48th Sq	1/0/0
2nd Lt. Albert Barber, 48th Sq	1/0/0
Total	11/1/0

Pilots of the 14th fighter Group, flying repeated sorties averaging 2 1/2 to 3 hours, also attacked enemy troops and vehicles with bombing and strafing missions. The frenzied operation was not without loss. During the missions of 10 July the 49th Squadron lost three pilots killed. Lt. Sidney Booth went down on a dive-bombing mission when his flight was jumped by 109s. Lt. Wallace Bland was strafing when his plane was struck by flak. He was seen to leave his P-38, but is believed to have struck the tail, as his chute did not deploy. In the same low-level action, Lt. Allen Knepper's aircraft was also struck by flak and crashed. Harry Crim (37th) remembered the front line patrols:

"We'd fly a combat air patrol over the battle line, carrying a 1,000 lb general purpose bomb and a belly tank. We patrolled the front line in radio contact with forward units to defend against air attacks, and to provide bombing and strafing support to the ground troops. From about 3,000 feet up we'd fly up all the roads leading to the front, and hassled with German Panzers quite often. One of our flights caught four tanks at a crossroad. They dive-bombed and heavily damaged all four. One that had been knocked over on its side had an aggressive gunner, and as our eight planes worked in a gunnery pattern on the tanks he put holes in seven of them. He didn't knock anyone down, but he was sure doing some good shooting."

Capt. Jim Stitt recalls the battle damage that the strafing missions were inflicting on the P-38s:

"They came back now and then looking like woodpeckers had worked them over. The only thing we could do to keep the planes ready for another quick mission was to throw a patch of some kind over the holes, hang the bombs, reload the ammunition, charge the guns, and send them back out. We handled the patching with stuff called dope and fabric. At low altitude, where we didn't need the turbos, we could get away with it. When the low-level combat demand slacked off a little bit our sheet metal people, headed by S/Sgt. Stan Hill, would come in and put on a neat metal patch with flush rivets to replace our glue and fabric."

The last *Luftwaffe* units, with a worn handful of aircraft, flew to Italy on 11 July. Their ground echelons fled toward Messina in every manner of vehicle, frequently attacked enroute by Allied fighter-bombers.

From Italian bases, German and Italian air units continued to contest the air over Sicily in an effort to aid the trapped ground forces. The German Army was conducting a fighting retreat toward Messina, where they hoped to be evacuated across the narrow straits to Calabria, on the toe of Italy.

14th Fighter Group pilots flew repeated daily sorties supporting Allied ground forces, and occasionally were engaged by enemy fighters. On 12 July, over central Sicily, the 48th Squadron ran into a mixed force of German and Italian aircraft, shooting down three (by Lts. John Saum, Daniel Africa, and Sid Weatherford) and damaging two more. Lt. Robert Herman was lost. His P-38 was seen to crash into the sea.

The next morning, while the 48th was strafing a motor convoy in Sicily, Lt. Jerry Stidham was hit by flak and killed in the crash of his P-38. Later that day, the 48th again encountered a mixed flight of enemy fighters. F/O Jack Homan downed a 109, and Lts. Yarberry and Robertson claimed one probable and one damaged. Lt. Donald Lister failed to return from this mission.

Lt. Herbert J. Walker (37th Squadron) inaugurated flights to Sicily on 13 July. Wounded while strafing enemy ground forces, he landed at the recently liberated Licata A/D for medical attention.

The Allied armies in Sicily were rapidly driving north, and with ample short range P-40s and Spitfires available to support the ground forces, the 14th Fighter Group was released from tactical duties, and began to range out to Italy on fighter sweeps and strategic bomber escort.

On 17 July P-38s of the 1st and 14th Fighter Groups conducted their deepest penetration yet, escorting bombers to attack railroad yards at Naples. The Italian response to this incursion was meek; only a handful of enemy aircraft were sighted. Wayne Manlove (49th Squadron) managed to get a few rounds into a Macchi 202 for a damage claim.

During an 18 July air-sea rescue mission over the Tyrrhenian Sea, between Italy and Sardinia, eleven P-38s led by Capt. Herbert Ross encountered a swarm of Ju. 52 transports. Eight pilots downed fifteen of the tri-motored Junkers. The victors were as follows:

Capt. Herbert Ross, 48th	2
1st Lt. Sidney Weatherford, 48th	2
F/O Jack Homan, 48th	2
1st Lt. Donald Leighton, 48th	1
1st Lt. Orson Smith, 48th	1
2nd Lt. Richard Jennings, 48th	1
2nd Lt. Lloyd Hendrix, 37th	4
2nd Lt. Paul Wilkins, 37th	2

Once again, the 14th Fighter Group was assigned to strategic operations, escorting medium and heavy bombers to Sardinia and Italy. Through the end of July and into August 1943 the group had no substantial engagements with enemy aircraft during these escort jobs, although they ranged as far north as Naples.

The 14th made another station change from El Bathan to a marginally better field at St. Marie du Zit, some 45 miles from Tunis. It had been a major base for enemy air units, and turned out to be a scrounger's heaven. Jim Stitt, 37th Engineering Officer, recalls the treasures of du Zit:

"We liberated German and Italian motorcycles by the dozens. I had a big German BMW, and it was a dandy. I rode it all over the area. We also had German half-tracks and German Jeeps [*Kubelwagens*]. The only problem was that when the Germans left they booby trapped and mined the area. And yet, if you knew what you were doing, you could get out there and scrounge equipment, avoiding the explosives.

Old Harry Crim was pretty good at finding that sort of thing and deactivating the bombs, as he had been in the infantry before aviation cadets, and knew how to locate mines. He'd spot a likely place for a mine, and he'd poke around with a wire until he located it, then he'd defuse it and throw it away. He and Wightman did that

The 37th Squadron salvage crew poses with Hanna's P-38 in the Sahara. (Fields)

Lts. John Wilkes (left) and Harry Hanna. (Norman

Arabs join the scavengers around Hanna's wreck. (Fields)

work. I can't tell you how many motorcycles they blew up, but they managed to stay alive in the process."

Flying B-17 escort to Naples on 1 August 1943, the 14th Fighter Group was up for over four hours. A few Italian aircraft intercepted the bombers, but fled rather than engage the P-38s. Capt. Carl Rudder (37th Squadron) managed to destroy a Macchi 202 for his fifth victory. The following day the 14th escorted medium bombers to Sardinia, and ran into aggressive 109s and Macchi fighters. In the swirling fight that followed the group destroyed or damaged seven while protecting the bombers. Claims were as follows:

Capt. William Hanes, 48th	1/0/0
1st Lt. Joe Miller, 48th	0/0/1
1st Lt. Orson Smith, 48th	0/0/1
2nd Lt. George Barcak, 48th	0/0/1
1st Lt. Lothrop Ellis, 49th	1/0/0
1st Lt. Carroll Knott, 49th	2/0/0

On 4 August the group escorted B-26 bombers to targets in southern Italy, and again encountered a mixed force of German and Italian fighters. A major dogfight ensued, in which the 14th downed eight enemy aircraft for certain without loss. Individual scores for the mission were as follows:

Maj. Forrest Barker, 37th	1/0/0
2nd Lt. Richard Atkinson, 37th	1/0/0
2nd Lt. Robert Highsmith, 37th	1/0/0
2nd Lt. Edward J. Lynn, 48th	0/1/0
1st Lt. Beryl Leikness, 49th	1/0/0
2nd Lt. Beryl Boatman, 49th	0/1/0
1st Lt. Anthony Evans, 49th	2/0/0
2nd Lt. Carroll Knott, 49th	2/0/0
2nd Lt. Wayne Manlove, 49th	0/0/1
Totals	8/2/2

A B-26 escort mission to Marina de Catanzaro, Italy, on 5 August was unopposed. However, on the return trip Lt. Lloyd Hendrix (37th Squadron) pulled too close to the bomber formation, and one of the tail gunners, harboring rumors of the Axis having captured a P-38, fired a warning shot. Hendrix veered away, then, thinking he had been recognized as friendly, began to resume his close formation with the B-26s, and was fired on again. This time his plane went down, and it is believed that he was killed.

Successive bomber escort missions for the 17th, 319th, and 320th Bomb Groups' B-26 Marauders followed through mid-August, yielding little opposition.

A few replacement pilots had arrived, and one of them (Lt. Walter Brower of the 37th) recalls his first combat mission—nearly fatal, but mostly embarrassing:

"It was a B-26 escort on 8 August. Fortunately it was a medium altitude flight, because I had a faulty oxygen mask and suffered hypoxia [oxygen deficiency]. I thought I was flying great formation, but later learned that I was all over the sky."

On 13 August the P-38s visited Rome for the first time. As Italian fighters menaced the B-17s, Lt. Russell Moomaw shot down a Macchi 202, and Lts. Jim Hollingsworth and Bob Gardner each damaged one. Flying time was five hours.

On 16-17 August, as the Allied armies of Patton and Montgomery closed in on Messina, large contingents of the enemy succeeded in escaping across the straits to Italy. German and Italian units had performed a masterful Dunkirk-like retreat and evacuation under an umbrella of flak, taking advantage of the hours of darkness. During the preceding week over 100,000 men, along with vehicles, tanks, and artillery crossed to Reggio Calabria, or ports further north. The entire 2nd Panzer Division with all its armor escaped to Italy to fight another day.

The 48th Squadron was on a fighter sweep along the southern coast of Italy when intense, accurate light automatic weapon fire was encountered. Lts. Jack Tarr and Harold Texter, flying at low altitude, were both hit and seen to crash offshore. An extensive Air-Sea rescue search the following day found only a German fighter pilot who had been downed several days earlier.

On 19 August the group made up part of the escort for a force of 162 B-17s. The heavy bombers hit a railroad marshalling yard near Foggia, on the eastern side of Italy. The raid was met by a concentration of some 70 enemy fighters that waded into the bombers. The 14th was heavily engaged, and Lt. Jack Moak (49th Squadron) was shot down. He bailed out successfully and was taken prisoner. However, the group scored heavily against the mixed force of German and Italian fighters:

Capt. Richard Decker, 49th	1/0/0
2nd Lt. Walter Hoke, 49th	1/0/1
1st Lt. Harold Harper, 49th	1/0/0
F/O Herbert Hickman, 37th	2/0/0
1st Lt. Jim Hollingsworth, 37th	1/0/0
2nd Lt. George Barcak, 48th	0/0/1
1st Lt. Don Leighton, 48th	1/0/0
Totals	7/0/2

As the war progressed, AAF commanders became increasingly intrigued with the long-range capabilities of the P-38, and escort missions of heavy bombers became the 14th's specialty, no doubt to the delight of the shorter range tactical fighter outfits. Harry Crim discusses the unique nature of the long-range, high-altitude escort sorties:

"The B-17 would cruise-climb so that they reached bombing altitude about half an hour or 45 minutes before initial point. We just stayed in the vicinity, as the B-17 was a slow flying bum to escort. At 24,000 feet they indicated about 120 mph, and we needed about 160 for maneuver capability. When the Fortresses reached their base altitude we would climb up to our escort altitude, and set up a zigzag pattern back and forth across the lead bombers so that our 160 matched their 120.

The Germans would have us on their radar about an hour or more before we got to the IP. You could hear it in your headset.

About 15 minutes before the IP you could expect the first probing attacks.

Usually the 109s would arrive in gaggles of ten to twelve, pull into a trail formation about 3,000 feet above our fighters, and just follow along. Every now and then one or two would dive vertically through the fighter formation. They'd start shooting at about 200 yards, and might fly right between you and your wingman. All you could do was kick some rudder and make them guess where you were going. When the Germans would build up their ratio to about five or eight to one they would get more aggressive. One might come down to our level and sit out there about 300 feet away, slide his canopy back, and wave at you. Sometimes a green pilot would try to turn out and take a shot at him, but the German would only bob up about 50 feet, and the green pilot would then have to correct for that maneuver. About that time two or three of the German's friends would be punching little round holes in the rookie's P-38. It's amazing to consider that this happens, because you just got through telling the new fellow that it could happen, and he goes ahead and suckers anyway.

By this time the bombers are in the flak, and we have a general free for all. You stay in for a time, and then plan to break out when your gas reaches a predetermined critical level. You do your breakout and go home.

At first our tactics called for us to hit the deck from altitude. When we did this, as many as six or seven 109s would follow each airplane down. We were fast enough that they couldn't catch us until we were on the deck and throttled back. But we had to do this in order to have enough fuel to get home. Then they would come in on our tail in a shallow dive. When one got within shooting range, we'd break right and stay in the turn until the overtaking 109 broke out to the left, which they'd do. Then we'd turn back to course and wait for the next 109. If the German followed you around the right turn, we would just pull it tighter and tighter until he had to break out. Right down on the deck he couldn't take the chance of snapping in a stall.

Later we developed a different and more effective way to break out of a fight with a 109. We learned that the 109's best climb speed was about 110 mph, and ours was 160. So if you were out of gun range of a 109 at the same altitude and the same speed, you turned your tail on him, put on 2,800 rpm and all the throttle you could stand, and held the airspeed at 160. In less than two minutes, if he followed, you could make a 180-degree turn and an overhead pass at him. Usually he'd half-roll and go home, leaving you to do the same.

Usually on the way back to base we'd start a rate of descent that would get us to 10,000 feet at the same time that that oxygen ran out, which it usually did."

During a 20 August long-range escort of B-17s to the marshalling yard of Aversa, north of Naples, enemy fighters were seen in the distance but did not attack. Some of the sixteen P-38s became separated from the formation as they returned to St. Marie du Zit. When the last of them landed after nearly five hours in the air, one was missing and presumed lost. Thus began the saga of Lt. Harry Hanna.

The 37th Squadron pilot had called his base for a fix. The direction-finding device was a crude navigational aid, an old SCR 522 radio fitted with a homemade direction antenna. Hanna was given a directional heading but never landed. "What happened," according to Freeman Fruge, a communications technician, "is that he had already passed over the base, not realizing it because of clouds, and our equipment had no way of telling if the pilot was coming or going. So the heading we had given him took him away from the base and into the desert." He finally ran out of fuel and belly landed deep inside Tunisia.

In the rough landing Hanna injured his knee, and an Arab who found him at the crash site helped the crippled pilot for some 12 miles to the small settlement of Sidi bou Zid. There were no telephones in the native village, so the camp at St. Marie du Zit, hearing nothing further, assumed that Hanna had been lost north of the field, probably over water. Several days had elapsed when Hanna came riding into the St. Marie du Zit camp on a burro, dirty and aching, but no worse for his ordeal.

With Hanna's directions, a crew from the 37th Squadron set out to salvage the P-38, and that was another adventure. Sgt. Lester F. Fields of the "scrounger squad" describes the scene and the salvage operation:

"The plane was exactly as the pilot had left it. The hatch was closed and, wonder of wonders, his parachute was still in the seat. Parachutes were hot items on the black market.

It was late afternoon by the time we got to the site, so we got busy while we still had some daylight left. While we were working, the sheik of a nearby tribe arrived riding his donkey with bodyguards on either side of him. He brought with him water, watermelons, chicken, hot sauce, and bread. The bread was round and flat like a pancake, and the idea was to tear off a piece and dip it into the hot sauce, and then suck the sauce out of the bread.

A little later another donkey came loaded with grass mats. Each was about twelve inches thick and eight by eight feet in area. Piled on each other they became beds. It was just like sleeping on a feather bed. Near dark the Arabs began collecting certain bushes that were used for a fire. While we were sitting around the fire one of the Arabs began brewing tea in a small teapot that held the equivalent of about two glasses. The only thing they would take from us was sugar for the tea, as they liked it thick and sweet like syrup. You can imagine how many pots of tea we had to brew, as there were 12 of us and about 20 of them, each of us getting a shot glass of tea.

Meanwhile, the Sheik was telling us about their life and customs. He spoke in French, and Leo Desrochers and Freeman Fruge translated... His power in the tribe was absolute—life and death over everyone. He was responsible to only one man, the Bey of Tunis. He told us everything that was going on in the war, most of which we had no knowledge. How he knew all this out in the middle of nowhere was beyond me....

The next day we began to strip the wreck in earnest. The Arabs came in handy, as we needed all the manpower we could get. To drop the landing gear we had to get under the wing and lift it as high as we could, then back a truck under the wing to hold it there while we cranked down the landing gear.

The serious parts that we were after were tires, wheels, and the leading edges of the wings containing the intercooler, batteries, radio, guns, ammo, instruments, and so forth. In order to remove the leading edge of the wing we had to remove uncounted Phillips head screws, and as I removed them I threw them away. One of the natives kept picking them up, and by the time I had the intercoolers off he brought me about eight pounds of screws in his robe.

On the last day, having stripped all we could from the plane, the Arabs brought us their favorite dish as a goodwill gesture. It was a rice dish called couscous. Everyone dipped his hand in the same pot and ate it with his fingers. As we loaded the truck they asked if they could have the rest of the plane, and were delighted when we gave it to them."

Freeman Fruge said that parts supply was always a major problem, and "stripping wrecks was our most important and reliable source of spares." Other members of the team who "harvested" spare parts from Hanna's P-38 (#82) were: Crew Chief T/Sgt. Floyd Osborn, Robert Hamaker, Julius Friend, Cecil Reineck, Clarence Brown, and Harold Durham. In post war years, the men often reminisced about their salvage effort, wondering if the skeleton of old #82 was still out there on the edge of the Sahara.

The exact same sort of reciprocal direction incident had occurred some three months earlier in the war when a 376th Bomb Group B-24 named "Lady Be Good" had over flown its base on the Libyan coast and come down in the desert. After waiting for a rescue that never came, the ten-man crew began to walk north toward the sea and died one at a time. The Liberator and the skeletons of the crewmembers were not found until some 17 years later.

On 23 August a dozen P-38s of the 14th Fighter Group escorted a Catalina of the 1st Emergency Rescue Squadron to look for downed airmen just south of Naples. While at low level in broken clouds, the OA-10 was jumped by several 109s that came out of the overhead layer. The Catalina fell in flames before the P-38s could react. When they did, Lt. Robert Gardner (37th) downed one Me 109, and F/O Harvey Scott damaged another. However, Lt. Russell Moomaw failed to return from the action. He was last seen headed into clouds, coolant smoking, with a Messerschmitt on his tail.

The Germans and Italians had created a major airdrome complex on the plains of Foggia, near Italy's eastern coast. Some of the fields had been bombed from high altitude by B-17s of the Twelfth Air Force. But on 25 August the 14th Fighter Group visited the Foggia complex twice. First, thirty-six P-38s escorted B-17s on a high-altitude bombing raid. That mission was followed by a low-level strafing mission involving two dozen P-38s. The latter mission caught several transport aircraft on the ground and destroyed seven Ju. 52s. The Axis defense of its vital air bases was surprisingly lame. Captains Herb Ross and Joe Miller of the 48th each shot down a Macchi 202, and all aircraft returned. Lt. Walter Brower, a pilot in the 37th Squadron, provides his memory of the historic sweep:

"I'm not sure who was leading the group, but he made his turn early, thinking he had spotted Cape Manfredonia. When he realized his mistake he did a 180 turn right through the formation. I never understood why no mid-air collisions took place. This radical maneuver alerted the Italian coastal artillery, and we were not only avoiding each other, but also the geysers of water that the shells threw up.

We made landfall at the cape, and spread out to cover as much territory as possible in the Foggia plain. At minimum altitude in a short time someone transmitted, 'Don't shoot him 'til he gets in the air.' At that time no credit was given in the MTO for aircraft killed on the ground. Shortly after that a Junkers 52 flew from behind a line of trees in front of me—a 90-degree deflection shot. I dropped the nose and fired a short burst into the wing root area, while at the same time another flight opened fire on the same target. They were at my level, converging on me from the right about 45 degrees. Had I continued, I would have flown into the fire of several P-38s. My sole interest at that time was survival, and I went full power, stood the aircraft on its tail, and immediately found myself all alone, and at a vulnerable altitude. As I recall, I did a lot of jinxing at full power and ended up going home alone. I never learned who the unfriendly friendlies were that nearly eliminated me that day."

Tunisia was littered with military equipment abandoned by the Germans and Italians. This was a factory fresh Focke-Wulf 190, apparently disabled before it could get its unit markings. It shows evidence of being picked apart by souvenir seekers. (USAF)

While escorting B-17s of the 97th and 99th Bomb Groups to Capua A/D on 26 Aug 1943, the 14th encountered 45-50 enemy fighters climbing to engage. With a rare height advantage, the P-38s dove on them, breaking up the attack, and the enemy aircraft scattered. But not before four Me. 109s were downed by 48th Squadron's Captains Herb Ross, Joe Miller, Sid Weatherford, and Lt. Edward Yarberry.

Maj. Gil Bright was appointed Executive Officer of the 14th Fighter Group, and a new arrival, Maj. William Leverette, took over command of the 37th Squadron. About the same time, Maj. Burton McKenzie assumed command of the 49th Squadron.

Lt. Gen. Carl Spaatz, Maj. Gen. Jimmy Doolittle, and Brig. Gen. J.H. Atkinson visited, dispensing congratulations to the group for a job well done. They also delivered a case of Canadian Club whiskey for each squadron, along with the news that some tours of duty would have to be extended because of the slow pace of arriving replacement pilots.

With the advanced base on Sicily, the 14th was increasingly called on for deeper forays into Italy. Successive missions on 27, 28, 29, and 30 August were all five hour plus sorties, one to a point north of Rome. The P-38s encountered heavy opposition at some targets. Claims were as follows:

1st Lt. Dick Campbell, 37th	2/0/1
2nd Lt. Paul Wilkins, 37th	0/1/0
1st Lt. Robert Gardner, 37th	1/0/1
2nd Lt. Don Clark, 37th	1/0/0
2nd Lt. John Joyce, 37th	1/0/1
Maj. Herb Ross, 48th	1/0/0
2nd Lt. Albert Barber, 48th	0/0/1
2nd Lt. Harrison Hannah, 48th	0/0/1
Capt. Lloyd DeMoss, 49th	1/0/0
1st Lt. Carroll Knott, 49th	1/0/0
1st Lt. Anthony Evans, 49th	1/0/0
2nd Lt. Aldo Deru, 49th	0/1/1
2nd Lt. Donald Leiter, 49th	0/1/0
2nd Lt. William Becker, 49th	0/0/1
F/O William Brewer, 49th	0/0/1
F/O Charles Richard, 49th	2/0/0
2nd Lt. Fred Bitter, 49th	0/1/1
2nd Lt. Harry Vogelsong, 49th	0/2/0
2nd Lt. Eugene Churchill, 49th	0/0/2
2nd Lt. Herman Kocour, 49th	0/0/1
2nd Lt. Albert Bess, 49th	0/0/1
2nd Lt. John Sandifer, 49th	0/0/1
Totals	11/6/14

Three pilots were missing in action after this flurry of missions. F/O Earl Dion (37th Squadron) was seen with both engines smoking and Me109s in pursuit as he parachuted. F/O John D. McCoy (49th) was shot down by enemy fighters southwest of Rome. Major Gil Bright, spotting a Macchi below him, went into a vertical dive from 24,000 feet. At 13,000 feet, in an apparent compressibility dive and totally out of control, he passed the Italian fighter. The tail of Bright's P-38 came off at about 7,000 feet, but he managed to parachute successfully, becoming a prisoner of war.

The human toll in Africa was also heavy. This is a military cemetery where the Germans buried friend and foe alike. (Dickenson)

5

The Invasion of Italy

A hit by 20mm AA opened up the wing of this 14th Group P-38. Repairs in North Africa were conducted in the open. (Stitt)

The liberation of Sicily and its airfields brought many Allied air units within easy striking range of Italy. The 14th Fighter Group established an advanced airbase at Lentani, Sicily, and from there they continued their bomber escort missions, and were prepared to support an invasion of the continent.

This time the Allies launched a three-pronged amphibious exercise to establish beachheads on the mainland of Italy; the most obvious place for an invasion was at Reggio Calabria, just across the Straits of Messina, where landings took place on 3 September 1943. Axis forces had anticipated this operation. More of a surprise was the simultaneous widely separated landings of 9 September at Toronto in the southeast, and at Salerno, just 20 miles from Naples, on the west coast. The latter was the largest, and was accompanied by an airborne assault.

In the three days preceding the Salerno invasion, the 14th sent sweeps over Naples area airdromes to eliminate enemy aircraft that might pose a threat to the combined British-American fleets. During the period 6-8 September they definitely destroyed ten enemy planes in aerial combat with no losses. Claims were as follows:

Maj. Carl Rudder, 37th	1/0/0
Capt. Robert Wilson, 37th	1/0/0
1st Lt. Beryl Boatman, 49th	1/1/1
2nd Lt. Wayne Blue, 37th	0/0/1
Maj. Herb Ross, 48th	1/0/0
2nd Lt. Albert Barber, 48th	1/0/0
2nd Lt. Harrison Hannah, 48th	1/0/0
F/O Fred Haupt, 48th	2/0/0
2nd Lt. John Harris, 49th	1/0/0
2nd Lt. Wilbur Vardel, 49th	1/0/1
2nd Lt. Harry Vogelsong, 49th	0/0/.5
Maj. Burton McKenzie, 49th	0/0/.5
Totals	10/2/4

On 7 September, 37th Squadron ground crews had a brush with disaster when a fire started during aircraft refueling. Although the inclination would have been to run from the nearby loaded

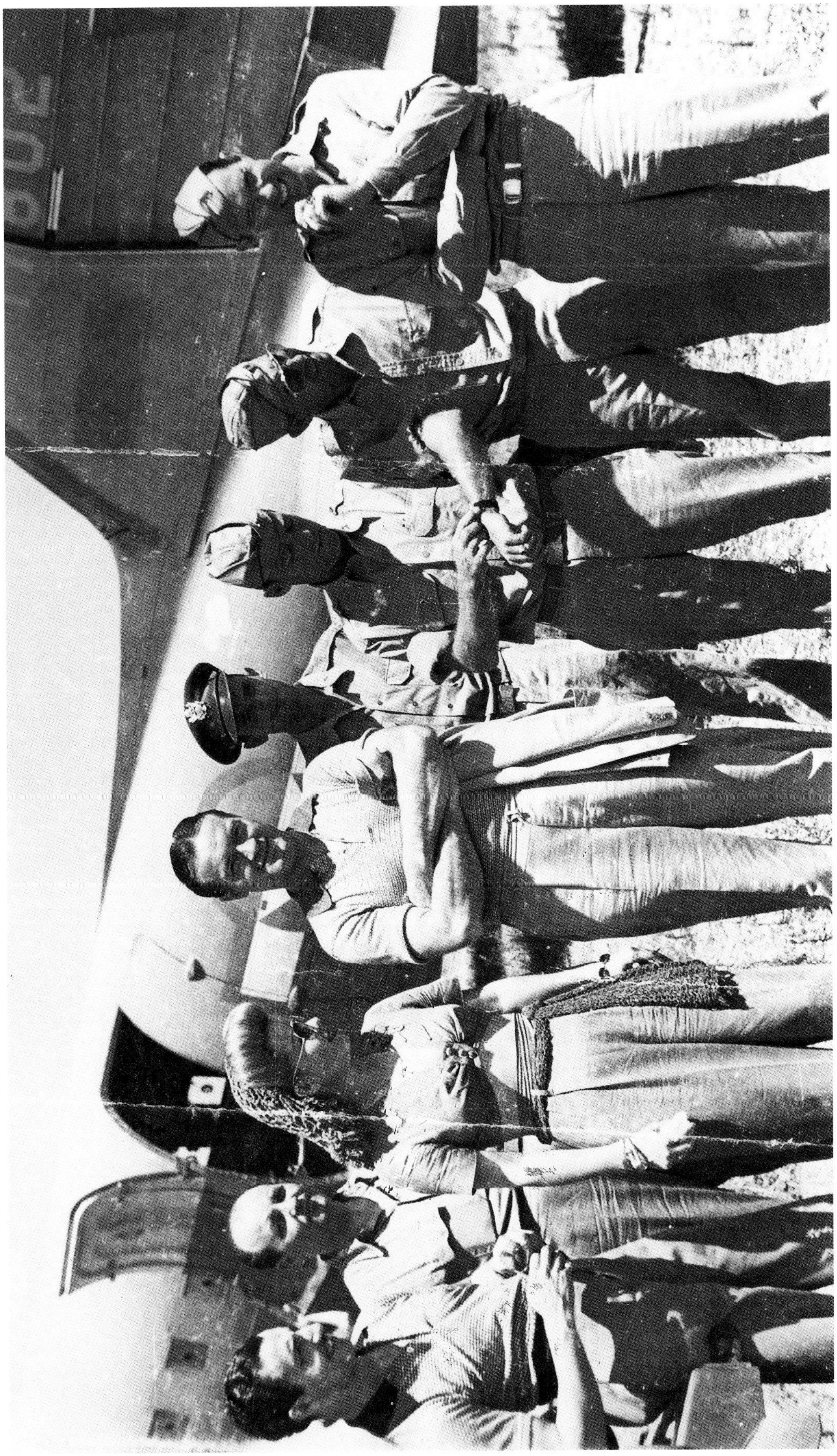

The King of the USO, Bob Hope, and his troop showed up on every battlefront in WW II. (L. to R.): Jerry Collona, unk., Frances Langford, Bob Hope, Gil Bright, Troy Keith, unk., and Robert Glendenning. (Stitt)

A Big Friend, with obvious tail damage, gets shepherded home by a 14th P-38. (Keel)

gasoline truck, S/Sgt Sparlin Conine played a fire extinguisher on the flames until they were successfully doused. Both the truck and a P-38 were saved, and Conine was later decorated with the Soldier's Medal for his bravery.

When the Salerno invasion was launched from sea and air on 10 September, 14th Group pilots flew as many as three sorties per day, covering the invasion fleet, and providing close support ashore. Harry Crim describes the missions:

"We did convoy and beach patrol using 1,000 lb bomb GP bombs and belly tanks. Here we were under control of a Navy ship just offshore for defense, and with forward units for ground work. Flying from Sicily, we could stay in the area for two or three hours if we didn't run out of ammunition."

A pair of famous Royal Navy aircraft carriers was providing additional close cover for the Salerno invasion: *H.M.S. Illustrious* and *H.M.S. Formidable*. Each had a contingent of American-made Grumman F4F Wildcat fighters, called Martlet by the British. Somehow the joint command had neglected to inform the joint air services of their presence. When a pair of 37th Squadron P-38s encountered Martlets near the fleet, the stubby, radial-engine fighters were first thought to be Focke-Wulf 190s. Walter Brower and Hank Alm spotted the strange looking aircraft, and Walter relates the story:

"We were vectored into a real bee hive in the Salerno-Naples area: aircraft of all types from the deck to 20,000 feet. Hank jumped a bogie that was at about 2 o'clock from his position and started throwing lead. I realized it was an F4F and yelled, 'Don't shoot, it's a Grumman!' Hank apparently thought I said 'German,' and continued firing until I yelled again.

We understood that the Navy type got back to its carrier, but when the arresting hook caught him it practically pulled the tail off the bird. Fortunately for the Navy jock and Hank, the majority of the rounds were behind the cockpit. Hank couldn't complain about his accuracy."

At the 14th Group's advance base at Lentini, Sicily, the aviation gasoline depot was made up entirely of 5-gallon fuel cans. (Dickenson)

Concurrently with the invasion of Italy, the Italian government surrendered to the Allies. Some 225 Italian Air Force crews flew their aircraft to Sicily, where they joined the Allied cause. It was a welcome but confusing turn of events, as the Germans merely took control over all those portions of Italy that they occupied, and the war continued.

In between the Salerno close support sorties, the 14th received a special request from General Bernard Montgomery for an unusual mission. 1st Lt Harry Crim tells the tale:

"On the morning of 13 September I was awakened early by a messenger from operations, who told me to take my wingman and an element and report to the British intelligence officer there. The four of us consisted of Lts. Dick Campbell, Leonard Conkle, Ken Waldron, and myself. We flew the twenty miles to Syracuse and landed. A British staff car was there to meet us, and took us to a 'desert' tent area in an olive grove. There were a series of tables laid out with detailed situation maps of Southern Italy. General Montgomery greeted us, and told us what he wanted.

The British had a landing in progress on the lower east coast of Italy near Taranto—a light armored force—and needed to know what the Germans had in the way of defenses, particularly heavy armor on the east coast of Italy, between the heel of the boot and the Foggia Airdrome complex. The mission was to fly low level to the heel of the boot, and then to follow the main coastal road some 180 miles north, to where the highway went inland to Foggia. Then we were to return by the inland parallel route to the heel and then back to Syracuse. In short, we were to sweep the area and report on armor, artillery, AA guns, and troop dispositions. We were given clipboards with maps so that we could easily record sightings as they appeared.

We decided that two of us would collect data and two would ride shotgun. To accomplish this assignment, we decided to fly at 500 feet and at 160 mph with two planes on each side of the road, and the other two line abreast separated by about one-half mile. This would give the data collectors time to see and record everything that was in the open, and the ability to see under camouflage nets. Also, this put us in a position where we could protect each other's tail. The whole coastal area is lightly populated, with a number of small villages having only one and two story buildings. We also agreed that in the event we were jumped by fighters we would head east out into the Adriatic, and then, after shaking the attack, come back to the coast and finish the mission.

We topped off our tanks and took off, flying at low level, and skirted the coast at the toe of the boot, then flew by compass across the Gulf of Taranto. We made landfall on the heel, picked up the highway at Maglie, and headed north. It was about noon, with a clear sky and no haze. We progressed up the coast, making notes of what we saw. Every now and then we would get some small arms fire or a shot from a Bofors AA gun, but they didn't seem to

The Axis retreat from Sicily forced them to abandon inoperative aircraft before they could be repaired. Left: A Me 109 at Lentini. Above: A Macchi 202 at Lentini with RAF insignia. (Crocker)

An unknown pilot sorts out his gear at Lentini landing ground, Sicily. (Keel)

Lt. Col. Oliver B. "Obie" Taylor joined the 14th as Commanding Officer when Troy Keith completed his combat tour. (USAF)

be able to react quickly enough to be effective, so we continued on at the planned speed.

Because we were flying toward a major German-Italian air force complex at Foggia (about 15 airfields), we became more and more tense as we passed Barletta and turned inland, some 20 miles from Foggia. There was a lot of air activity. We kept seeing pairs of fighters, but they didn't see us at our low altitude. Finally we passed Cerignola and reached the Carapella River, which was our turnaround point. We swapped sides and flew back down the inland road net, making notes as we went. Needless to say, we not only looked at the ground, but we watched the air, particularly to our rear. No one attacked us from the air, for which we were thankful.

Returning to Syracuse at low level, we landed and were taken to Montgomery's headquarters, and spent the better part of two hours going over our findings with his staff. The landing was made, and the British dashed north and took the entire coastal region up past Bari to Barletta. It was a major gain in territory and position, and hastened the breakout at Salerno.

The high command must have thought the mission was successful, as each of us was awarded a Distinguished Flying Cross."

The 14th had begun routinely raiding Foggia's airfields, and on one such mission on 18 September they caused heavy damage. Strafing one of the satellite fields, twenty-three P-38s destroyed seven Ju. 88s, two Me. 110s, one Fw 190, and one Me. 109 on the ground. They also shot up a 88mm gun battery, several trucks, and a number of railroad freight cars. Lt. John Garbett (37th) bagged a Ju. 52 that was taking off as the raiders arrived. Lt. Martin Faust (49th Squadron) was hit by intense, accurate medium AA, and perished in the crash of his plane.

A routine command change occurred near the end of September, as Lt. Col. Troy Keith headed home, turning over leadership of the 14th Fighter Group to Lt. Col. Oliver B. Taylor (nicknamed Obie). As a first lieutenant Keith had been a charter member of the 14th in 1941. At the time of his relief he had flown 50 combat missions.

October 1943 brought with it adventures to new and exotic places for the group. Some they would visit frequently, while others they hoped never to see again. On 3 October the 14th had its first mission to the Island of Corsica. Enemy aircraft were sighted, but attempted to evade combat. Lts. Don Clark and Robert Highsmith, and F/O Harvey Scott of the 37th engaged fleeing Me. 109s, and claimed one destroyed and two damaged.

The following day, a contingent of the group departed for a special detached assignment to Gambut, Libya, near the Egyptian border. Lt. Col Taylor led twenty-three P-38s and seven C-47 transports. The latter were loaded with seventy-seven members of the ground echelon, along with supplies and equipment. The purpose of the exercise was to provide air cover to Royal Navy ships in the Greek islands near Turkey. The RAF lacked fighters with suitable range, and the 1st and 14th Fighter Groups each provided some long-range Lightnings.

C-47 transports airlifted 14th ground crews to and from Gambut, Libya. (Mauss)

Lt. Bob Gardner (37th) saddles up at Lentini, Sicily.

Operations in this region had been the brainchild of Winston Churchill, who had long been enchanted with the idea of invading Europe through the Balkans. President Franklin Roosevelt and the Joint Chiefs of both Britain and the U.S. had vetoed such an invasion, but Churchill, nonetheless, had placed a small force on Leros, near fabled Rhodes. The British had counted on a garrison of Italian troops to help them, but the Italians had no more stomach for war, and the British troops were isolated, and coming under German air attack. The Royal Navy was sent to protect or extract them, and found that it needed air protection that only the U.S. Army Air Force could provide.

On 4 October the 14th Fighter Group's air echelon located one of Gambut's landing grounds just as darkness was settling and landed, albeit at the wrong field. Harry Crim used his landing lights to get down, then kept them on to give some guidance to others, and maintained radio contact from his cockpit. One P-38 was damaged, with its nose gear wiped out, and the outfit spent a cold night at the wrong place. They got sorted out the next day, and found their temporary base a dirty, dusty piece of earth on the edge of the desert.

Jim Stitt, part of the ground echelon airlifted to Gambut, describes the living and operating conditions:

"We pitched our pyramidal tents with the sides rolled up and had C-rations.... The dust and sand were flying everywhere and into everything. It got by the dust filters of the engines. It got into the radios and the actions of our machine guns. The sand also got into our food and water.

When we got back to Tunisia we had to change every engine on every plane that had been there. Sgt. Fruge had a lot of repair work to do on his radios, and Lt. Ives and Sgt. Scharn had to pull all the guns and blow the sand out of them."

Lt. Col. Taylor described the assignment at Gambut:

"Our combat operations, which finally began on the 6th, were entirely planned and controlled by the British; we merely advised

The wind blew and the dust flew on the shore of the Mediterranean and the edge of the Sahara at Gambut. P-38s took off eight abreast to limit the dust clouds that caused taxi and departure accidents. Landing was another matter. (USAF)

them of our capabilities and limitations, made pilot and aircraft assignments in the specified numbers and, of course, flew where we were told to go. All in all, our operations over a four-day period totaled two fighter sweeps and thirteen fleet patrol missions—a total of about 110 sorties."

The Royal Navy squadron in the southern Aegean Sea consisted of one cruiser and four destroyers, and was frequently far from its reported position, and was reluctant to respond to radio requests for location from the 14th. The first three days of missions were relatively uneventful, except for some occasional flak. However, 9 October turned out to be an extraordinary day in the annals of the 14th Fighter Group. Maj. Bill Leverette, CO of the 37th Squadron, takes up the story as he related it in part to author-historian Eric Hammel:

"At 10:30 hours I departed with nine P-38s from Gambut. Shortly after takeoff, two planes were forced to return because of engine trouble, leaving four P-38s of my Red Flight, and three of Lt. Wayne Blue's flight.

We went all the way on the deck to stay under German radar on Crete, and sighted the British warships at almost exactly noon, fifteen minutes before our scheduled rendezvous. The ships were approximately 15 miles east of Cape Valoca, on the Isle of Scarpanto. I contacted them on their frequency, and was told that they were under attack. I could see that the cruiser was smoking from the stern.

I led my P-38s up to 6,000 feet, and began a counterclockwise circle around the ships, just out of range of any nervous AA gunners. As we reached 8,000 feet, halfway through the first circuit Lt. Homer Sprinkle called out, 'Bogies at one o'clock!' They were slightly higher, and approaching the ships from the northwest. And there was a cloud of them.

I immediately added power to gain speed, and climbed and changed course to pass slightly behind them in order to make a positive identification. It quickly became clear that they were Junkers 87 Stuka dive-bombers. There were 25-30 of them in roughly three flights. Before we could get within firing range, even though we were closing fast, several of them tipped over in their dive-bombing runs on the British ships. At least one hit was scored on a destroyer, which broke in two and began to sink.

As we closed on the Stukas, I told Lieutenant Blue to hold up his flight momentarily in case there were more enemy aircraft—possibly fighters following the first group. With my flight I immediately closed on the left rear quarter of the Stukas. Before the Germans knew we were there, I attacked the nearest enemy

Some of the 14th pilots on detached service at Gambut discuss the "Stuka Shoot" of 9 October 1943 near Leros island, in the Aegean Sea. (USAF)

An example of the German Ju 87 Stuka dive-bomber the 14th caught attacking British warships near Leros island. This captured aircraft bears RAF markings. (Lambert via E. McDowell)

airplane ahead of me with a short burst of the fifties from about twenty degrees. Smoke poured from the engine....

The Stuka pilots who still had bombs jettisoned them as soon as the shooting started. Several of my pilots also reported later that they thought a number of Stukas jettisoned their fixed main landing gear as well.

I broke to my left, and attacked a second Stuka from his rear and slightly below. After I fired a short burst from about 200 yards, this airplane rolled over and spiraled downward steeply.

I turned back toward the formation, and as I did, I saw both Stukas I had already fired at hit the water. I opened fire at a third just as the rear gunner fired at me. His gun immediately ceased firing, and I saw the pilot bail out, although I did not see his parachute open. The gunner did not jump.

Continuing on into the enemy formation, I attacked my fourth Stuka from an angle of 30 degrees. I observed cannon and machine gun fire hit its engine, and I saw large pieces of cowling and other parts fly off. The engine immediately began smoking, and the Stuka nosed down.

I broke away upward to my left, and reentered the enemy formation. Another Ju. 87 was nearly dead ahead, and I opened fire again with my cannon and machine guns. The canopy and various parts of this Stuka flew off, and a large flame shot out of the engine and along the wing root. The gunner jumped out of the airplane as I passed it.

Continuing into the formation, I was approaching the sixth target from below and to his left rear, but on a crossing course that would take me over to his right rear. Since I was closing too fast, the only way I could bring my guns to bear was to roll the P-38 tightly left to an almost inverted attitude. I opened fire at very close range, and saw concentrated strikes on his engine, which began to smoke as I broke away. My element leader, Lt. Harry Hanna, saw this airplane hit the water.

Maj. Bill Leverette, 37th Squadron, led the seven-plane flight on 9 October 1943. (USAF)

Lt. Homer Sprinkle was killed in the crash of a two-seat P-38 at St. Marie Du Zit, shortly after participating in the Gambut operation. His passenger, who also died, was Sgt. Julius Friend. (USAF)

I attacked the seventh Stuka from straight behind and slightly below. The rear gunner fired at me, but stopped as soon as I fired a short burst. As it nosed down slightly, I closed to minimum range and fired a full burst into the bottom of the engine and fuselage. Some Ju. 87s were thought to have wooden props, and this one acted as though its prop had been shattered, as it abruptly and uncontrollably pitched downward. It seemed that I was instantly looking broadside at a nearly vertical Stuka directly in front of me. Intuitively I jammed the control yoke forward as hard as I could. I heard and felt a thump as I went by the falling aircraft. Looking back, I saw what I feared was my left tail section falling, but it was intact. The falling object was probably the Stuka pilot or gunner catapulted out of their seat by the negative G force of the plunging airplane.

Later on the ground, the damage to the edge of my propeller blades proved to be very light. We reasoned that my props had cut into the tail of the German's rudder and fin. Fortunately, he fell faster than I did, or I would have plowed headlong into him.

We pursued the survivors until they passed over the Isle of Rhodes, and several were shot down during the chase."

The attack and pursuit had only lasted about fifteen minutes, but apart from saving the British Navy squadron further damage, the seven P-38s had downed a confirmed sixteen Stukas, and a Ju. 88 that appeared on the scene at the wrong time. Credits for the aerial action were: Major Leverette, seven victories and two damaged; Harry Hanna, five destroyed and one probable; Homer Sprinkle, three destroyed and one probable; Lt. Robert Margison, one Ju. 87; and Lt. Elmer LaRue, one probable. Lt Wayne Blue destroyed the twin-engine Ju. 88. All of these participants would ultimately be awarded decorations; Leverette would receive the nations second highest award for valor, the Distinguished Service Cross.

Roll Call in the mud and cold outside Bizerta before embarking for Italy. (USAF)

There was no further action for the Gambut contingent. But before they could depart, they were engulfed by a Sahara sand storm. Lt. Col. Taylor was briefing for another mission when it hit:

"Stepping out of the tent, we saw this awesome dark mass approaching us from the south. We were told that it was a sirocco, and that we were looking at a solid wall of sand."

Taylor considered trying to take off on instruments, but even with ground crews leading the aircraft it was impossible to miss chuckholes. He got lost on his motorcycle heading for the RAF command post:

"From about 1400 through the day when Jerry had the sky to himself was an agonizing experience for me," Taylor recalled, "as I listened to fleet reports on the radio requesting any possible assistance, as they were under heavy attack. I seem to remember that they lost one more destroyer. I heard those radio calls all night long in my sleep"

The Gambut unit had barely reassembled back at St. Marie du Zit when the crash of a two-seat P-38 took the lives of Lt. Sprinkle and Sgt. Julius Friend. Their comrades buried them at the American Cemetery in Tunis.

As September wound to its conclusion, the 14th resumed its long-range escort duties, reaching as far north as Torino, in the shadow of the Alps. It was a seven-hour mission, with no opposition and no losses

On the ground, the Germans evacuated Sardinia, and by 3 October had left Corsica. About this same time Allied ground forces entered Naples, on the west coast of Italy, and Foggia on the east. German land and air units were in retreat, but not beaten.

With Foggia in British hands, advanced units of various Allied squadrons, including the 14th Fighter Group, began to take over the former enemy facilities. The move of the bulk of the ground echelon and its supplies and equipment was by ship from Bizerta, and took some 25 days. The ultimate destination for the group was Foggia Satellite Field No. 7 at Triolo, Italy, near San Severo. Living accommodations had gotten rather comfortable after three months at St. Marie du Zit, and now they had to be recreated at the new base. Walter Brower recollects on the shantytown nature of the housing:

"I lived in tents throughout my tour with the 14th Fighter Group. There was some improvisation in Italy. We used the sides

The harbor of Naples and fabled Mount Vesuvius come into view. (USAF)

An Italian warship sunk in Naples harbor. (USAF)

of drop tank crates to give rigidity to the tent walls. White bricks had been procured for the floor, but I'd rather not say how that happened. A couple of marble slabs made a good entryway, and the door was the entry door from an Italian passenger rail car complete with window.

Our fuel supply was 100 octane aircraft gasoline fed from a fuel tank set high on a frame outside the tent. The control was a needle valve in the floor where a half brick was missing. The stove was standard GI. The burner was a curved copper fuel line with small holes about an inch and a-half apart, buried in an inch or so of sand. It was a fairly efficient unit, however, it would hardly meet OSHA standards today. The night the pilots arrived at San Severo we were setting up our tents under blackout conditions. Some group apparently fired up their stove a bit early, and the mechanism wasn't stable. At any rate, the tent went up in flames, and all we could think of was that we hoped no *Luftwaffe* raiders were in the area, as we made a great target."

With more replacement pilots arriving, the last of the old North Africa hands completed their combat tours and departed for the States. The group also began receiving J-model P-38s, the latest in the Lockheed Lightning line.

Escort missions during late October were scattered about Northern Italy, but there was no contact with the *Luftwaffe*. Although November escort missions ranged as far as Marseilles, France, in the west, and Sofia, Bulgaria, in the east, German air defenses remained dormant.

Despite the lack of opposition, another casualty occurred without explanation on 9 November when Lt. William Green went missing between Corsica and Sardinia.

It wasn't until 1 December 1943, during a mission to Torino, that the 14th encountered enemy aircraft when Lts. Warren Jones, William Becker, and George Monnier tangled with Messerschmitt 109s, downing two and damaging one.

On the following day near Marseille, Lts. Ronald Ashmead and John Meidinger (48th Squadron) shot down a pair of FW 190s.

The ground war in Italy had witnessed great gains by the Allies since the September landings. But the Allied armies had bogged down in the mountainous narrow portion of Italy between Gaeta (just north of Naples), on the Tyrrhenian Sea, and Termoli, on the Adriatic—approximately 70 miles. Crossed with rivers, the high country favored defense, and the German Army had dug in there to make a winter stand on what was labeled the Gustav Line. The battle of Italy had become a stalemate.

Late in 1943 the Germans drew their Italian air defenses further north to concentrate on major industrial, supply, and communications centers, partly in recognition of reverses on both the eastern front and in Italy. However, it was also due to the proximity of growing Allied air power in southern Italy, and new bases being built in Sardinia and Corsica. The *Luftwaffe* might cope with strategic bombing and the few long-range escorts (the three P-38 groups), but they could not also deal with the 10 short-range fighter-bomber groups of the AAF, and the many squadrons of the Desert Air Force now in Italy.

The Allied air forces countered with a new strategy for their combined air forces. Starting about 1 November 1943, the Twelfth Air Force and the RAF's Desert Air Force became the tactical air arms supporting the joint ground forces. They retained most of the short-range fighters: Spitfires, Hurricanes, P-39s, P-40s, P-47s, and A-36s. The mission of attacking Germany's strategic war production was assigned to the newly formed Fifteenth Air Force. All six four-engine bomber groups then in theatre, as well as the three long-range P-38 groups (1st, 14th, and 82nd) likewise were absorbed by the new Fifteenth Air Force.

On 7 December the 14th was directed to escort a pair of C-54 transports enroute from Alexandria to Morocco—an unusual assignment. The passengers included President Franklin Roosevelt and Prime Minister Winston Churchill bound for the historic Casablanca conference. Thankfully, the operation was conducted without incident.

14th Fighter Group missions during late December took them deeper into enemy territory, and there *Luftwaffe* resistance stiffened. On 14 December squadron leaders Maj. Bill Leverette and Maj. Burton McKenzie shot down a pair of Me 109s over Greece. Three days later Lt. Paul Wilkins (37th) bagged another near Lake Veneta. However, Lt. Eugene Pitre was seen to go down in the same action.

It was not until 20 December during a B-17 escort mission to Eleusius A/D, near Athens, that the 14th had a major engagement. Lt. Col. Oliver Taylor, leading the group and flying with the 49th Squadron, provides his recollection of the event:

"Having quickly designated which portions of the enemy formation each of my flights would engage, I swung my flight in behind our target, a flight of four 109s—a *Schwarme* in enemy parlance. At the proper moment I lined one of them up in my sights, pressed the trigger button, and nothing happened!

In an instant I realized that the pilot whose ship I had borrowed for the day had the various buttons on the steering column rewired to suit his own personal predilections—a not entirely uncommon practice among our seasoned pilots. My frustration led to a lapse in my judgment, and to a disregard of my own policy on impulsive straying, as I stayed with the Germans until I could discover which buttons fired which guns. They simply were not going to be allowed to get away scot-free just because of something so stupid as my fouled up button situation. During my frenzied search for the right gun control combination I did damage one Jerry and probably destroyed another.

Having by now solved the button mystery, and finding myself practically on top of another Me 109, a bit above him and to his right rear (but unaware that he was nearly in a vertical dive), I caught him with a long burst of both machine guns and cannon full in the cockpit area. It quickly filled with smoke; the shattered canopy and a side panel flying off, and the shells visibly exploding inside, were evidence that he was mortally wounded. He seemed to be disintegrating in slow motion.

Just a split second later, I realized that I was unable to maneuver my ship, and that I was heading straight down. Everything that followed must have occurred in a matter of seconds: no response to the controls; increasingly violent vibration of the entire ship; extreme bucking of the steering column; airspeed indicator showing a blurred 550 mph as the needle seemed to spin by; and altimeter indicating less than 10,000 feet, as its needle also was doing a spinning act.

Somewhere along the line I literally had flashes of unrelated events pass before my mind's eye, including childhood scenes. Just before I blacked out I recall deciding to try retarding my throttles and pushing forward on the wheel, but don't know whether I did so or not. At about the same instant it occurred to me that I must have been getting awfully close to the ground, considering speed and altimeter lag.

I woke up to find myself pointing straight up, hanging on my props, just beginning to stall at about 20,000 feet. Recovering from the stall, I saw my squadron flying beautiful formation just above me. Getting a firm grip on myself, I very calmly, in well-modulated tones, told them where I was, and to make a 360 degree turn and form on me. They acknowledged my call and proceeded to try. The next thing I knew P-38s were whizzing by me, followed by a call: 'Colonel, if you would raise your flaps it would be easier for us to form on you.'

I not only had my flaps extended, but also was just barely making flying speed. With a very red face I cleaned up the ship, was joined by the others, and headed for home."

Claims for that date are as follows:

Lt. Col. Oliver Taylor, 14th	1/1/1
2nd Lt. Recard Wilhelm, 37th	1/0/0
2nd Lt. Eugene Stahl, 37th	1/0/0
2nd Lt. Robert Hoke, 49th	1/0/0
2nd Lt. Herbert Schoener, 49th	1/0/
2nd Lt. Robert Seidman, 49th	3/0/1
F/O Jack Lenox, 49th	0/1/1
Totals	8/2/3

There were no losses on the Athens mission, but it was a close thing, according to Walter Brower:

"We were doing a normal weaving to maintain our position with the B-17s somewhere over the Adriatic. Bob Margison crossed over and came uncomfortably close. It thought he was playing his usual tricks, trying to shake me up, but I did not communicate with him. He did this a second time, and on the third crossover I had to change altitude to avoid him. I still remained off the air, maintaining radio silence. On his third crossover Bob continued on his turn, was slightly descending, and continued on toward the Yugoslav coast, but his flight turned and kept formation with me.

Bob disappeared, and we went on the mission and returned. When we got back to our home station he met us. It turned out that he had an oxygen leak, and had passed out from hypoxia. When he woke up he was at 4,000 feet cruising up the Yugoslavian coast, with flak bursting all around him. He was fortunate to be flying the P-38, as nothing else would have been that stable and maintained level flight under those conditions with no hands on the controls."

The group ended 1943 operations on 30 December, escorting heavies to Verona, Italy. Many enemy fighters were seen at a distance, but only a handful attempted interception. The 48th Squadron engaged, and Lt. Harrison Hannah was seen to destroy two, while Lt. Robert Cowie claimed another. However, Hannah was forced down and became a POW, and Lt. Chester D. Erwin did not return, and was listed as missing.

There was no mission scheduled for the next day, so despite recent losses, the group celebrated the arrival of the New Year with spirits, food, and all the fixins. Since landing in North Africa thirteen months earlier, they enjoyed marginally better living accommodations, and could see solid progress in the war. The establishment of periodic visits to rest camps in Alexandria, Egypt, and on the Isle of Capri also brightened the outlook of both officers and enlisted men.

Triolo airfield, Italy, was the final home for the 14th Fighter Group. Some buildings even had walls. (USAF)

The first hard liquor ration for enlisted men finally made it through the supply pipeline from the States. Celebrating the event are these 37th members (L. to R.) Standing: Stuart Ballard, Tom Long, Louis Volbrecht, Lester Cummings, and Ray Lyle. Kneeling: Willard Luce, Charles Clark, Earl Steininger, and Dayton Stone. (USAF)

6

Going Deep

In January 1944 the 14th Fighter Group escorted bombers deep into German occupied Europe whenever the weather would permit. There were just 17 escort missions, and some of those hit secondary locations, or had to return because of heavy weather obscuring the primary targets.

On 3 January, during an escort mission to Villa Perosa, in Northern Italy, a flight of Macchi 202s fell on the 49th Squadron and escaped before there was time to react. (All of the Italians had not surrendered, and some continued to fight on the fascist side.) Lt. David Fritz was missing after the brief encounter, and Lt. L.D. Wells of the 48th did not return for unknown reasons.

On the 7th the group conducted a long escort to Weiner-Neustadt, Austria, in company with the 1st Fighter Group. The target was the Messerschmitt assembly plant. The *Luftwaffe* contested this raid, and while most of the action was with the 1st Group, the 48th Squadron managed to get in its licks on a pair of Me 110s. Capt. George Richards, leading the squadron, claimed a probable, and 1st Lt. Max Wright got a kill.

A major engagement took place on 10 January, when 25-30 aggressive defenders (possibly including Bulgarian Air Force pilots) attacked heavy bombers under the 14th's care. The encounter took place as the raiders approached Sofia. Claims for the day were as follows:

P-38 Lightnings weave contrails as they escort a formation of Fifteenth Air Force B-24s to Vienna. The vapor trails and the winter cloud layers often obscured targets. (USAF)

Lt. Col. Oliver Taylor, 14th	1/0/0
1st Lt. Robert Margison, 37th	1/0/0
2nd Lt. Paul Wilkins, 37th	1/0/1
2nd Lt. Cleveland Tatum, 37th	1/0/0
1st Lt. Tom Smith, 37th	0/0/1
2nd Lt. Dale Tyler, 37th	0/0/1
2nd Lt. Robert Cowie, 48th	1/1/0
2nd Lt. John McGuyrt, 48th	0/1/0
2nd Lt. Ralph Sebring, 48th	0/1/0
2nd Lt. John Grant, 49th	1/0/0
2nd Lt. Robert Hoke, 49th	1/0/0
2nd Lt. Roy Liles, 49th	1/0/0
1st Lt. Harold Simmons, 49th	1/0/0
2nd Lt. Jack Schetler, 49th	0/0/1
2nd Lt. Rupert Sparks, 49th	0/0/1
Totals	9/3/5

The group suffered one loss: Capt. George Richards, leading the 48th Squadron, dove to the assistance of a P-38 that appeared to be in trouble and was not seen again. Another pilot spotted a parachute that might have been Richards. Lt. Melvia Waldrop had an engine shot out, but soldiered on, and made it back the near 450 miles to San Severo.

The escort mission of 13 January was of relatively short duration, the target being Rome's airdromes. The *Luftwaffe* had been absent from this area for some weeks, but showed up in force when the 14th Fighter Group appeared. Both German and Italian fighters engaged all squadrons. In the swirling dogfights that followed 2nd Lt. Ralph Sebring got one the hard way in a head-on collision with a 109. The German ship disintegrated, and Sebring's P-38 lost ten feet of one wing. He was last seen losing altitude and fighting to control his ship, and there was some hope that he might have bailed out. However, he did not return. Claims for the day were as follows:

Lt. Cleveland Tatum, 37th Squadron, and his P-38. (USAF)

2nd Lt. Paul Wilkins, 37th	1/0/0
2nd Lt. Cleveland Tatum, 37th	0/1/0
2nd Lt. Kenneth Sullivan, 37th	1/0/0
1st Lt. Nathaniel Raley, 48th	1/0/0
2nd Lt. Michael Wagner, 48th	1/1/0
2nd Lt. George Wood, 48th	0/1/0
1st Lt. Ray Kopecky, 49th	0/1/2
2nd Lt. Robert Hoke, 49th	0/.5/0
2nd Lt. Herbert Schoener. 49th	0/.5/0
F/O Orse Brewer, 49th	0/1/0
2nd Lt. Ralph Sebring, 49th	1/0/0
Capt. Frank Collins, 49th	1/0/0
2nd Lt. John Forrest, 49th	1/0/0
2nd Lt. Roy Liles, 49th	0/0/1
2nd Lt. James Riley, 49th	0/0/1
Totals	7/6/4

The 14th returned to Austria on 16 January. The target of the bombers was Klagenfurt. Lt. Enoch Lemon recorded details of the mission in his diary:

"Just as we neared the target, someone broke radio silence by calling, 'Ten bogies are making passes at the rear bombers!' The bombers were strung out for miles. We did a 180 turn, and headed back along the bomber stream. Next thing I knew there were Me 109s all around us.

Smitty [1st Lt. Thomas Smith] was leading Blue Flight. Blue and Green flights made a turn into some 109s that were coming in on us from behind. As I completed the turn, I saw Smitty pull up into a climb and get in a short burst on one of the Germans. It just kept coming, and rammed Smitty with its right wing between the tail booms, knocking out his right engine....

The 109 went end over end, with pieces of airplane and wings falling apart. Coolant black smoke and flying objects were in evidence as the 109 rolled over into an inverted spin... Smitty was streaming white coolant and heading down."

The duels between the *Luftwaffe* and the 14th continued until withdrawal, and in the final analysis, the 37th Squadron had downed two 109s (Smith's "victim," and one by Lt. Morgan Mathews), and probably destroyed another two (by Lts. Porter McClaine and Robert Zimmerman). However, there had been a price to pay. Lt. R. F. Williams (48th Squadron) was seen bailing out of his aircraft and entering a cloud base, while Lt. Ken Stahl spun in and was killed. Several other planes were shot up, but made it back. Lt. Tom "Dub" Smith should have been a casualty after his mid-air collison with the Messerschmitt. Here he recalls the seemingly dire situation:

"I looked around and could see enemy fighters all around, and realized I would be very easy pickings, so I decided to jump out before any of them had a chance to make a pass at me. I told my flight that I was bailing out, and would see them after the war.

I released my canopy, unfastened my safety belt, rolled down the window, and took off my helmet and oxygen mask. Realizing that a map might be handy, I started pulling them out and discarding until I found one of the area I was in. I then pulled off my gloves to make it easier to grab the ripcord, and started practicing grabbing it to make sure there would be no slipup when I bailed out.

I was making 100 to 110 mph, losing about 300 feet every 15 minutes when I discovered that by turning into the dead engine I could gain altitude at a rate of about 200 feet every time I made a 360-degree turn. I continued this maneuver all the way back, as I did not want to get below 10,000 feet for a possible bailout....

My good engine was running at an extremely high temperature, and when it got real hot and started detonating, I pulled the throttle back to cool the engine. But then I would lose altitude. I had little hope that I would ever get back, and was looking for a likely place to belly land.

During this whole time it was necessary for me to hold the rudder with both feet, as it required too much pressure for me to hold it with just my left foot....

My right rudder tab control cable had been severed. It was so cold that my feet and hands were nearly frozen. The radio was also frozen....

Finally, I came out over the coast near Fiume at about 10,000 feet, and it seemed as if everyone down below started opening up with 88mm flak. Having no canopy, I could hear the 88 rounds go past me, and heard it when it burst, often much too close. The air became so turbulent it almost turned my ship over. To escape the AA I did a diving turn into a cloudbank. However, at about 150 mph the elevator started vibrating so badly that I feared it would rip off. When I slowed and came out of the clouds I was hidden from the AA gunners by a lower cloud layer.

After banging on my radio with a jackknife it lit up like a pinball machine, and I managed to call for a homing and, getting a reply, I decided it was worth taking a chance to get back to base. I told them to be ready with a Walrus [ASR aircraft] if I had to land in the sea. [Adriatic].

When I was within 20 miles of the Italian coast my good engine quit due to overheating. I called in my position and started to let down. At about 6,000 feet the engine caught again, apparently having cooled off.

From any angle, the P-38 of Lt. Thomas "Dub" Smith is a wreck that should not have flown, but he brought it back from Austria on 16 January 1944 after a mid-air collision with a Me109. (USAF)

P-38s of the 14th Fighter Group carried an array of ordnance depending on the mission:

250-pound high explosive bombs. (Stitt)

1,000-pound high explosive bombs. (Mauss)

Fragmentation clusters above disposable fuel tanks. (USAF)

I called the homing station again and told them it must be my lucky day, as the engine had started again, and said that I was going to try to make the base. I came over the field at about 4,000 feet, still undecided if I would bail out or belly land. When I tried to release my feet from the rudder the ship would go into a steep bank and spiral to the right. That would throw me into the path of the elevator if I jumped.

I made a practice landing in the air, reducing speed to 90 mph, and saw that it might be possible to hold up the nose sufficiently to land if I didn't bring it in too fast."

Here Dub Smith's story is taken up by Flight Surgeon Dr. William Curtis:

"I was standing down on the line under the control tower when the boys yelled at me to come up. Smitty was on the radio, saying that he was approaching, and in about five minutes he showed up at the east end of the runway barely visible....

The cross piece [horizontal stabilizer] between the two tail booms was fractured, and the ends were hanging at odd angles. He was about 1,000 feet.

I talked to him, and said that I thought he would be better off to go up a little and jump. He replied, 'I'm afraid I wouldn't get out. I'm going to bring it in on the belly.'

He went back out over the town of Foggia, turned back, and made a perfect belly landing on the grass. By the time I could go from sitting in the ambulance to where the plane stopped, he was standing at the side of his P-38 trying to light a cigarette. Gasoline was everywhere. I yelled at him to stop, then loaded him into the ambulance and let him have a cigarette."

On 20 January Lt. Arthur Duff had a mechanical failure, and he was forced to bail out over water near Nettuno, Italy. His dingy was seen inflated, but a search failed to locate the pilot.

For the entire winter the Allied drive in Italy had been stalled before the Gustav Line, a series of mountainous fortifications. In an attempt to break the stalemate, Allied strategists conceived an amphibious end run behind enemy defenses coming ashore on 22 January 1944 on low ground in the vicinity of Anzio, on the Tyrrhenian coast. The landings were generally unopposed, and for a time it seemed that the Allies had flanked the Gustav line and opened the road to Rome. But as beachhead forces advanced, German units holding the high ground struck back with unexpected ferocity. For a time it seemed to be another Gallipoli, as Allied units were first driven back, and then shelled heavily by enemy artillery.

In describing the tenuous military situation at Anzio, Winston Churchill said, "We had hoped to land a wildcat that would tear out the bowels of the Boche. Instead we have stranded a vast whale, with its tail flopping about in the water!"

Only Allied air and sea power prevented the Germans from overrunning the narrow beachhead. Short-range fighters of the U.S. Twelfth and the British Desert Air Force protected the air over the invasion fleet and the beachhead, while the long-range 14th escorted heavy bombers in striking airdromes in Italy, and even Southern France. However, the P-38s were eventually called on to conduct support missions in the Anzio area in an effort to stem the movement of German reinforcements that were threatening the slim bridgehead.

On 22 January P-38s of the 14th Fighter Group conducted strafing missions on the roads leading to Anzio. They destroyed many vehicles, but as usual, the low level work was subject to intense flak and small arms fire. Lt. John Lindstrom of the 48th was hit and forced to belly his P-38 in near Ajaccio. Lt. Paul Wingert of the 49th was hit several times, and seen to turn away from his flight toward Anzio. Here is his story:

"I knew from the way my ship jumped that I had been hit on the right side. I saw a big bump on top of my right engine, then a red glow coming out of the hole in the middle of the hump. There was an even bigger hole on the bottom, and smoke was pouring out. My hands did a war dance all over the cockpit, getting

Lt. Larry Mars, 37th Squadron. (Stitt)

Capt. Jim Stitt, Engineering Officer of the 37th Squadron, and later the 14th Group, astride one of his Lightnings. (Stitt)

everything to that engine shut off and the prop feathered. In those first few seconds I still hoped to save the ship. Just in case, I got all unfastened and ready to get out.

I was just getting the left engine going again and trimming the ship when smoke started to come into the cockpit. I immediately pulled the emergency canopy release and started to get out. However, I was going too fast, and the rush of air at that speed left me only part way out of the cockpit, and pinned me back against the rear of the canopy.

I managed to get partly back in the cockpit, and pulled the control column back to kill my speed, while at the same time I got my feet on the seat, so that when I slowed a bit I could give a kick and push with my hands. I remember faintly the fire starting to come up in my face just about that time. I left so quickly, I have no recollection of what took place until I realized I was falling headfirst. From then on, every little detail is very plain.

At first I was going so fast that my arms were pinned to my sides; then, as I slowed down, I reached up and gave the ripcord a terrific yank. It came clean out, and flapped around in the breeze, almost hitting me in the face. I waited for what I thought ought to be long enough for the chute to open, and then I wondered if it was stuck. The earth seemed to be coming up awfully fast....

The thing still hadn't opened, so I tried to pull the pack out... then it started to go out, and somehow the shroud lines got wrapped around my legs. I thought that that was about the end, and looked back to see a streamer of white flapping behind me. I was sure it was the end, and then the thing opened....

I lit right in an American camp and got a lot of razzing, because I landed almost in the chow line and just in time for supper."

The next day Lt. Col. Oliver Taylor led a mission north of the Anzio beachhead to hunt German traffic. The P-38s carried 1,000 lb bombs, and the first assignment was to hit a railroad bridge around Rimini. After the attack Lt. Enoch Lemon had a "hung" bomb. (One that would not release.) Despite heavy flak he decided to try a second run, admitting "this was a crazy idea." As he jinxed away from the target heavy AA fire from 88s began to bracket him and his wingman. They dove to the deck and managed to get away.

Oliver Taylor found little worthy of their effort as they cruised valleys at low level:

"I observed a column of thirty or forty animals—horses and or mules—and a few uniformed attendants moving along a narrow trail on the side of a mountain. The thought of attacking them had not even occurred to me. Just then a plaintive Texas drawl came over the radio, 'Colonel, please don't shoot the horses!'"

When the day of low-altitude, heavy flak was over, two 48th aircraft had landed at another base. Two more, containing Lts. Waldrop and Viertel, were missing, and Paul Wingert, hurt but alive, was being flown back to Triolo in a Piper Cub from the Anzio beachhead.

Recent losses had reduced the 14th Group's complement of aircraft so badly that only two squadrons were available for escort missions, so a contingent of pilots from the 49th Squadron was transported to England by B-17 in order to ferry back new Lightnings.

On 27 January 1944 the 14th Fighter Group escorted heavy bombers to Salone de Province Airdrome, France. Only 27 aircraft were operable, so the 48th Squadron stood down for the day. With

Lts. George Wood and Robert Hames (48th) collided over Triolo on 14 March 1944, the wreckage falling on the airfield. Both were killed. (USAF)

Lt. Col. Taylor leading the group, the rendezvous with the B-17s took place just off the French coast. 1st Lt. Walt Brower, leading the 37th Squadron, recalls the situation:

"As we approached the target we encountered cloud cover just below our altitude. The bombers were barely skimming under the clouds, and the group leader decided to go under the clouds. This concerned me, because I figured we would be good targets for fighters, and we knew they were in the area. So I did a 360-degree turn, picking up speed, and went under the clouds at a good rate of speed. Shortly after, sure enough, German fighters popped through a hole into the formation.

There was one German after another piling into the organization, and I remember meeting a FW 190 head-on. He rolled on his back just as he approached me, and I depressed the nose and fired, and never knew whether I got him or no, but I don't know how I could have missed him, because he was such a big target. I can't forget the pretty colors of the 190, blue and gray."

Lt. David Vann managed to get his battered P-38 back to Triolo despite a mid-air collision with a FW 190. (USAF)

T/Sgt Sparline Conine braved the flames from a crash to move a P-38. (USAF)

The action was fast and furious, P-38s and German aircraft flicking off shots. The 14th stayed near the bombers as ordered, and scored many hits, but few certain kills. Claims were as follows:

Pilot	Claims
Lt. Col. Oliver Taylor, 14th	0/0/1
1st Lt. Norm Jackson, 49th	1/0/1
2nd Lt. Robert Seidman, 49th	1/0/0
1st Lt. Robert Hoke, 49th	0/0/1
1st Lt. Herb Schoener, 49th	0/0/1
1st Lt. Walt Brower, 37th	0/0/1
2nd Lt. Morgan Mathews, 37th	0/0/1
Totals	2/0/6

The group lost two 49th pilots, Lts. Harry Greenup and James Riley, during the melee, and Riley was assumed killed. On the long return the group landed on Sardinia to refuel. The P-38s of Lts. Schoener and Grant were too badly damaged to continue on, and Lt. John Grant was treated for wounds received in action. The balance of the outfit returned to Triolo after a total logged time of over seven hours.

On 30 January the group saw some 20-25 enemy aircraft during an escort mission to northern Italy. But the *Luftwaffe* showed no inclination to tangle with the P-38s, banking away as the 14th turned into them. Lt. Max Wright (37th) managed to get a shot at a Focke-Wulf 190 and destroyed it.

On the last day of January 1944 the 14th was so short of aircraft—the 48th had just five operational—that it could only muster 26 P-38s for an escort mission to Klagenfurt, Austria. The Germans avoided combat, and there were no losses. Still the mission was a chore—five-plus hours of cold boring cockpit time. 1st Lt. Enoch Lemon, leading a flight in the 37th Squadron, committed his impressions to a diary:

"We went NE to Yugoslavia, then north to the target. We looked for all hell to break loose as we got near the target. Intelligence reported 50-60 plus enemy aircraft in this area, so we climbed to 29,000 feet. Boy it was cold as hell up there, and my electric gloves and boots did not work.

We stayed just below the contrail layer; that way, if anything tried to climb above us, we could see them. My hands and feet felt like chunks of ice.

About this time the 49th called out bogies. Everyone dropped tanks and got ready. We saw something down around the bombers, so we dived to 27,000 feet. But it must have been P-47s—they didn't try any attack—and we couldn't get close enough to tell exactly what they were. Single-engine though. Anyway, it was some warmer down there, and my little fingers began to thaw and sting.

The bombers hit the target, and we escorted them back. We had been all keyed up and nothing had happened. About halfway home—out over the water—we couldn't hold it any longer. The major [Leverette] started to dive slightly and climb, then began a 360-degree turn. I decided to do a roll with my flight while the major was in a turn and couldn't see me. Ha! It helped relieve the tension....

Doesn't look like I'll ever get a shot at anything, but I'm not bitching. There are plenty in the Klagenfurt area, so I may get more shooting in the future than I want."

Capt. John McGuyrt became 48th CO early in 1944. (USAF)

February 1944 was another month wherein bad weather limited flight operations, and made the living at Triolo unpleasant. However, the chow had improved, as local merchants began to work with the group, supplying fresh meat, butter, and eggs. Still, the unit history complained of 15-cent eggs.

Escorts for B-17s and B-24s continued, reaching out to Northern Italy and deep into Germany. Regensburg and Steyr were two of the targets. The *Luftwaffe* seemed reluctant to come to grips with these air raids, a few enemy aircraft were seen. February claims were as follows:

Lt. Col. Oliver Taylor, 14th	0/1/0
2nd Lt. Lawrence Mars, 37th	1/0/0
Lt. Col. William Leverette, 37th	1/0/0
1st Lt. Robert Margison, 37th	1/0/0
2nd Lt. Jack Harrow, 37th	0/0/1
1st Lt. Morgan Mathews, 37th	1/0/0
2nd Lt. Robert Cowie, 48th	1/0/0
1st Lt. Max Wright, 48th	0/1/0
2nd Lt William Schleich, 48th	0/1/0
Totals	5/3/1

There had only been one loss on the escort missions. 1st Lt. Donald McMahon, an RAF veteran who had flown a previous tour of 92 sorties in Spitfires, was shot down and declared missing after being hit by flak on 14 February. Enoch Lemon heard his radio farewell: "I'm going to have to belly this son-of-a-bitch someplace in the Po Valley. I'm okay. Will you feed Mike for me...I'll see you after the war." Mike was his dog.

During that same escort mission to Verona on 14 February, engines began to act up at high altitude. Enoch Lemon had gathered a series of cripples, and he himself was only able to use his left engine intermittently:

"As we were leaving the target area and heading home, I spotted a lone B-24 way below the other bombers. He was obviously in trouble.... Just as I turned to check on him I got a glimpse of something shiny way behind the Liberator—a closer look, and I spotted a pair of Fw 190s making a tail end pass.

I was mad by this time and all keyed up. I had a feeling maybe I wouldn't make it back, so I'd try and take as many 190s with me as I could before I went down.... I called on the radio to the others and broke around to intercept. Even if I was just on a single engine, I couldn't see them shooting down a crippled B-24.

So I turned into the right engine in a break in order to not waste time, and tried to roll over to the left for a pass. But she didn't want to move. I had to kick left rudder hard, and had aileron all over to the left. She started over, but by now I would have to make a diving turn upside down and pull like hell for lead. I was coming upside down, firing like crazy. I got hits on the lead FW 190, and when he saw me he was surprised—he just split-S'ed. I almost ran into the second one before he saw me, and he tried to split-S as I went by him in high-speed buffet and stall. The last I saw of them they were heading away in a split-S dive.... We saved the B-24."

The cold weather of Italy and the high altitudes needed to navigate over the Alps had created maintenance problems not previously encountered in North Africa and the Mediterranean. Jim Stitt, 37th Engineering Officer, explains:

"We began having trouble with high altitude engine operation due to the fact that our carburetor air intake temperature was so ungodly cold. On the new planes the intercooler doors had been moved from the wings down between the oil coolers, and they worked very well. In fact, they worked too well. The big new radiator had so much capacity that it could drop the carburetor air intake temperature down to the point that we were not getting good fuel vaporization. We modified our planes by installing intercooler doors. They were set in front of the intercooler to close off the passing of the air to control the temperature. Control cables were run through the radiator and worked off the flap motor. They worked just fine, and eventually we educated our pilots on the operation of the doors, and taught them how to maintain proper carburetor air inlet temperature.

We also had a problem of freezing oil in the oil coolers. That was kind of a sneaky thing, because when the oil started to freeze the oil temperature gauge would go up, and the natural reaction of the pilots was to open the oil cooler door a little more. If you did that, the additional air through the coolers would freeze the oil solid, and there would be no oil, so you could lose an engine very quickly. The pilots picked up on this very quickly, and eventually we operated our P-38s at high altitude without trouble."

The location of the P-38's gun camera was moved from the nose to an underwing ordnance pylon, as shown by M/Sgt. Chester Choate and Capt. Lee Ives. (USAF)

Lt. Enoch Lemon, 37th Squadron. (USAF)

Engineering officers and enlisted men similarly resolved other maintenance problems discovered during combat operations by the 14th Fighter Group, and their modifications were channeled back to Lockheed.

The few gun cameras that existed had originally been mounted in the nose of the gondola of the P-38. When the guns were fired, the vibration was such as to make the pictures almost worthless. Jim Stitt moved the camera to a location in the under-wing bomb shackle, resolving the vibration.

Similarly, a modification of the external auxiliary fuel tanks was found necessary. Under certain conditions of speed and attitude the detached fuel tanks could rotate back and upward, knocking a hole in the flaps as they left. The addition of sway braces resolved that problem.

Ground attack sorties were flown only on 10 February, as the 14th was assigned to dive-bomb various targets in central Italy. As was usually the case, the dangerous low-level operations took a heavy toll, one of the heaviest in unit history. Four pilots from the 48th were lost and believed killed: Lts. Raley, Dalrymple, and Darnold, and F/O Bowerman. Lt. Jackson Schetler of the 49th was also downed, but survived and returned the following day.

In March 1944 the ground campaign continued to be stagnant—the irresistible force vs. the immovable object. Allied troops held the Anzio lodgment, and had sufficient air and naval support so that they could not be expelled. But neither could the Germans be budged from the high ground overlooking Anzio, or from the Gustav line. These seemingly impregnable enemy defenses ran from the Adriatic Sea to the Tyrrhenian Sea near Gaeta, and then north around the Anzio lowlands. The hinge of the German line was the heights around the town of Cassino. Above the town loomed the ancient Abbey of Monte Cassino. Occupying the monastery, the Germans looked down on Allied forces and, despite repeated and costly infantry assaults, could not be dislodged. The Allied air forces were called on repeatedly to bomb the town and the adjacent monastery, and the 14th Fighter Group flew four short escort missions from the Foggia area to put a top cover over the bombers. These were pleasant milk runs, but frustrating, because the fighter pilots could see the bombs making rubble of the Cassino area, but still German soldiers held out deep in the ruins.

March had begun with the same weather patterns that had afflicted flight operations in February. Missions were assigned by Fifteenth Air Force field orders; 14th Fighter Group held briefings; pilots nervously anticipated the sortie, then inclement weather over the target area caused a cancellation. 1st Lt. Enoch Lemon (37th Squadron) recorded the frustration attendant to such operations:

"7 March 1944: We had started on three missions before we finally got this one. We were briefed early this AM, and didn't have any breakfast. Mathews woke up at 5:00 and said it was time to get up, and I decided to stay in bed until he called the other boys.... I woke at 5:45, and Matt said that briefing was at 6:15, so we rushed around and got dressed, and we were briefed and took off at 7:25 without eating.

Col. Oliver Ford, 14th Group, was lost on 15 April 1944. (Jackson)

The target was sub pens at Toulon, France, escorting B-17s, and refuel at Sardinia on return. The weather seemed pretty good compared to other times; it was about 8/10 overcast from 5-7,000 feet. We went out below 8,000 feet to Corsica, where we rendezvoused with the B-17s. I was leading green flight, and as we met the fortresses at 17,000 feet, my tail-end Charlie [last man in flight of four] fell out. We hit contrails at 22,000 feet, so we climbed to 25,000 and began weaving over the bombers. By this time they were almost to the IP [initial point] when they turned and started back due to weather and clouds, which were too bad for bombing.

We went on toward Toulon for a while, looking for trouble, when we heard the bombers call and say that an FW 190 was playing around near them. As we started hunting for him, my element leader said that he had to go home, possibly on one engine. I asked his wingman to accompany him, and that left me alone....

I rolled out and rejoined my squadron, and saw the 190, with Leverette trying to sneak up behind it. I decided not to try to turn into him for fear he would piss off before Leverette could get him, and would let him go unless he dove at me. He did, then I broke into him at just the right instant, for he could not get a lead on me, nor I on him. He rolled trying to get a lead, but went over me, and as I turned back he split-S'ed.

I could see him plainly, with black crosses on the wing tips—one of Goering's boys. We followed him down a ways, but he went into a cloud and out of the contrails, so we lost him.

The trip back was uneventful, and we did not refuel at Sardinia. We hit the coast of Italy a little north of the lines and got some heavy caliber flak, but got out of it in a hurry. I had a darned good time, because I was flying by myself on the way home, and was all over the sky, diving doing wing-overs and making passes at the rest of the squadron. Ha! I was full of piss and vinegar, and had to get it out of me some way. Logged 6:00 today."

Lt. William White (37th) and "Pistol Packin' Mama." (USAF)

On 14 March disaster visited Triolo, when a pair of P-38s collided at low altitude. 2nd Lts. George Wood and Robert Hames were both killed in the crash of their aircraft. As a result of the crashing aircraft, the concussion knocked down several ground

P-38s of the 14th Fighter Group make a low level pass over Triolo air base. (Stitt)

"Big Bruiser II" was Wayne Blue's P-38, and then Porter McClaine's before it was lost over Rome. The 37th ground crew is (L. to R.) T/Sgt. Marcel Tomlin, Crew Chief, and Sgt. Tolvo Oja. (USAF)

personnel as they tried to run from the hurtling wreckage. Flaming gasoline injured one man, who was dragged from the fire by Cpl. John Farley. For his selfless act Farley was later awarded the Soldier's Medal. T/Sgt Sparlin Conine did a repeat of his courageous performance in North Africa by again disregarding the flames from the crash and moving a parked P-38 out of danger.

Weather prevented any long-range escort missions until 17 March, when the 14th Group visited Austria. Enemy aircraft were seen, but they kept their distance. On the return trip Lt. Roy Liles (49th) developed engine trouble over Yugoslavia, and was seen to parachute successfully, but was never heard from again.

On the following day all three Lightning groups were sent on a sweep of the Maniago A/D complex in northeast Italy. The P-38s flew some 350 miles at just 30 feet over the Adriatic Sea in an attempt avoid radar detection, but German fighters were above them as they swept into the area. In a swirling dogfight that lasted over a half hour, the massed formation of P-38s downed or damaged 20 enemy aircraft. 14th Fighter Group claims were as follows:

Lt. Col. William Leverette, 37th	1/0/0
1st Lt. Charles Townsend, 37th	1/0/0
1st Lt. David Vann, 37th	0/1/1
2nd Lt. Wesley Hancock, 37th	0/1/0
1st Lt. Lawrence Mars, 37th	1/0/0
2nd Lt. Joseph Garrity, 37th	0/1/0
Capt. John Sandifer, 49th	1/0/0
Totals	4/3/1

Several pilots came home with battle damage, a few on one engine, and some with just 10 gallons of gas remaining, but all returned.

Escort missions to Steyr, Austria, and Verona, Italy, produced no contacts until a second trip to Steyr on 26 March. Lt. Enoch Lemon (37th) had taken off behind the rest of the group, and had lost them in cloud layers. Along with another 37th P-38, he tacked on to the 1st Fighter Group, and managed to get in a duel with FW 190s. He hit one and claimed it as probably destroyed. There were no losses among members of the 14th.

On 29 March the 14th escorted B-24s to Bellumo, in northern Italy, and while defending the bombers the 48th's Capt. Max Wright and Lt. Robert Griffith each shot down a 109. 2nd Lt. William Tucker was seen to parachute near Verona for unknown reasons.

The following day the 14th escorted B-24s to Sofia, Bulgaria, and observed a mix of fighter aircraft thought to be Axis leftovers provided to the Bulgarian Air Force, including Messerschmitt 109s, Focke-Wulf 190s, a Macchi 202, one FW 189, and a Reggianne 2000. The air defense units seemed, according to the official history, "lacking in attack formation, coordination, and experience." Lt. Charles Townsend of the 37th became separated from his squadron during the mission, and was heard to call for a homing but did not return. Claims by the 14th Fighter Group are as follows:

Capt. Max Wright, 48th	1/0/0
1st Lt. John McGuyrt, 48th	0/1/0
2nd Lt. Robert Boettger, 37th	0/0/1
2nd Lt. Cleveland Tatum, 37th	0/0/1
Capt. Ray Kopecky, 49th	0/0/1
2nd Lt. Warren Semple, 49th	0/0/1
2nd Lt. Louis Benne, 49th	0/0/1
2nd Lt. Phil Goldstein, 49th	0/0/1
Totals	1/1/6

The arrival of more replacement J-model Lightnings was the highlight of the month. The military supply pipeline also found

Some of the pilots of the 48th Squadron pose in April 1944: (L. to R.) Standing: William Church (KIA), John Meidinger (KIA), Harold Thysell, John Lindstrom (EV), John McGuyrt, and Nathan Abbot, CO. Kneeling: Milo Gnewikow (EV), William Shannon, Clarence Jones, Arnold Dickenson, Michael Wagner, and William Blocker. (Dickenson)

During spring 1944 missions over Rumania, the 14th Group encountered radial engine enemy aircraft that were assumed to be Focke-Wulf 190s. They were, in fact, IAR 80Cs manufactured in Rumania, the only indigenous fighter to serve in the Balkan air forces. (Lambert)

enough space to ship some Coca-Cola, long a distant memory for veterans of North Africa. The initial allotment was one bottle per man.

The spring weather of April 1944 saw a marked improvement in flying conditions over the continent, and the 14th Fighter Group sallied forth on twenty escort missions. The only mission that was aborted for sour weather conditions was a planned airdrome strafing attack. Half of each squadron would stand down while the rest flew. This routine had each pilot logging 10 to 12 sorties per month.

During several of the escort operations the *Luftwaffe* showed up in greater numbers than had been witnessed in months, and exhibited aggression long dormant. The mission of 2 April 1944 to Steyr, Austria, involved some 548 bombers. It turned into a swirling dogfight for the 14th, as they were assigned to provide withdrawal support. The targets were airdromes, the Daimler-Puch aircraft parts plant, and a ball bearing factory. 1st Lt. Enoch Lemon, leading the 37th Squadron, provides his view of the battle:

"We had made a few turns over the bombers, and I now only had ten planes, as two more had just headed for home. [Whenever one aircraft had a mechanical problem that required an early return, another always accompanied the cripple.] The 48th Squadron called out bogies below the bombers and went down after them. I

Maj. Nathan Abbott (wearing flight helmet) and his ground crew pose with their ship (L. to R.): Victor Mousseau, Abbott, James Summerlin, and Doc Hunter. (Ethell)

stayed up for a good look around and dropped belly tanks, getting ready to go down and cover when someone said, 'Look at the 110s coming in!'

I glanced at 7 o'clock and began to turn into them, before I really knew what they were. They [Messerschmitt 110 and 210 twin-engine, two man fighters] were coming in level to the B-17s and closing fast. I knew I didn't have time to come around behind them, or they would get the bombers, so I dove head-on at them.

The first wave was Me 210s, about 16-20 of them. They saw us coming, and dove to get under me and succeeded, but they went down very steeply. The second formation of Germans was about twenty-five Me 110s, and they tried to dive also, but we headed them off, and they began firing at us. I opened up, spraying lead into the formation, trying to split them up. They went in all directions....

I did a wing over and came in on the tail of four 110s that split in pairs. I got on the closest two, and saw that their rear gunners were shooting at me. I said, 'You son of a bitch!,' and pressed the button. My tracers hit home, for there was a flash of strikes just behind the cockpit, and the gunner quit firing. I closed and let him have it. Pieces peeled off its left engine, and it began pouring out black smoke. Then I saw his left wing start to come apart and disintegrate from the tip inward.

The radio call sign for the 49th Squadron was "Hangman." Hence, the officers club at Triolo was "Hangman's Hangout." Posing at the front door are Lts. Don Hughes (KIA) and John Thomas. (Luttrell)

I switched to the other one that had turned to the left and started firing. There was a large flash under his left wing that looked like one of his rockets exploded, then his engine began to smoke and I peeled off." [German air defense units had begun to employ rockets that were lobbed into bomber formations.]

Pilots of the 49th Squadron in front of their tent at Triolo: Lts. Robert Seidman (KIA), Jackson Schetler, and John Schill (KIA). (Jackson)

By this time all three squadrons were engaged with both twin and single-engine German fighters, and the unit formations had been pretty well broken up by the duels. Enoch Lemon looked around for the rest of his squadron, and saw both 109s and 110s diving with P-38s on their tails. He fired at two more 110s, then began to gather his chicks together.

Twenty bombers had been lost to intense accurate flak and the swarms of German fighters; however, the loss would have been much greater had it not been for the escorts. The running battle had involved all three P-38 groups, and the P-47 equipped 325th Fighter Group. Between them they claimed the certain destruction of 36 enemy aircraft. The 14th Fighter Group, with Lt. John McGuyrt leading, had no losses, and their victory claims were as follows:

2nd Lt. Philip Goldstein, 49th	1/0/0
1st Lt. Arthur King, 49th	1/0/1
2nd Lt. Richard Fowler, 49th	0/0/1
1st Lt. Harold Simmons, 49th	0/0/1
1st Lt. Enoch Lemon, 37th	2/0/1
F/O Albert Ginder, 37th	0/0/1
2nd Lt. John Ingram, 37th	1/0/0
1st Lt. Frank Phillips, 37th	1/0/0
1st Lt. Cleveland Tatum, 37th	1/0/0
2nd Lt. William White, 37th	1/0/0
Maj. Nathan Abbott, 48th	1/0/0
2nd Lt. John Lindstrom, 48th	3/0/0
2nd Lt. Arnold Dickinson, 48th	1/0/0
2nd Lt. Clarence Jones, 48th	1/0/0
1st Lt. John McGuyrt, 48th	2/0/0

2nd Lt. John Meidinger, 48th	1/1/0
1st Lt. William Shannon, 48th	1/0/0
2nd Lt. Harold Thysell, 48th	1/0/0
2nd Lt. Michael Wagner, 48th	1/1/0
Totals	20/2/5

For its outstanding performance on 2 April 1944, the 14th Fighter Group was awarded the Distinguished Unit Citation.

On the following day (3 April), with Lt. Col. Taylor leading, the 14th escorted bombers to Budapest, Hungary, but met comparatively little resistance. Capt. Max Wright (48th) scored the only victory when he destroyed a Messerschmitt 210. Lts. William Palmer, Jack Lenox, and George Monnier of the 49th Squadron damaged several reluctant Me 109s.

The great refinery complex at Ploesti, Rumania, was the target on 5 April. Hit many times in the past, its engineers worked miracles of repair, and it was still producing fuel for the German war machine. Only a dozen enemy fighters were seen, but none encountered. On the return leg Lt. John Lindstrom, 48th Squadron, reported that he was apparently leaking gasoline and could not make it back to Italy. He bailed out over the mountains of Yugoslavia.

Carried as missing in action, Lindstrom became the first of many 14th pilots who would be rescued and aided by Yugoslav partisans. Two competing guerilla factions had never surrendered to German occupation. They battled the Germans and each other for the entire war. But given the chance to assist downed Allied airmen, they generally performed heroic feats. In 1944 the Allies established clandestine missions on the mountainous Adriatic coast, and from these bases they extracted airmen who had evaded capture. Lindstrom came out on 17 June 1944.

The rail marshalling yard of Maestre, adjacent to Venice, was the target of bombers on 7 April, and Lt. Col. Taylor led the 14th's escorting fighters. Single-engine enemy aircraft attacked the bombers, but attempted to avoid engagements with the P-38s. However, the 14th pursued and extracted a toll. Claims were as follows:

1st Lt. James Martin, 48th	1/0/1
2nd Lt. Myrville Thornberry, 48th	1/0/1
1st Lt. Morgan Mathews, 37th	0/1/0
1st Lt. William Becker, 49th	1/0/0
2nd Lt. Louis Benne, 49th	2/0/0
2nd Lt. Wilson Oldhouser, 49th	0/1/0
2nd Lt. Warren Jones, 49th	2/0/1
Capt. John Sandifer, 49th	1/0/0
1st Lt. Robert Seidman, 49th	1/0/0
Totals	9/2/3

The 49th's Lt. Wesley Crow developed engine trouble and left the engagement, but failed to return to Triolo. 2nd Lt. Richard Zimmerman (48th) gave a "Mayday!" signal over the Adriatic, but could not be located. A later ASR patrol also proved negative.

Another new batch of factory-fresh J-Model Lightnings arrived, and the last of the H-models was retired. A pair in the 48th Squadron, numbers 4 and 7, each had accumulated 100 missions and over 700 hours, thanks to the expert care of devoted ground crews.

During April, several pilots who had achieved the 50-mission goal departed for a well deserved rest, and new pilots arrived. Lt. Col. Bill Leverette was one of those who got his stateside ticket. Major Forrest Barker, back for his second tour of combat duty, replaced him as CO of the 37th Squadron. Col. Oliver E. Ford, Jr., slated for a command position, joined the 14th Group. Another recent arrival, actually on detached service from the Fifteenth Air Force, was Maj. Nathan Abbott. He had about 1700 hours in single engine fighters, but after a quick checkout in a P-38 he had flown as wingman, and scored his first victory on 2 April. He was soon assigned as CO of the 49th Fighter Squadron.

On 12 April the group provided target and withdrawal support for B-17s bombing an aircraft plant in Fishamend, Austria. German fighters attacked, and in the engagement that followed the 14th downed three enemy fighters without suffering a loss. It was the final mission for Bill Leverette, who tallied his tenth and last victory, a rocket-carrying Me. 110. Major Nathan Abbott, new 48th CO, and 2nd Lt. Arnold Dickenson also downed twin-engine enemy aircraft.

An escort mission to Gyor, Hungsry, on 13 April was uneventful, but the P-38 of Capt. Ronald Ashmead developed a fire, and he was obliged to bail out over the Adriatic. His wingman, 2nd Lt. Bill Starbuck, circled Ashmead until an ASR Walrus arrived for

The leadership of the 14th Fighter Group in May 1944 (L. to R.): Maj. Nathan Abbott, 49th CO; Col. Oliver B. Taylor, group CO; Maj. Ken Gaskin, 37th CO; and Maj. Frank Robinson (KIA), 48th CO. (USAF)

a successful rescue. It was Ashmead's final mission before being rotated back to the U.S. The Adriatic was an immense body of water, but Allied air and sea power controlled it so thoroughly that both ASR ships and aircraft were able to operate with considerable impunity.

On 15 April the 14th Fighter Group was given the assignment of target and withdrawal support for B-24s attacking Bucharest, Rumania. "The sky was full of cumulonimbus clouds," 2nd Lt. George Walter recalls, "and as sixteen of us came around one cloud we saw about forty 109s and 190s." Enemy fighters of the *Luftwaffe* and the Rumanian air forces engaged and a bitter dogfight ensued as the P-38s sought to protect the Liberators. Claims were as follows:

1st Lt. Robert Hullsiek, 37th	2/0/0
1st Lt. Larry Mars, 37th	1/0/0
1st Lt. Porter McClaine, 37th	1/0/0
1st Lt. Cleveland Tatum, 37th	1/0/0
1st Lt. Frank Phillips, 37th	1/0/0
1st Lt. Jack Harrow, 37th	0/1/0
2nd Lt. James Mitchell, 37th	0/1/0
2nd Lt. Philip Goldstein, 49th	0/0/1
Totals	6/2/1

The mission consumed almost six hours, with bad weather covering the return route, and the encounter had been costly. Lts. Robert Zimmerman, John Ingram, and Joseph Garrity of the 37th Squadron were all lost when enemy aircraft attacked them from above. Only Zimmerman survived to become a prisoner. Col. Oliver Ford, flying with the 49th Squadron on his introductory combat mission, was heard over the radio briefly but never returned.

The escort missions of the 16th and 17th to Rumania and Yugoslavia were both devoid of action. The *Luftwaffe* seemed to be licking its wounds. Returning from Belgrade, Lt. Enoch Lemon said, "We looked all over Yugoslavia for something to shoot at but couldn't find a thing."

Not until 20 April did the 14th have another encounter with enemy aircraft. They were escorting B-24s in the Trieste area. A number of distant German fighters were sighted, but only a handful showed any aggression. Lts. John McGuyrt and Michael Wagner each downed Me 109s for the 49th Squadron. Capt. Norman Jackson and Lt. Harold Simmons bagged another pair for the 49th. There were no losses.

On 21 April, while escorting bombers to Bucharest, the 14th had better hunting. Some 35-40 single engine enemy fighters went after the B-24s. The attackers were a mix of Me 109s, FW 190s, and what the 14th Group history referred to as Italian Fiat G. 50s. It seems likely that the aircraft were in fact Rumanian manufactured IAR 80C radial engine fighters that bore a resemblance in profile to the old G. 50. Claims were as follows:

Col. Oliver Taylor, 14th	2/0/0
2nd Lt. William Church, 48th	1/0/0
1st Lt. Marvin R. Elston, 37th	1/0/0
Maj. Kenneth Gaskin, 37th	3/0/0
1st Lt. Porter McClaine, 37th	1/0/0
1st Lt. Frank Phillips, 37th	2/0/0
2nd Lt. Ken Sullivan, 37th	0/1/0
1st Lt. Cleveland Tatum, 37th	0/1/0
Totals	10/2/0

The mission was marred by the loss of 1st Lt. Richard Wilhelm (37th Squadron), who was believed shot down and killed by a Messerschmitt 109.

Bucharest had been a brawl on 21 April, but when the Fifteenth Air Force returned just three days later there was no sign of enemy aircraft. The 14th weaved in vain over its B-24s and marveled at the calm. Crossing Yugoslavia, a Liberator pilot broke in on the 14th's frequency: "P-38s, you are the best and most beautiful sight we've ever seen."

One of the fighter pilots responded, "Oh, I bet you tell that to all the fighters." It was a rare moment of humor in the deadly skies.

During the final week of April 1944 the 14th Fighter Group escorted bombers to Padua, Piombino, and Toulon. Northern Italy seemed devoid of air defense, and while enemy aircraft were seen in the distance at Toulon, France, they were reluctant to attack. On the last day of the month a few German fighters were spotted

Capt. Harold Simmons had previously served with the 50th Fighter Squadron, and managed to catch up to the 49th in Italy. This is his second P-38, dubbed "Sweet Lorraine." (Ethell)

near Milan. They just milled about at high altitude, "shooting up their ammo. They sprayed it out in big strings across the sky," said Enoch Lemon, "not even aimed in our direction." Such behavior caused him to reason that they had to be out of ammo or gas, or be shot up to return. Otherwise they would be punished. Indeed, ever since the Battle of Britain, Hermann Göring had heaped abuse on his fighter corps, frequently accusing them of cowardice. "They don't like to fight if they have less than a 2 to 1 advantage," Lemon observed. As the odds began to shift in favor of the Allies, it only made tactical sense for the *Luftwaffe* to pick its fights.

Despite a lack of enemy action in this last week of April there was one loss. Maj. Forrest Barker, 37th Squadron CO, was on the radio briefly to say that he was having engine trouble. It was hoped that he had parachuted successfully, but he was never seen again.

The month of May 1944 brought excellent flying weather, permitting the 14th Fighter Group to conduct combat operations on 22 days. The warm dry weather also freed Allied surface forces from the mud that had helped to bog down the ground campaign. With a mighty mid-May offensive the Allies finally dislodged the Germans from Cassino, the obstacle that anchored the Gustav line. While tactical air units pounded German defensive positions and battered their supply lines, the 14th generally concentrated on its long-range escorts. However, many of those missions were attacks on the German supply system in Northern Italy—rail yards, bridges, and highways—the interdiction of which foreshadowed the abandonment of the Gustav defenses.

Among the 19 escort missions assigned to the 14th, five were to Rumania and two to southern France. On the 5, 6, and 7 May they flew to Campino, Bucharest, and Ploesti. In the latter two instances enemy fighters engaged the bombers, and had numerous encounters with the Lightnings of the 14th Group.

There was no air opposition on the 5th, but heavy accurate flak:

"I was enjoying the scene of the beautiful Danube River," recalled Norm Jackson, 49th Squadron, on his last mission, "when my plane suddenly jumped and rang like a bell. The air was suddenly full of flak bursts, and I later discovered several shrapnel holes in my P-38.... The AA over Ploesti was the heaviest I had seen. Several bombers exploded or went down in flames.... On the return trip we tried to slide in under some B-17s, but a trigger-happy gunner started shooting at us."

Possibly contributing to the attitude of the gunners was a long-standing, widespread rumor of the German's capturing a P-38 and putting it back in flying condition. Claims for 6 May were as follows:

1st Lt. Michael Wagner, 48th	1/0/2
1st Lt. Walter White, 48th	1/0/0
2nd Lt. William Blocker, 48th	0/1/0
2nd Lt. Donald Wimmer, 48th	0/1/0

Officers of the 48th Fighter Squadron: Maj. Emmett Wilson, XO; Lt. Frank Resweber, maintenance; and pilots Capt. Jack Meidinger and Capt.. John McGuyrt. Meidinger was shot down and killed over Yugoslavia in 1945. McGuyrt was an ace and squadron CO at the end of his tour. They stand on Pierced Steel Planking, a U.S. innovation utilized on unpaved airfields on every battlefront. (Dickenson)

Pilots of the 49th Fighter Squadron pose for a formal portrait in May 1944 (L. to R.): Standing: Thomas Purdy, Quentin Teige (KIA), Richard Fowler (POW), John Lewis, James Tipton, George Johnson (KIA), Jackson Schetler, Gunvald Thorsen, John Cullen (KIA), Walter McConnell (KIA), Moses Long, Lawrence O'Toole, William Palmer, and Warren Jones. Seated: Edger Hammerlein (KIA), Warren Semple (KIA), Harold Simmons, Jack Lenox, Louis Benne (PCW), Wilson Oldhouser, Nathan Abbott, John Schill (KIA), Houston Musgrove, Clyde Jones (POW), Wesley Jule (KIA), and Phil Goldstein. (Photo taken by Norman Jackson)

2nd Lt. Thomas Yarwood, 48th	0/1/0
2nd Lt. Arnold Dickenson, 48th	0/1/0
2nd Lt. George O'Connor, 48th	0/0/1
Totals	2/4/3

Claims for 7 May were:

2nd Lt. Clyde Jones, 49th	2/0/0
2nd Lt. Wesley Jule, 49th	1/0/0
2nd Lt. Quentin Teige, 49th	1/0/0
2nd Lt. Richard Fowler, 49th	0/0/1
2nd Lt. Phil Goldstein, 49th	1/0/0
Totals	5/0/1

Losses on the three consecutive missions to Rumania consisted of Lts. Robert Griffith and Earvie Cloyd, both of whom became prisoners of war.

Wiener-Neustadt was the target for Fifteenth Air Force B-24s on 10 May, and the 14th put up 52 Lightnings to provide penetration coverage. The 328 heavy bombers were also escorted by the P-38 equipped 1st and 82nd Fighter Groups, along with the 31st and 325th Fighter Groups, newly equipped with the North American P-51 Mustang. Lt. Col. Oliver Taylor, leading the 14th Group, remembers the hectic overture to an encounter with the *Luftwaffe*:

"As I became increasingly puzzled by the absence of substantial numbers of enemy aircraft, with none at all in evidence down below near the bombers, I sighted contrails [vapor or condensation trails] approaching from the northwest high above us. They were too far away for me to make out the ships themselves, but the contrails indicated that there were about a dozen of them.

I immediately decided that the situation called for a departure from our normal policy of sticking very close to the bombers, which waaas a bit difficult in this situation since they were so strung out.... The few enemy aircraft we saw were quite a bit higher, and at some distance from the bombers. Therefore, I told the 37th that we would go up to meet the contrails. We would use our spiral climb, which enabled us to go straight up without getting too far from the bombers (horizontally), while at the same time avoiding some cloud formations. Although I had used this maneuver perhaps a half dozen times over several months, this was the first time I had tried it in a combat situation.

Things suddenly started happening all at once. First, I became aware that my ship was mushing uncomfortably, and that my own contrails were getting loose and sloppy. Our climbing turn was not all that tight, so it had to be the altitude, which I noticed was over 32,000 feet. In a single ship you can adjust pretty well to the changing flying characteristics, even up to our ceiling of about 40,000, but with a formation of sixteen ships to worry about, it could become rather sticky if much rapid maneuvering should be required. Second, at that moment the little black specks up there leaving the contrails suddenly came into focus. What had first appeared to be a formation of only about a dozen ships turned out to be really a mass formation of at least twice that number! They looked like swarming bees....

While we were thus stymied, swarms of the enemy began attacking us from all sides. This was just too much, especially when good ideas on how to cope with the situation were so slow in coming to me. As the attacks developed I received a call from Lemon, who was leading the tail-end flight. I no longer recall his message, but seem to remember that there was a touch of impatience in his tone, probably inspired by his anxiety over my snafuing his chance to complete his fiftieth mission successfully."

1st Lt. Enoch Lemon takes up the story at this point:

"Colonel Taylor began climbing to attack, which was wrong, for they were in contrails and 3,000 or 4,000 feet above us, and it wasn't long before we were pulling contrails, making it easy for them to follow our every move.

They took advantage of the altitude and attacked, causing us to Lufbery [a defensive circle maneuver]. I had about three head on passes with 109s. I climbed through a thick contrail, and as I broke out one was tooling along beside me at about one o'clock. Well,

Lt. Ed Hemmerlein displays some trophies taken from German aircraft. He crashed and died of his injuries on Corsica a few days after this photo was taken. (Jackson)

Maj. Ken Gaskin shows his ground crew how he bagged a Jerry. (USAF)

I pulled out for a shot, and my wingman saw that the 109 started pouring black smoke and went into a steep dive, seemingly out of control—I had broken off to get back into the Lufbery, and didn't watch to see what had happened. I was looking up and watching for more passes, for I was on my last mission and wanted to get back.

After having to break several times I came out headed for two 109s at 90 degrees that were firing at three P-38s. I began firing and calling to the 38s to break. I followed through to 70 degrees, getting direct hits and closing until he went under my wing, where we lost him. My wingman, Hancock (with 45 missions), was firing at the second one at the same time and it exploded. He had tacked on to me during the first fight when he had become separated from his flight.

We were in the Luf for about 30 to 40 minutes, and I was getting tired of being shot at, but Colonel Taylor would not break out. So I screamed over the radio for all P-38s to follow me. I was breaking out, and sure enough they followed me. Several were low on gas and letting everyone know it. Getting out of a Lufbery Circle is a dangerous undertaking, for if no one follows, the bastards on top will dive and pick you off before your own planes can help."

Colonel Taylor recognized the plight that he and the 37th had gotten into, and relates his version of the event that Lemon described as a Lufbery and Taylor called a spiral:

"Feeling that Lemon should have assistance from someone else, while I was *non compos mentis*, I called the 48th and, being told that they were not busy, asked them to come over and 'brush some of the flies off of us.' As they approached and began to draw off some of our attackers, I told the 37th that I was going to break out of our spiral and to follow me....

Needless to say, I got very little sleep that night, as I wondered if I had lost my marbles that day. I was keenly aware that it was simply luck that we lost only two ships, and not necessarily due to battle action at that. I was particularly at a loss to explain what had been Jerry's problem, for I would have delighted to have caught him in the same fix as the one I got the 37th into. It was a beautiful setup for a grand old turkey shoot."

The tally for the day's air battle over Austria reflects the defensive nature of the battle: lots of damage claims, as P-38s flicked off shots at the superior numbers of enemy fighters. Several members of the 14th got a piece of a Jerry:

1st Lt. Enoch Lemon, 37th	1/1/1
1st Lt. Wesley Hancock, 37th	1/0/0
2nd Lt. Paul Winston, 48th	1/0/1
1st Lt. Walter White, 48th	1/0/0
2nd Lt. Charles Ingram, 48th	0/0/1
2nd Lt. Selmer Underdal, 48th	0/0/1
2nd Lt. William Lavery, 48th	0/0/2
1st Lt. Michael Wagner, 48th	0/0/2
Capt. William Palmer, 49th	1/0/1
2nd Lt. Warren Jones, 49th	1/0/0
2nd Lt. John Penning, 49th	1/0/1
2nd Lt. Paul Wingert, 49th	0/0/1
1st Lt. John Cullen, 49th	0/0/1

1st Lt. Houston Musgrove, 49th	0/0/1
2nd Lt. Gunvald Thorsen, 49th	0/0/1
Totals	7/1/14

Despite being seemingly outnumbered and attacked from above, the 14th had suffered no combat losses. However, enroute to Austria that day, 2nd Lt. John Jones of the 37th Squadron had developed trouble in his right engine. He aborted, and advised the others that he was heading back to Triolo. Coming down the Yugoslav coast, the bad engine caught fire, and he was obliged to bail out. Partisans corralled him almost immediately, and after several days, delivered him to one of their clandestine landing grounds, where he was picked up by a C-47 and returned to Bari, Italy.

Successive missions on 12, 13, and 14 May 1944 were designed to support the ground offensive below Rome. All were against targets north of the front lines.

The escort mission of 12 May to bomb airdromes in the Reggio and Bologna areas met with no opposition, but a lot of cloud cover. There were two losses from the 48th Squadron: 2nd Lt. Herbert Aldrich and 1st Lt. Paul Winston failed to return.

On the following day, the 14th Fighter Group escorted bombers to hit rail marshalling yards at Parma and Modena. The *Luftwaffe* made a feeble attack, with two fighters attempting a pass at the bombers and then diving away. There were no claims and no losses.

By 14 May Allied forces were breaking out of the Anzio perimeter. The tactical air forces threw a blanket of aircraft over the battlefront, and the strategic air forces flew missions to neutralize German airfields in northern Italy. The 14th Fighter Group was assigned to sweep airdromes in the Udine area of northeastern Italy. 2nd Lt. Larry O'Toole of the 49th Squadron describes the tense two-hour approach up the Adriatic, with forty-eight P-38s flying at low-level to avoid radar detection:

In addition to the open-air conditions, the complexities of an engine change on a P-38 are obvious in this view. (Stitt)

"This was an extremely difficult task over a long period,, because of the danger of losing your concentration and hitting the water. It became very nerve wracking. I found that if I concentrated and put the airplane just where I wanted it above the water, and set my altimeter on zero, it really helped a lot. Not long after, out to the left, I saw a huge geyser that must have gone up a hundred feet. One of the P-38s had gone in [2nd Lt. William Lavery]. Hitting the water at 275 to 300 mph meant that the pilot was killed instantly. Of course, nothing was said. We were under strict radio silence, and the mission continued.

I was flying Lt. Siedman's wing. He was leading my squadron. As we neared the target we checked our gun switches, dropped about 20 degrees of flaps to obtain the best firing angle, spread out some, and started across the airdrome, firing at everything in our path. I remember shooting at a boxy piece of what looked like construction equipment. It probably contained a machine gun nest. I hope I took it out.

At this point someone called out, 'Red Two, you are on fire!' I was Red Two. I looked in my rear view mirror, which was just above my head on the canopy, and saw that my left engine was pouring black smoke. I had always believed that in such a situation on the deck, the best thing to do was to pull straight up in a loop with full power to get as much altitude as possible and bail out at the top. But I was 500 miles from home, in enemy territory, and the natives were definitely unfriendly. So I didn't play the odds. I gambled, pulled the left throttle and mixture control back, feathered the prop, and prayed. Praise the Lord, the smoke started to subside and the fire went out.

I made a slow 180, keeping as low as I could to keep out of radar. I had to pull up over every tree line and back down on the deck. Then I started calling for some help, 'Red Leader, this is Red Two. I'm on single engine, and I could use some help!' Finally someone replied, 'Aw shut up. Red leader is down.' I really felt awful. My leader down in enemy territory, and I'm calling him for help."

1st Lt. Robert Siedman, leading the charge across Villaorba, had spotted a line of German Junkers 88 bombers on the tarmac, and proceeded to strafe them. He pulled up at the airport perimeter to pass over some telephone or power lines, and at that point he was hit by light AA, and his P-38 burst into flames. His mates last saw the Lightning in a high-speed belly landing that seemed to preclude Sideman's survival.

Colonel Taylor, and Lts. Goldstein, Harrow, Honeycutt, and Phillips all shot up German aircraft on the ground, unsure as to whether some were derelicts left in the open to encourage strafers. 1st Lt. John Schill jumped a Ju. 88 flying near the airport and shot it down. Larry O'Toole pursues his narrative of the mission:

"I continued my tree hopping and back down on the deck again, heading for the Adriatic, and expecting to be jumped by enemy fighters at any moment. But thank God, I was not. On one engine I would have been a sitting duck. When I reached the sea, I got as low above the water as I could with a maximum speed, probably about 175 mph. But my troubles weren't over. I forgot about coastal flak towers, and one of them began firing at me. I veered away from it, and luckily was not hit. A few minutes later a pair of P-38s from another squadron picked me up and started escorting me down the Adriatic until I was about 20 or 30 minutes from the base.

My single-engine landing (my first) went okay, and I was towed back to the ramp. I don't remember how many hits my plane took, but the one that caused the fire had severed an oil line, with oil hitting the red-hot turbo blades. Had it been a gasoline fire I may not have survived. If I had lived, I probably would have been a POW."

2nd Lt. George Walter, 37th Squadron, has a humorous recollection of the attack on Villaorba:

"We all made one firing pass and headed out toward the Adriatic. I can remember coming out of a tight left turn and seeing a very tall bell tower sticking up from this little town. As everybody else did, I got a real good shot at the tower, and then pulled up over it and came on home. Later that week the gun camera film was shown. We weren't really supposed to go out shooting up Italian towns, but as soon as they started showing the gun camera pictures, it was obvious that everyone had a view of the bell tower, and we began to get a little nervous until the colonel's film came up and, sure enough, he had a picture of the bell tower too. That let us off the hook."

The loss of Lavery and Siedman (on his 50th sortie) had been a considerable price to pay for the meager results obtained. It was apparent that getting to that 50-mission goal was not easy, and extending a tour, or coming back for a second, was stretching one's quota of luck.

The 14th was back in the escort business on 15 and 16 May, with neither losses nor victories. The 37th Squadron's war diary reported that they had chased P-51s "all over the sky" before discovering that they were friendlies. From a distance, the early model P-51 Mustang bore a remarkable resemblance to the Messerschmitt 109.

Over 700 heavy bombers were dispatched to hit the Ploesti refinery complex on 18 May 1944. Enemy aircraft attacked the bomber stream, but did little in the sector guarded by the 14th Fighter Group. Only a handful were seen, and just a single Me 109 was engaged and downed by Lt. Tom Yarwood, 48th Squadron. Lt. Paul Wingert was seen going down through a cloud layer over Bulgaria for unknown reasons. He had survived a bailout over Anzio in January, but did not return from this mission.

Escorts to northern Italy on 19 and 22 May were uneventful. However, Lt. Andrew Sziich (37th) lost power on takeoff and was killed. Lt. Larry O'Toole, 49th Squadron, was waiting his turn to depart and witnessed the crash:

"It kept rolling and rolling, and finally, off the end of the runway, hit a ditch, flipped over, and burst into flames. I had to taxi out and take off over the burning airplane. Not a good feeling. I chased after my squadron halfway across Italy, and I was beginning to think I wasn't going to find them, when finally I spotted the formation and joined up. I don't remember anything about that particular mission, but when I got back my crew chief, S/Sgt. Dick Hunter, said, 'Lieutenant, when you looked over and saw that burning P-38 you turned white as a sheet.'"

A rare strafing mission was on field orders for 23 May. The assignment took the 14th to Ferrara airdrome, a three-hour plus mission. The low-level approach surprised the enemy, as several aircraft were being serviced when the P-38s broke over the field. Five aircraft were believed destroyed on the ground, several were damaged, and a nearby locomotive was strafed. Lt. Jack Lenox (49th Squadron) caught a single Messerschmitt 109 at low altitude and destroyed it. All P-38s returned to base.

The 14th was back in the Weiner-Neustadt area on 24 May, escorting B-24s to Wollersdorf Airdrome. The Germans may have withdrawn from the air defense of northern Italy, but displayed aggressive tactics in protecting their interests in Austria. With Colonel Taylor leading, the group ran into many enemy aircraft, mostly twin-engine types. All claims were made by the 49th Squadron:

1st Lt. Wilson Oldhouser	2/0/0
1st Lt. Louis Benne	1/0/0
1st Lt. John Cullen	1/0/0
2nd Lt. Richard Fowler	1/0/0
2nd Lt. Jack Lenox	1/0/0
2nd Lt. John Louis	1/0/0
Capt. William Palmer	1/0/0
1st Lt. Thomas Purdy	1/0/0
2nd Lt. Clyde Jones	1/0/0
Totals	10/0/0

Lts. Quentin Teige and John Penning of the 49th Squadron, both of whom failed to return, were last seen engaged with enemy aircraft.

Piacenza A/D was attacked by B-24s on 25 May, and the 14th Fighter Group provided top cover and withdrawal support. It was reported that the bombers flew a good tight formation going into the target, but straggled badly on retirement. Lt. Larry O'Toole describes the action:

"About the time the bombers reached the target area we met a force of about twenty-five Me 109s and FW 190s. We dropped our belly tanks and dove to attack. Suddenly I looked up to the right, and saw a pair of FW 190s coming down on us from three o'clock high. They were always above us, it seemed. I called out the two bogies twice, and that's all the time I had. In a few seconds they would be on our tails firing.

There was really no decision to make; I turned sharply into them, and started firing machine guns and cannon. One of the enemy fighters fell off and down, while the other kept coming at me, and me at him. I saw hits on the 190 as we closed on a near collision course. We weren't 40 feet apart when we passed, looking at each other in 90-degree banks, cockpit to cockpit.

I had been climbing all the while, and just after we passed my plane stalled completely, and I went into a spin. I recovered and could see no other enemy fighters, so I started looking for my squadron. Suddenly I saw a Me 109 coming toward me a few hundred feet above. I pulled up and to the right to intercept him, started firing cannon and machine guns, and got my first victory. I don't believe the enemy pilot ever saw me.

I started looking for my squadron again, but my troubles were just beginning. I must have gotten careless, because suddenly it was as though I was sitting in the center of a hundred bright copper colored high-tension power lines. They were tracer bullets. What I did next defied all logic, but maybe it saved my life.

Instead of making a violent break, I let my left wing start to drop, hoping the enemy pilot would think he had killed me. The firing stopped. When I got to a 45-degree bank, I pulled up into the most violent, steep climbing turn I could manage while applying maximum power. I was sure the P-38 had the zoom ability to stall him out well before I stalled. It worked. I never saw the enemy fighter again.

Thick white smoke was coming from my left engine. When I tried to look into my rearview mirror mounted on the canopy, I found it had been shot off. I feathered the bad engine and set course for home, hoping I didn't meet any more Germans while on a single engine....

When I got back my airplane drew quite a crowd. Every one of the six propeller blades was riddled with bullet holes. I could stick my fingers in bullet holes in the wings on each side of the cockpit. Someone threw me an eight-inch pipe-like piece of the tail section he had just lifted out. Looked like it had been hit by a cannon round.... The white smoke had come from engine coolant."

While O'Toole was engaged in his own private war, the rest of the group was also in a melee. Claims were as follows:

2nd Lt. Clarence Jones, 48th	1/0/0
2nd Lt. Vaughn Herdell, 48th	0/0/1
Maj. Nathan Abbott, 49th	1/0/0
2nd Lt. Phil Goldstein, 49th	1/0/0
2nd Lt. Warren Jones, 49th	1/0/1
2nd Lt. Larry O'Toole, 49th	1/0/1
2nd Lt. Warren Semple, 49th	2/0/0
2nd Lt. Ed Hemmerlein, 49th	0/0/1
2nd Lt. Jack Lenox, 49th	0/0/1
2nd Lt. Jackson Schetler, 49th	0/0/1
2nd Lt. John Lewis, 49th	0/0/1
2nd Lt. Jack Harrow, 37th	1/0/0
2nd Lt. Albert Ginder, 37th	0/1/0
Totals	8/1/7

One P-38 did not return to Triolo. Lt. Richard Fowler was seen to parachute in the vicinity of the Po River, was captured, and became a POW.

An escort mission to the rail marshalling yard at Lyon, France, on 26 May was uneventful, except for the usual staging, which took place through Corsica. As the 46 Lightnings were departing from Serragio airfield, Lt. Edgar Hemmerlein (49th Squadron) ground looped and crashed on takeoff. He climbed clear of the burning wreck with his clothes on fire, and died of his injuries in the hospital the following day.

The group returned to France the following day, as they escorted bombers to Nimes. The mission was 1300 miles roundtrip, and involved over ten hours, with a refueling stop in Corsica. German fighters were observed at a distance, but were reluctant to attack the B-24s. One FW 190 got careless and was shot down by Colonel Taylor. There were no losses, but Lt. George Walter came near being a casualty:

"I must have had my head up and locked that day, because I made a navigational error, and instead of landing back at Triolo, I discovered I was going south across the toe of Italy, and was just about out of gas. I got on the horn and started yelling 'Mayday,' and I finally got directed to a bombed out airstrip on the southern tip of Italy, right across the Straits of Messina from Sicily. A place called Reggio Calabria. The field was waist high in grass, and covered with bomb craters. But I did manage to get down, and was just about out of gas when I rolled to a stop.

The town was in control of the British, and there were some American officers there. They had an Italian work force doing odd jobs, like keeping the railway running. They took me to town, wined me and dined me, and put me up for the night, and I marveled in the luxury these guys were living in. In order to get word back to my group I went to a British radio station and gave them a message to send.

The next morning I went down to preflight my ship, and found that they only had about 60-70 gallons of gas, and a couple of ex-Italian Air Force people were straining it through a chamois for me. This was just enough to get me to an RAF Spitfire base, where I got enough fuel to get back to base.

I came in over Triolo at minimum altitude, pulled up and did a roll, and looked down at my parking place. Darned if my ground crew wasn't there sitting on their toolboxes, waiting for me. After I landed, and amid much celebration, a message was delivered that Major Bowman, Operations Officer, wanted to see me at group headquarters.

He was a 'paddle foot' (formerly rated, but now a ground officer), and he didn't say, 'Glad to have you back. Are you Okay?' All he did was rip a strip off me for not letting them know where I was. I tried to explain that I had attempted to get a message through, but nothing would satisfy him, and he let me know that I was in big trouble. Maybe that was what held up my promotion, as

Taunting any Nazi who got close enough, the 49th's Lt. Phil Goldstein named his P-38 "Jew Boy." (Jackson)

I didn't get my first lieutenant bars until July, right before I went back to the states. For a while I thought I was going to be the oldest second lieutenant in the Air Force."

An uneventful escort mission to Austria was flown on 28 May, and once the group was released from its shepherding duties they went down to strafe roadways, as well as a rail line running south of Banja Luka, Yugoslavia. Several trucks and a number of boxcars were destroyed despite the difficult terrain. The mountainous road wound up a narrow canyon, obliging the pilots to turn continuously, sometimes flicking off shots while in a bank.

They were ordered back to the same area to hunt for more targets the following day, and found an ample supply: six locomotives and over 100 rail cars. The latter were loaded with troops and munitions, it appeared, from the secondary explosions. Again, the mountainous terrain made it difficult to concentrate one's aim for any length of time. Lt. James Martin, who had recently learned that he had become a father, was killed when he flew into a mountain.

The month of May 1944 was closed out with escort missions to Wels, Austria, on the 30th and Ploesti, Rumania, on the 31st. There was no enemy opposition and no losses.

7

Beyond Rome

In the last days of May 1944, Allied ground forces linked up below Cassino, and the German Gustav Line was finally broken. As American troops from Anzio surged north toward Rome, German commander General Albert Kesselring began a retreat with his forces to the next natural barrier, the Arno River. There, near the neck of the Italian Peninsula, his units dug in to defend what was called the Gothic Line. Days after the German retreat the Allies reached Rome, and the entire city was liberated on 5 June, an event overshadowed in the war news by the epic invasion of Normandy, France.

The capture of the Eternal City meant little to the strategic Fifteenth Air Force. It continued attacks on airfields and communications in northern Italy while reaching deep into France, Austria, Germany, Rumania, and Hungary. In support, the 14th Fighter Group flew 21 missions during the month of June. Only one was a scheduled strafing mission.

On 9 June the 14th had penetration escort of heavy bombers into Munich, Germany. It was a maximum effort, with 20 aircraft per squadron. Another group was slated to take over once the target was in sight. However, a heavy undercast prevented any visual navigation. It was a long mission (500 miles), and the P-38s had to weave above the slower bombers. Fuel began to be a concern, as Larry O'Toole of the 49th Squadron recalls:

"Soon there was a call about running out of fuel, and then another. And it kept up. Somebody said, 'We'll never make it back.' [There was some belief that Germans monitoring the channel were also claiming to be low on fuel.] John Schill was leading our squadron and the group that day, and he kept telling them he didn't see the target cover (our relief), and that we would have to hold on for awhile. He absolutely would not consider leaving the bombers unprotected at the most critical part of the mission, just before the enemy fighters always attacked.

"The Fighting Irishman" with its 49th Squadron crew (L. to R.): S/Sgt. Hunter, Lt. Larry O'Toole, Cpl. Merack, and Sgt. May. (Ethell)

The Abbey of Cassino, long an obstacle to the Allied drive in Italy, stands above the ruins of the town. (Stitt)

Suddenly, directly in front of us we saw a huge cloud of enemy fighters. I had never seen so many. The Germans had put up everything that would fly. Schill ordered 'drop tanks,' and we all started firing at the enemy in a head-on attack. Of the 50 or 60 Germans, I would guess that nearly all of them rolled over and dove down to escape our concentrated firepower. I saw no attacks on our bombers, as some P-38s dove after the Germans, but most of us stayed with the bombers. As soon as the target covering force appeared we took off for home. All of us made it back"

There were no claims and no losses this day, but the five-hour plus mission was a success, since there were no bombers lost to enemy fighters while the 14th was escorting.

The *Luftwaffe* and its allied air forces were conspicuous by their lack of aggressiveness until an escort mission of 11 June to Giurgiu, Rumania. As the group's forty-seven P-38s provided target and withdrawal support, some two-dozen enemy aircraft attempted to attack the bombers. The 48th and 49th Squadrons engaged with the following results:

2nd Lt. William Starbuck, 48th	0/1/0
2nd Lt. Richard Pitner, 48th	0/0/1
2nd Lt. Clyde Jones, 49th	1/0/0
2nd Lt. Donald Luttrell, 49th	1/0/0
2nd Lt. Thomas Purdy, 49th	1/0/1
Capt. Wilson Oldhouser, 49th	1/0/0
Totals	4/1/2

There were no losses, nor were there any on the escort mission that followed.

The group had gone half a month without a single combat casualty, but all that changed dramatically on 14 June 1944 over Hungary, as they provided escort for B-24s to the Petfurdo oil refinery. Don Luttrell (49th Fighter Squadron) describes the mission as it unfolded:

"We rendezvoused with our bombers on schedule and, as we were well back in the bomber stream, they were not by any means the first aircraft to arrive at the target. As a matter of fact, by the time they arrived the earlier groups had been in and hammered the refinery quite well, and it was burning furiously. There was a cloud of black smoke coming up off the target to 22-25,000 feet, and it was miles across. As the bombers turned in on the initial point to make their home run, and this target was well defended—as almost invariably it was—we pulled out and went across, and met them on the other side. We did this because in reality there was no use of our taking the flak, as we didn't contribute anything to the bomb run, and certainly the enemy fighters were not subjecting themselves to the AA....

The smoke column was miles across. Lou Bennie was leading the squadron, and I was flying number two in one of the flights.... The other two squadrons went around the smoke column to the east, and the 49th went west, so we were separated widely....

It was a milk run. The sky was blue and beautiful, and we were sitting there watching the bombs drop down into the target, and commenting among ourselves on the good job the B-24s were doing; perhaps we were not looking around as well as we should have, when suddenly someone called out, '51s at nine o'clock!' Of course, fifteen heads immediately turned in that direction, and a voice that I knew to be Clyde Jones' said, '51s hell! Those are 109s!'

Suddenly the 49th had the entire *Luftwaffe* all to itself. I have never seen so many black crosses on so many planes. They were on us instantly. Benne called 'Drop tanks!' and began to climb and turn into the enemy as they passed through our formation."

1st Lt. Lou Benne, leading the 49th that day, summoned the other squadrons as he began firing at Me 109s. He saw one go down, then called his own outnumbered unit to form a Lufbery circle. As Benne destroyed a second 109 his P-38 was hit by a fusillade of fire. The right engine was damaged, the left engine caught fire, and a 20mm round entered the cockpit, injuring his left shoulder and shattering the instrument panel. There was nothing for Benne to do but bail out of the stricken P-38. His chute had just barely opened when he hit the ground and was immediately captured. Don Luttrell continues with his view of the action over Hungary:

Old No.61 had a series of 37th Squadron pilots. Crew Chief Robert Taylor kept it flying. (Walker)

The refinery at Budapest, Hungary, sends a column of smoke skyward after one of many attempts by Fifteenth Air Force bombers to knock it out. The B-24 is "Calamity Jane" of the 451st Bomb Group.

"I will never forget the melee that evolved. Many times I have been scared. Any intelligent man gets tensed when exposed to danger, but in this case I remember that I went into the scrap chewing gum under my oxygen mask, and when I came out my mouth was so dry that the gum was strung back and forth between my teeth. Going in I was freezing to death. There was a heater hose in the P-38 that blew warm air, and I was blowing it down my boots and up my gloves. When I came out of the fight I was burning up.

There were airplanes everywhere. They were firing at us, and we were firing at them. I was trying my best to do things like drop my tanks, switch my gas selectors, get my gun sight on, get my mixture to rich, get my RPMs up, and all the detailed actions you have to take to make an airplane a weapon while trying to stay alive.

I was following Clyde Jones quite closely. We were in a right turn, and he rolled over and turned back to the left. As he did, a 109 came down from above with great speed and advantage. And the next thing I knew Clyde is nothing but a ball of fire. You could not even see the outline of the airplane, nor could you tell it was a P-38. All you could see was a ball of flame. It fell off and disappeared.

Col. Daniel S. Campbell took command of the 14th in July 1944 after Obie Taylor completed his combat tour. (USAF)

The 109 that shot Clyde—and I'll never know why it was he and not I—continued to pull up. I rolled slightly to the right and gave him the same treatment he had just given Clyde. So Clyde was gone, the German was gone, and I was up there by myself looking for company."

Assumptions of Clyde Jones' death were unwarranted, as it turned out. Here is his account:

"I looked back over my shoulder, and there was a 109. If you've seen a Me 109 in the movies firing guns, it becomes flame from wingtip to wingtip, and even out of the nose—a pretty horrible sight. At the same time everything in my airplane disappeared. The instrument panel was gone. To rationalize what happened, we carried a canister behind our seat. It was a firebomb to destroy the airplane in the event we went down in enemy territory. Also, our oxygen lines and gas lines ran very close together on the left side of the cockpit. One or more rounds of German ammunition must have hit the fire canister, and then the oxygen and gas lines, causing an explosion.

In an effort to escape the gunfire I twisted the wheel, kicked the rudder, and went into a vertical dive. Fire was everywhere in the cockpit. My gloves were so burned I could not get a grip on the emergency release for the canopy. By using both hands I managed to pull the release, and the canopy went.

We didn't have ejection devices then, and didn't know to release our seat belt and shoulder harness before we popped the canopy. So I was sucked into a 500 mph slipstream to the extent of the seat belt. I managed to get my fingers under the release, and was thrown clear of the airplane. Some portion of the boom struck me on the head above and behind the ear. I was knocked unconscious, and when I came to I was quite low. I pulled the ripcord, and was in the chute only a short time before hitting the ground. My airplane was almost directly under me, and I barely missed the fire. I could hear the ammunition going off. Since my legs were injured I pulled them up as I hit the ground—a bad idea. I landed flat on my butt, and injured my spine and couldn't walk."

Far above Clyde Jones the air battle swirled. Don Luttrell continues:

"I rolled back to the left and could see all this action going on, but it was better to be over there with some friends than out here all by myself, when there's 75 Me 109s swarming around. So I got back in the melee. We had no leader, because Benne had been shot down. I believe Moose Musgrove broke us out of this thing. He said 'Follow me!,' and turned out of the Lufbery and into the sun climbing."

The 14 June air battle over Hungary had been costly. The 49th Fighter Squadron had lost five pilots: Louis Benne, Clyde Jones, Bill Williams, John McLaughlin, and Wesley Jule. Jule was killed in action. The others were taken prisoner and released at the end of the war, except for McLaughlin, who apparently died in captivity. Several of the remaining ten pilots came home with battle damage. The P-38 of Swanson Short was so battered—some 50 bullet holes—that he would have been added to the casualty list had he not hidden in the cloud of smoke over Petfurdo to elude the swarming enemy aircraft. Strangely, Don Luttrell's airplane didn't have a scratch.

Clyde Jones, injured but alive, was found by farmers and a pair of soldiers almost immediately after parachuting. He was assisted by some, and threatened by a lynch mob until a Hungarian Army officer took over. John McLaughlin and other U.S. airmen joined him shortly. Taken to a hospital near Budapest, they later witnessed a horrific Fifteenth Air Force bombing attack that destroyed some of the hospital buildings, and as they prepared to be moved, Lou Benne was found among the wounded. Many moves later all of them ended up in a *Luftwaffe* prisoner camp (Stalag Luft 3), where they were liberated by General Patton's forces in April 1945.

The furious 20-minute dogfight of 14 June 1944 had involved only the 49th Fighter Squadron. Despite their disadvantage in position and being outnumbered, they had extracted a heavy toll from the enemy fighter force. Victory credits were as follows:

1st Lt. Louis Benne	2/0/0
1st Lt. Tom Purdy	2/0/2
1st Lt. Houston Musgrove	1/1/0
2nd Lt. Swanson Shortt	3/0/2
2nd Lt. Jack Lenox	3/0/0
2nd Lt. Moses Long	1/0/0
2nd Lt. Don Luttrell	1/0/0
2nd Lt. John Thomas	1/0/0
1st Lt. John Tipton	0/1/0
2nd Lt. George Johnson	1/0/0
Totals	15/2/4

As a postscript to the air battle, subsequent research has revealed that the enemy was not the *Luftwaffe*, but the Hungarian Air Force equipped with Messerschmitt 109s by Germany.

The day after the Hungary mission (15 June), the group was dispatched in the opposite direction on another long mission. The target was the Orange/Caritat A/D complex near the City of Avignon, in southern France. This was a strafing job, with one squadron to fly high cover while the other two attacked the airfields, then looked for targets of opportunity during departure.

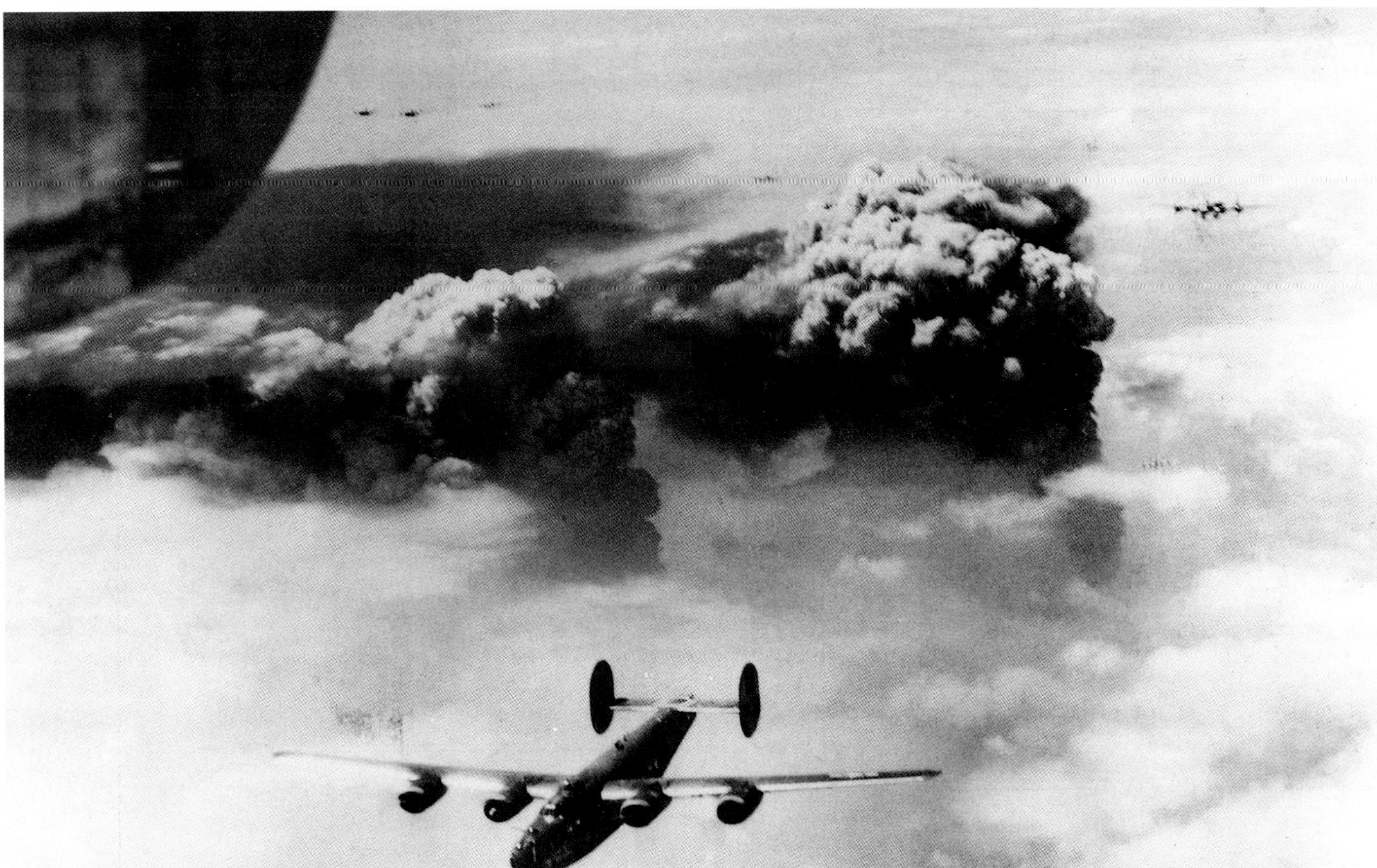

Clouds obscured the Ploesti, Rumania, oil refinery complex on 15 July, but B-24s bombing through the undercast hit the target, starting fires that sent smoke columns to 23,000 feet. P-38 pilots escorting the bombers reported that the smoke could be seen from 200 miles away. (USAF)

Trouble reared its head early, as Lt. Bill McClain, 37th Squadron, had mechanical difficulty with both engines when only a few minutes from the target. He was seen to crash land successfully near the town of Valreas and leave his aircraft.

With Lt. John Schill leading, the group swept down on the airdrome and destroyed or damaged nine enemy aircraft on the ground. A single airborne Me 109 was encountered by Lt. John Lewis, and claimed as a probable. On departure, the local rail line to Marseille was abused, with damage to two locomotives and a number of boxcars. When the group reformed for the return to Italy two more P-38s were missing: Lts. Robert Powers (37th) and Warren Sempl (49th). Neither pilot was ever found.

The two-day loss of eight pilots cast a gloom over the 14th Fighter Group. In some ways it was harder on the ground crews, who were devoted to "their" panes and pilots. Lt. George Walter recalls how his crew chief, T/Sgt. Robert Taylor, worried about him:

A trio of 48th Squadron pilots pose smiling and relaxed. They are (L. to R.): Lts. Arnold Dickenson, Ward McCombs, and Rusty Seilert. McCombs went down over Hungary and became a POW. Rusty Seilert was killed over Southern Germany. (Dickenson)

"Bob was a Roman Catholic, and decided that I should have a St. Christopher medal to carry with me whenever I was flying, and so presented me with one. It was about the size of a silver dollar, and he insisted that I pin it inside my flight suit or pocket so I wouldn't lose it. I was very happy to oblige. He always checked to make sure that I had it with me. One morning it turned up missing. We couldn't find it. I thought there for a while that Bob was going to stop the war until we located that medal. Fortunately, however, it had slipped down in my knee pocket, and was under my escape kit and all the other junk that I carried in there, and Bob agreed to let the war proceed."

The tragic losses over France on 15 June were somewhat mitigated by the return of Bill McClain two months later. After bellying his plane into rural France, he had immediately been rescued by resistance units and hidden from searching German patrols. Ultimately he became a member of the Maquis underground, and fought alongside them until the Allied invasion of southern France in August 1944. After an American armored unit liberated him, Bill was taken to Toulon and flown back to Italy.

During the balance of June the 14th Fighter Group participated in eight more escort missions that involved occasional strafing. The targets were widely dispersed in northern Italy, Austria, Southern Germany, France, Yugoslavia, and Hungary. There were no engagements with enemy aircraft until the last day of the month near Blechhammer, Germany, when small numbers of *Luftwaffe* fighters appeared. The only credits were for a kill by Lt. Richard Pinter (48th Squadron), a probable by Lt. Ed Tindell of the 37th, and damage claims by Maj. Frank Robinson (48th) and 2nd Lt. John Jones, 37th Squadron. Don Luttrell, of the 49th, is certain that he bagged a 109, but didn't claim it:

"We encountered seven to nine Germans. We were above them, and they were below and climbing. I spotted a 109 slightly below me dead ahead, and closing with me very rapidly. I attempted to lower my nose to get a shot at him, and could see that he was trying to raise his nose to fire at me, but our closing rate was too fast for both of us. He would pass directly underneath me by just a few feet. When I realized that I wouldn't be able to fire at him, I estimated his time of passage underneath me and pickled both of my drop tanks right in front of him. I rolled up on my left wing in an attempt to see what happened, but I didn't see him. I could only stay for a second, then had to turn back. I couldn't make any kind of claim, but I believe to this day that I got a Me 109 by dropping my spare tanks onto him."

Casualties during June were thankfully limited. Lt. Swanson Shortt was killed on 20 June when his P-38 crashed at Triolo airfield, and Lt. John Wakeman was lost on 22 June during an operation near Bologna, Italy. Wakeman survived, escaped after capture by a German SS unit, and then evaded recapture with the help of Italian partisans. He returned to U.S. Army control in September.

There had been a troubling annoyance during the month of June 1944 in the form of P-51 Mustangs making passes at formations of P-38s. By this point in the war, four groups that

This group of 37th Squadron ground crewmen appears to be enjoying their stay in Italy (L. to R.): Standing: Les Fields, Leroy Lenert, Stan Hill, Fred Colton, and Chris Stanton. Kneeling: Frank Witt, Shorty Wiley, Arthur Bonsdale, and Ray Lewis. (Stitt)

had formerly flown Spitfires, P-40s, and P-47s had converted to the North American Mustang. Apparently, the P-51 boys were feeling their oats, and lacking substantial contact with the enemy, had taken to buzzing the three Lightning groups. The good clean fun was not appreciated by the P-38s pilots, who frequently broke toward what they believed were approaching Me 109s. Fortunately for the P-51s, there were no casualties resulting from this aerial horseplay. The Mustang drivers were not always as fortunate when making passes at the heavy bombers. B-17 and B-24 gunners shot at friend or foe if either came too close.

Recent casualties—fourteen in May and ten in June—had seemed inordinately high to the members of the 14th Fighter Group. But they would pale by comparison to the losses suffered in July 1944, when 19 pilots were killed or missing in action from various causes. Still, the official group history reports that morale remained high. Perhaps part of the reason was the ministrations of the medical staff. Doctor William Curtis, the 37th Squadron's Flight Surgeon, comments:

"You know I really didn't practice medicine. My biggest job was to tell the boys how good they were, so that after having the hell scared out of them on Tuesday, they would fly again on Wednesday and Thursday."

Lt. Mike Brezas (left) and Capt. Ernest Rehm, Flight Surgeon (48th Squadron), at an awards ceremony in August 1944. Brezas was on his way to becoming the leading ace of the 14th Fighter Group. (Dickenson)

The 14th ranged far and wide in search of the enemy during the first week of July 1944, with consecutive escort missions to Hungary, Yugoslavia, Rumania, France, northern Italy, and Germany. Only the mission to Trieste, just 3 hours 45 minutes of flying, could be called a milk run. Enemy fighters were seen, but proved elusive. Only a lone FW 190 was claimed as destroyed, and that was over Yugoslavia by Maj. Frank Robinson. Just one casualty occurred with the loss of Lt. Billy Turner, who turned back with mechanical trouble on 3 July but failed to return to Triolo. He came down along the coast of Yugoslavia and was taken prisoner.

On 8 July 1944 the 14th Group was assigned a fighter sweep over Vienna, Austria, an area defended by the *Luftwaffe's* veteran JG 27. Only the 48th Squadron was engaged, and chased enemy fighters in battles ranging from 25,000 feet down to 2,000. Lts. Michael Brezas and Don Wimmer each bagged a 109, and each damaged two more. Lt. George O'Connor claimed a 109 as probably destroyed. However, F/O Bernard Martin and 2nd Lt. Henry Mitchell were both lost, Martin to flak.

By mid-July Colonel Taylor had completed his combat tour, and was preparing to depart for the States. Two new senior officers had arrived for roles in the command structure of the 14th. Col. David S. Campbell was slated to take over as commanding officer, while Lt. Col. Thomas B. Whitehouse assumed the role of deputy commander. Both flew on the escort mission of 14 July to Budapest, Hungary, but as flight leaders. 1st Lt. John Schill, a seasoned veteran nearing the end of his combat tour, led the group's 48 Lightnings. Leadership in combat was dictated by experience and exhibited skill, not rank.

As a formation of 30 to 40 enemy aircraft approached the bomber stream from 27,000 feet, part of the 14th Group went on the attack, while others remained with the B-24s. In the ensuing engagement, Maj. Frank Robinson, leading the 48th Squadron, downed a Messerschmitt 110, while Lt. Michael Brezas claimed two FW 190s and a single Me 109. Lt. Don Luttrell damaged another Me 109.

However, the mission proved very costly for a variety of reasons. According to Larry O'Toole (49th Squadron):

"A new pilot flying John Schill's wing collided with him in a huge ball of fire. I recall seeing the fireball but not the collision. These things make you feel awful when you witness them. Schill was such an outstanding professional. I hardly knew him, but we saw his performance in the air over and over, and admired him. It felt good when he was leading the group." Both Schill and Durbin perished.

Shortly after the enemy was engaged, Lts. Frank Higdon and Gustav Strom (48th Squadron) disappeared, and neither was ever heard from again. Lt. Ward McCombs, another 48th pilot, was seen parachuting after an engine burst into flames. He became a POW.

A five and one-half hour escort to Ploesti on 15 July yielded uncertain results due to heavy cloud cover over the target, and a complete absence of enemy air defense squadrons.

On 16 July the 14th escorted B-24s to Austria. It was rare that German fighters did not rise to the defense of Austro-German air space, and this day was no exception. A number of single-engine fighters hovered on the fringes of the bomber stream, awaiting a good opportunity to attack. In each case P-38s turned into the 109s and 190s, forcing an engagement. Three P-38s sustained damage, but all returned. Claims—all from 48th Squadron pilots—were as follows:

2nd Lt. Richard Pinter	1/1/0
1st Lt. William Church	1/0/0
2nd Lt. Cody Stout	1/0/0
2nd Lt. Robert Welsh	0/0/1
2nd Lt. Nello Infanti	0/0/1
Totals	3/1/2

An escort mission to southern France on 17 July involved nearly six hours of flying time for thirty-six P-38s, but was totally uneventful. However that same evening, during a night training exercise for new pilots, an anti-aircraft defense unit put its searchlights on a flight of 14th Group aircraft and tracked them for some time. One of the young pilots, Lt. Leon Neubeck, was so blinded by the intensity of the lights that he crashed and was killed.

The 14th Fighter Group conducted a fighter sweep over Munich on 19 July as both B-17 and B-24 heavies attacked. A handful of Focke-Wulf 190s were spotted, and in a running dogfight three were downed, one each by 48th Squadron Lts. Henry Van Horn, Boyce Langley, and Michael Brezas. 1st Lt. Walter White damaged a 109. After two P-51 groups arrived to assume escort duties the 14th was released, and went down to strafe targets of opportunity over Austria and northern Italy.

The widespread action was not without its cost. Lt. Donald Van Gilder was lost during the engagement with enemy aircraft. Lts. David Wilson and Aurelian Jekot, 37th Squadron, collided near Munich, and both were forced down to become prisoners. Lt. Richard Thompson (49th) and Cody Stout (48th) collided near San Giorgio, Italy, and both were killed.

Nor was this the end of a tragic day of mid-air collisions, as Lts. Oliver Bryant and Walter McConnell, 49th Squadron, touched P-38s over Germany. Bryant's plane was only slightly damaged, but McConnell was in serious trouble:

"My right engine was damaged, and the prop bent so that it wouldn't feather. My squadron commander immediately sent a ship to escort me home. However, my bad prop was windmilling, and I was unable to keep the ship from spiraling to the right; I was losing about 500 feet altitude per minute. So I sent the escort back to the squadron, telling him that I would probably have to crash land.

At about 11,500 feet the bad prop stopped windmilling, and I found that I was able to maintain altitude by using 50 inches of manifold pressure and 2,800 rpm on my good engine. This held my air speed at 120 mph....

Just as I was crossing the coast of the Adriatic I saw a single-engined aircraft coming toward me from about 8 o'clock, so I ducked into a cloud layer at about 8,000 feet. I was unable to climb back out of the clouds, and I didn't want to sacrifice my altitude to get below them. So I stayed on instruments for about an hour and a half, came out of the clouds just off Ancona Point, and turned to a heading for Triolo.

As I started my approach my landing gear refused to come down. I started pumping, but ran out of gas before I could get them down, and had to belly in to a wheat field about five miles from the base."

On 20 July the group was on escort duty in northern Italy when enemy aircraft were engaged in the Udine area. In a brief dogfight, Lt. Michael Brezas shot down a Me 109, while Lts. Don Wimmer and Nello Infanti each damaged one. There were no losses.

The 14th escorted heavy bombers to Brux, Germany, the following day, and again the 48th encountered most of the action, as some 40-50 *Luftwaffe* fighters went after the bombers. There were no losses, and claims were as follows:

2nd Lt. Michael Brezas, 48th	0/0/1
1st Lt. Don Wimmer, 48th	0/0/1
2nd Lt. Dock Welch, 48th	1/0/0

Lt. Don Luttrell and his P-38J, named after his red-headed wife. (Luttrell)

1st Lt. Walter White, 48th	1/0/0
2nd Lt. Richard Pinter, 48th	0/0/1
2nd Lt. George O'Connor, 48th	0/0/1
2nd Lt. George Johnson, 49th	0/0/1
Totals	2/0/5

22 July 1944 proved to be a noteworthy day in the history of the 14th Fighter Group. They flew two missions: one an uneventful 16-plane escort to Ploesti, and the other an action filled, five and one-half hour trip to hit airfields in Rumania. The targets of the latter operation were Buzau and Zilestia, with a shuttle flight to Russia. The 14th provided top cover, while the 82nd Fighter Group strafed. Thirty FW 190s (likely IAR 80s) and a few Me 109s were encountered, and proved "capable and aggressive," according to the post mission briefing. From deep in Rumania the 14th flew on to a prearranged landing at an airbase in Mirgorod, in the Russian Ukraine. Henry Van Horn recalls the battle and the hectic aftermath:

"Over the target we got into a hell of a fight. When enemy fighters jumped us I was unfortunate to find myself alone after breaking into four 109s coming in from behind me. I saw I was in for it, so I hit the deck and headed for Russia alone. My radio was out, so I couldn't call for help.

Three 109s stayed on my tail close enough for me to see the white prop spinners. I dumped flaps and racked around to the right, and they missed me. I guess their gunnery wasn't so hot, or I would have had it then and there. I caught one as he chandelled up, and gave him a good burst. I saw hits, and he rolled over and started down from about 200 feet. I didn't see him hit, so it couldn't be confirmed.

My gas was getting low, and I began to sweat getting over the front lines. When I saw the Dnieper River I was more at ease, but I was running out of gas, so I landed on a wheat field some twenty miles from my destination.

When the Russian peasants came out of the little village to see what was going on they were just like those you read about in books and see in movies. They all wore plain clothes, and some were barefoot; they were wary. I stood on the wing of the P-38 and waved them over. When they finally became convinced that I was American and not German they became very friendly. They gave me food and water, and took me to the mayor of the town, who was very helpful in getting word to Mirgorod that I was safe.

I spoke with a lot of them, who understood a little English, and they let it be known that they liked America very much. It was the dream of some to come to America. The mayor took me to his home, and his wife had a big dinner in progress. That night we had a big feast and drank vodka (as long as I could take it), and the village girls put on a dance for me. The girls were healthy and nice looking. I stayed with the mayor that night, and the next morning a mechanic arrived with some gasoline so that I could fly on to Mirgorod."

Lt. Leroy Strader (37th) survived combat, but was lost on a ferry flight over the Bay of Biscay on 10 August 1944. (Walker)

As they flew over Russia, the P-38 pilots were particularly struck by the degree of devastation to some towns. However, the Russians were friendly and helpful according to 48th Squadron pilot Walter White:

"We were surprised at the number of Russian women in uniform. A Russian girl who was a 3rd Lieutenant, and who had learned English at a university in Moscow, was our liaison. The Russians were very curious and anxious to learn about our planes and operations, but were unwilling to give out any information about their own equipment. They expressed the desire to come up to American standards of living and production."

Claims for the day were as follows:

Lt. Col. Tom Whitehouse, 14th	0/0/2
2nd Lt. Charles Leonard, 37th	1/1/1
2nd Lt. Darrel Stoyke, 37th	0/1/0
2nd Lt. Fred Branscombe, 37th	0/0/3
2nd Lt. Michael Brezas, 48th	2/0/0
1st Lt. William Church, 48th	0/1/1
1st Lt. Nello Infanti, 48th	2/0/1
1st Lt. Boyce Langley, 48th	1/0/0
Maj. Frank Robinson, 48th	1/0/0
2nd Lt. George O'Connor, 48th	1/0/0
1st Lt. Walter White, 48th	1/0/0
1st Lt. Don Wimmer, 48th	2/0/0
2nd Lt. Harold Thysell, 48th	0/1/0
2nd Lt. Henry Van Horn, 48th	0/1/0
2nd Lt. Dock Welch, 48th	0/0/1
Totals	11/5/9

Losses for the day included Lts. Don West and George O'Connor of the 48th missing over Rumania. West was killed in action, but O'Connor lived to tell of his adventure. After having his right engine damaged he managed to down a FW 190, but found many enemy aircraft on his tail. He witnessed his canopy being shot off and his instrument panel shot up, and decided to "evacuate the premises."

He descended in his chute into a cornfield, and was soon surrounded by soldiers and farmers, and taken to one of the airfields that had recently been abused by the 82nd Fighter Group. Interrogated by a German officer, he was provided details regarding personnel of the 48th Squadron, including a pilot roster, in an effort to induce his cooperation. A Rumanian officer did further interrogation before O'Connor was taken off to a POW facility near Bucharest, where he joined approximately 100 other American airmen. As advancing Russian ground forces neared the city and the Germans retreated, the *Luftwaffe* bombed the POW buildings. The Rumanians capitulated, and protected their American and British guests until repatriation could be arranged.

Weather held the Mirgorod contingent on their Russian base for a few days. Then they flew short-range sorties, patrolling roads and shooting up German ground units, finally strafing a German airdrome at Milec, Poland. The 37th and 48th believed they had destroyed a dozen enemy aircraft of various types and damaged several more. All subjected the rail targets to a heavy strafing.

During the period that the major portion of the 14th was on detached service to Russia, the balance of the group flew escort missions to Linz, Austria, and Turin, Italy. Capt. James Smyth (37th) was missing over Austria, but was later confirmed as a POW.

Returning from the Russian shuttle mission on 26 July, the 14th flew over Rumania once again, and bagged a pair of Ju 52 transports. Lt. Col. Tom Whitehouse and Lt. James Mitchell got the credit.

The reassembled group flew an escort to Rumania on 28 July that resulted in the unexplained loss of Lt. David Reid (37th), missing near Niksic, Yugoslavia.

The final two days of July involved additional escort missions to Rumania, with no claims for enemy aircraft and no losses.

After its historic Russian shuttle mission, the 14th was allowed to stand down for the first two days of August 1944. There was routine training and maintenance, a Betty Grable movie, and for some, sleep to recharge their batteries.

On 3 August the group flew two missions: an escort to Frederichshafen, Germany, and a fighter sweep over Yugoslavia. There were no aerial encounters, but the gang had a circus shooting up locomotives, barges, and tugs in Yugoslavia. There were no losses.

A fighter sweep of the airdrome at Valence was flown on 6 August, with the P-38s dropping fragmentation bombs to damage grounded aircraft. The *Luftwaffe* did not appear, but flak was intense, as usual, and claimed Lt. Robert Simpson of the 48th, whose aircraft crashed on the field. Simpson and a 14th weather officer, Lewis Gould, had been high school and college chums back in Michigan. Just before the mission of the 6th departed, Simpson gave his ring to Gould, and in one of those precognitive episodes—rare but not unheard of in wartime—said "Send this home. I won't be back."

During a mission to Germany on 7 August, the *Luftwaffe* showed its face for the first time in many days. The 48th Fighter Squadron mixed it with some Me 109s. 1st Lt. Michael Brezas scored two kills, and Lts. William Church and Dock Welch claimed one each. Lt. Roy Sielert was killed in action on this mission.

Operations on 9 August to Budapest, Hungary, and 10 August to Ploesti, Rumania, produced nothing but mission credits. There were no losses. However, a veteran pilot of the 37th Squadron, 1st Lt. Leroy Strader, was lost on the 10th. He had left Britain to ferry a specially modified P-38 designed for bombing (called a "Droop Snoot") back to Italy. Somewhere along the circuitous route he vanished.

8

Operation DRAGOON Southern France

Dubbed operation DRAGOON, the invasion of France along its Mediterranean shore took place on 15 August 1944 in the Provence region, near Cannes, and St. Tropez, east of Toulon. The invasion fleet numbered in the hundreds, including battleships and aircraft carriers. Despite the naval air cover, the 1st and 14th Fighter Groups were temporarily transferred to Corsica, from whence they flew frequent support missions. From the airbase at Aghione, Corsica, they were just 100 miles from the beachhead.

The invasion plan called for preliminary landings the night of 14 August, along with the drop of paratroops just behind the beachhead. D-Day would take place on the 15th, following a bombardment of coastal fortifications.

On 13 August the 14th Fighter Group was directed to strafe airdromes just inland from the planned invasion area. These airfields had been visited before and had yielded little. The otherwise excellent German intelligence had not detected the buildup of naval strength, and they were spread too thin to provide substantial air units at this part of Hitler's Fortress Europe. The mission of the 13th involved a takeoff in the late afternoon from Corsica. The theory was that *Luftwaffe* aircraft would be caught on the ground. Don Luttrell, leading the 49th Squadron, recalls the day:

"The 49th was to strafe the Orange airdrome, while the 37th and 48th provided top cover. Things went routinely. We were right on the deck all the way, and hit the target dead on. But intelligence was bad [or German capability was limited], and there was not a single aircraft on the field, nor in any revetment. But the AA defense was waiting.

They opened up on us like it was the Fourth of July. The mission report described it as intense, accurate light and heavy flak. One of our P-38s got hit right over the field, and I saw Lt. Don Tracy pull up slightly, a big stream of fire coming from under the aircraft. He rolled over, the nose dropped, and he hit the ground inverted, rolling up into a ball of fire about a half-mile long.

Our strafing done, we escorted the other two squadrons to Valence. They had the same kind of luck; no airplanes on the ground, but an alert antiaircraft defense. They lost at least one plane, because I saw the explosion [Lt. Clarence Thompson, 37th Squadron]. On the way out I shot up two gun positions and a radar tower that I just happened to stumble across, and we came out of France with at least two losses and nothing to show for it. [There had been a third loss, Lt. Elmer Torgeson, 37th Squadron.]

T/Sgt Charles Mauss with the 14th Group's B-17. Retired from bombing operations, it served as a transport until a disastrous event on Corsica. (Mauss)

On the way home, due to the late takeoff, darkness fell, and we arrived at Corsica after dark. It was a clear night, and the wind was absolutely calm—and therein laid the problem. The first aircraft landed with no problem, but we were landing on a dirt strip, and usage had created a fine layer of talcum-like dust. When the early arrivals landed their prop wash stirred up the dust into a cloud that didn't go anywhere, but just hung over the field. From that point on, the rest of the squadron couldn't see where to land. It was a horrible situation.

One of our pilots, Lt. Lloyd Bro, put his landing lights down, mistook the top of the dust cloud for the runway, and landed about fifteen feet in the air. When the P-38 stalled out it came crashing down, and pieces flew all over that end of Corsica. He was unharmed, but the aircraft was destroyed....

I managed to get on the ground safely by heading toward the runway lights from way out and setting up a slow, constant rate of descent. When I entered the dust I just held my heading and rate of descent, and hit the runway between the runway lights. On the roll out I could make out one or two runway lights ahead to maintain direction. Once down I had to kill my landing lights, because the light shining back from the dust blinded me."

The strafing mission of 13 August had, indeed, cost the lives of three pilots. The only good news was that the invasion fleet was relatively unmolested by the German air force.

Starting 14 August, the group flew constant daylight patrols over the Allied fleet, never encountering a single intruder. Beginning on D-Day, the P-38s flew sortie after sortie, bombing coastal defenses and highway junctions that might funnel German reinforcements to the beachhead. These patrol and close support missions continued through 20 August, until the invasion was moving inland behind retreating German forces. Throughout the period from 14 to 20 August the group conducted hundreds of sorties from Corsica, with pilots putting in two or three trips per day.

Three more P-38s went down on the dangerous low-level missions of 14 August: Lts William Tippett (48th) and Walter McConnell (49th) were killed in action, and Moses Long (49th) was taken prisoner after crashing near Montfrin, France. Nor were all the losses due to enemy action, as Don Luttrell recounts:

"On 16 August Wayne Woody (49th Squadron) was scheduled to lead a flight of four to dive-bomb a target in France. Takeoff was at five o'clock in the morning, still very dark. For dive-bombing missions you had a belly tank on one side and a bomb on the other side. Sometimes you would get out to the airplane, and the belly tank would be on the left side and the bomb on the right side, or vice versa. It was important that you look to see which side had the gas tank, as once you got in the air, if you didn't remember, you couldn't see exactly what was where.

This kind of mix-up is what happened to Woody. He took off with the belly tank on the left and the bomb on the right. After he got in the air, not being able to visually check, he switched both fuel selectors to the bomb side, and both engines quit. He was at about 3,500 feet when this happened, and there was a heavy mist on the edge of the water. He turned back toward the field. We don't know if he tried to switch back to a fuel tank, but he never got his engines restarted. His wingman followed him down to 2,000 feet and lost him in the mist. He didn't answer the radio. The other two planes went on and completed the mission, and Woody's wingman came on back to report him missing. At daylight a ship went out to search, and found debris and an oil slick."

Maj. Franklin Robinson, commanding the 48th Fighter squadron, was killed in action over France during a later mission that day. And the deaths of Woody and Robinson were just the beginning of the most disastrous day in the history of the 14th Fighter Group.

T/Sgt Robert Taylor (37th) stands next to the wreckage of a P-38 on Corsica. (Walker)

Men and equipment were constantly being shuttled from Triolo, Italy, to the advanced base at Aghione, Corsica, in the group's B-17 used as a transport. On 16 August, as the old Flying Fortress approached Aghione for a landing, it suddenly went straight up in the air, stalled, fell off on the right wing, and then crashed and burned fiercely.

Dr. Bill Curtis dashed to the crash site, entered the wreckage twice, and pulled two men to safety. He was trying for a third rescue when flames drove him back. He then set about administering first aid and plasma to the survivors. Doc Curtis would later be awarded the Soldier's Medal for his heroism.

A P-38 with disposable fuel tanks lifts off for a long-range mission. (Stitt)

Doctor Bill Curtiss was present on Corsica when the B-17 crashed, and he attempted to rescue the injured. (Stitt)

Only three men escaped the wreckage, and one of them died later in the hospital. The living survivors were Cpl. William Campbell, a mechanic with the 49th Squadron, and Sgt. Eugene Gemmel, an aircrew member of the 48th Squadron. Thirteen officers and enlisted men died in the accident. The incident added to the general belief that Aghione was "jinxed."

In the following days the group continued sorties over southern France that were largely strafing, along with patrolling for what was assumed would be the inevitable appearance of the *Luftwaffe*. The closest they came to an aerial encounter was a lone Junkers 88 twin-engine bomber that was spotted near Toulouse A/D on the 17th. Col. Dan Campbell dispatched it. On that same mission, 2nd Lt. Daniel Haley of the 49th was lost to flak near Balgnac, France.

After two more days of fruitless patrol, the P-38s were ordered back to their bases near Foggia, Italy, but not before flak claimed two more P-38s. 2nd Lt. Stephen Lannan, 37th Squadron, was hit by ground fire near Arlis, France, and bailed out from 2,000 feet. He was close enough to a German Panzer unit that he had just strafed, that he was fired on as he was descending, a bullet clipping one of his shroud lines. He landed within a quarter mile of those troops, but ran and managed to hide. The next day he met locals who put him in touch with the French resistance. They took him to an area just liberated by Americans, and he was returned to his outfit.

2nd Lt. Darrell Stoyke (37th) went down while at low altitude on 19 August in such a way that he was considered killed in action.

The second invasion of France was over, and the invaders ashore were chasing the Germans north when the 14th departed Corsica for Foggia. With little respite, the group returned to their long-range escorts. The first was to Lubau, Austria, protecting a force of B-24s. Even here, deep in enemy territory, the *Luftwaffe* seemed reluctant to take on anything but unescorted bombers or stragglers. Lt. Col. Tom Whitehouse downed a Focke-Wulf 190, the only one that got close enough for an encounter. Lt. Mitchell Cwiek (37th) failed to return, and turned up a POW.

The month of August was concluded with eight more escort missions to northern Italy, Czechoslovakia, Germany, and Rumania. Only the mission to Kurim, Czechoslovakia, involved an encounter with the *Luftwaffe*. The 48th Squadron claimed several enemy aircraft as follows:

1st Lt. Michael Brezas	2/0/2
2nd Lt. Robert C. Groom	1/0/1
2nd Lt. George Partin	1/0/0
2nd Lt. Dock Welch	1/1/0
Totals	5/1/3

August had mercifully ended with the heaviest losses in the history of the 14th Fighter Group in World War II. It had suffered 27 casualties, and only two of the missing turned up as prisoners of war, while one evaded capture.

The only optimistic event of the gloomy month was the capitulation of Rumania, a German ally. The country surrendered as Russian troops crossed its border. On 31 August transports were dispatched to Bucharest to gather dozens of Army Air Force crewmembers, including 14th Fighter Group pilots that had gone down in Rumania and become POWs.

Miss Peggy Long was the American Red Cross representative at Triolo. She met returning missions with coffee and donuts. Here she helps feed Lt. Dock Welch, 48th Squadron. He was KIA on 15 November 1944. (USAF)

9

Twilight of the *Luftwaffe*

September 1944 was relatively relaxing compared to the frantic pace of August, when over a thousand individual sorties had been flown. In September Fifteenth Fighter Command only ordered 18 missions for the 14th Fighter Group, and these involved some 570 sorties. While none could be called milk runs due to the inherent dangers of mere flight in high performance aircraft, they were notable for the total absence of aerial combat. The *Luftwaffe* and its Balkan allies had seemingly abandoned the skies over Hitler's realm.

On 2 September the group was assigned to patrol the highway and rail line from Belgrade to Nis, Yugoslavia. They found long columns of motor transport and some rail traffic. Twenty-nine P-38s flying at treetop level through the mountainous country destroyed 21 locomotives and 82 freight and passenger cars, along with some 80 trucks of various types. There was intense, accurate small arms fire from determined German troops, resulting in hits on four P-38s. Lts. Neal Maloney and Alan Mohr of the 37th were missing in action. Mohr was killed, and Maloney was never found. Lt. William Church of the 48th Squadron was also lost. He had completed his 50-mission quota, and volunteered to continue in combat when he was killed on this, his 74th combat sortie.

Also lost was Lt. William Hopman (48th). Hit at low level near the village of Mokliste, the P-38 caught fire, and he was forced to crash-land. Suffering some burns, but no serious injuries, he sought the sanctuary of hill country, finding a shepherd who gave him food and water, and allowed him to spend the night in his crude hut. The next morning Hopman was linked up with partisans who brought him to Sofia, and arranged for his evacuation back to Italy. He returned on 29 October, and brought with him a dog tag of Bill Church, who had been buried by the partisans.

The 14th was back over Yugoslavia the following day, seeking river transport on the Danube. Twelve of the P-38s diverted to strafe Kovin A/D. They discovered many aircraft on the ground, including a squadron of Ju 87 dive-bombers apparently loaded and preparing for a mission. The pilots swept over the field and destroyed 21 Stukas, noting that several exploded spectacularly. The bag also included four single-engine fighters, a pair of twin-engine bombers, and two utility aircraft. A flight of just three P-38s stumbled onto an airdrome near Bavaniste, and discovered many camouflaged and well dispersed Ju 52 transports. After four or five passes it was believed that at least ten of the tri-motors were destroyed. There were no losses.

48th pilots Lts. Bill Hopman (left) and Robert Groom (sporting a souvenir Yugo cap and dagger). Hopman went down over Yugoslavia on 2 September 1944, but was aided by partisans in his escape. Groom also was MIA over Hungary, but evaded capture. (Dickenson)

Many brand new L-model Lightnings arrived at Triolo to join the Js on operational duty. The few remaining Gs were retained for training and parts. The major improvements in the L were the addition of dive flaps and a servo boost for ailerons. The experienced pilots longed to utilize these modifications in aerial combat turning situations, but would wait weeks to do so.

As the handful of veterans returned, packets of newly minted pilots also arrived to release those who were completing their tours, and to flesh out the strength of the group. In fact, there were so many replacement pilots that it was some weeks before they could be worked into combat missions. In the interim, they conducted training flights. What a contrast to the desperate days in North Africa, when men and equipment were constantly in short supply. The U.S. horn of plenty was now turning out P-38s and the pilots to fly them in record numbers. Attrition was a German dilemma, not an American problem.

One of the veterans who returned for a second tour was Capt. Bob Hullsiek, who became operations officer for the 37th Squadron.

The young replacements arriving at Triolo experienced the inevitable spate of rookie mishaps:

2nd Lt. George Reiman took off for a test hop on 17 September, and the wreckage of his plane was later found near a B-24 base. No one had seen him go down. He had flown just five missions at the time of his death.

2nd Lt. Robert Anderson had engine trouble, and bellied his P-38 in near the Bari Road. The P-38 was a wreck, but Anderson managed to escape injury.

2nd Lt. Robert Slatkow had a near fatal encounter with hypoxia: "I was flying along at 23,000 feet, and began to feel slightly faint, and the instruments became blurred. I guess I passed out, because

Maj. Emmett Wilson and Lt. Mike Brezas display the 48th Squadron scoreboard and the unit insignia in October 1944. (Dickenson)

the next thing I knew I was at 15,000 feet in a dive. I pulled the plane up and, not seeing any of my squadron about, I decided to return to base."

2nd Lt. Sterling Brubaker recalls his introduction to the 48th Squadron:

"On a cold, wet, and dreary evening I was ushered into a tent and pointed to a bunk. A wool-lined leather flight hat lay on the bunk. I glanced around to the other silent occupants of the tent, barely discernable in the dim light. 'Does that hat belong to any of you?' Silence, bordering, I thought, on hostility. I soon learned that the hat belonged to the recent occupant of that bunk, a popular and well respected pilot named Church, who had recently been killed.

Their conscious loss and anger over that loss was being played out as resentment that I should take his place. Within a few weeks two of my three tent-mates vanished over German territory, and when the third spent a night at an emergency field off the Yugoslav coast, I began to get a bit superstitious about that particular tent. It seemed to be jinxed."

During the month, long-range escort missions were flown over an expanse from Germany to Greece. Munich, Belgrade, and Budapest were frequent targets of the bombers, but only once did the 14th see the *Luftwaffe*, and that was just a pair of FW 190s too distant to be engaged. The escort sorties were uneventful, except for that of F/O Gerald Hanson on 21 September. Bound for Budapest with his 37th Squadron, he experienced the failure of first one engine, and then the other. Obliged to parachute, he came down in Yugoslavia. Initially, a peasant family cared for him, but then the local militia, allied with the Nazis, took him into custody. He was billeted at the town of Tivno when partisans attacked. They freed him, and made arrangements for his return. It was a month later to the day that he got back to the squadron.

Late in September, Allied ground forces broke through the Gothic Line at Rimini, and Marshall Kesselring's troops began a fighting retreat to the Po River country of northern Italy.

Poor weather curtailed flight operations in October 1944, with only seventeen missions. Just one was a designated strafing mission, while some strafing was also done enroute back from escort missions.

The most notable exercise of the month was the strafing attack against a German airdrome at Salonika, Greece, on 6 October. It was a four and one-half hour round trip that covered nearly 1,000 miles. Sweeping across the airfield, 35 Lightnings destroyed 18 assorted enemy aircraft, and damaged nine others. A small vessel armed with flak batteries was also attacked and sunk. The response from automatic weapons, thought to be 20 and 40mm, was intense and accurate, and took its toll. The following pilots were missing in action after the raid: Lts. John Jones and William Milton, 37th Squadron; Lts. Lloyd Bro and David MacArthur, 49th Squadron; and Lt. Richard Schmidt, 48th Squadron. Only Jones and Bro,

This Droop Snoot P-38 of the 82nd Fighter Group led formations of the 14th Fighter Group on level bombing missions. The Lightning had been modified for a bombardier and a bombsight in the gondola's nose. (Stitt)

both of whom parachuted into Salonika Bay, survived to become prisoners of war.

In between escort missions to northern Italy, Austria, and Germany there were the inevitable operational accidents. On 8 October Lt. Paul Ragusa (49th) lost an engine on takeoff and, although jettisoning his belly tanks, came back to earth in a blazing crash. Trapped in his P-38, Ragusa would certainly have died had not several enlisted personnel braved the fire and exploding ammunition to rescue him. Those gallant souls were: M/Sgt. Lewis Crooks, T/Sgt. Leonard Davisson, T/Sgt. Ross Swinford, T/Sgt Brownie Wybroski, and S/Sgt. Michael Onderchanin. All would eventually be awarded the Soldier's Medal for their heroic actions.

After escorting B-24s to Blechhammer, Germany, on 13 October, the group went down to strafe Szombathely A/D in Hungary. The attack destroyed or damaged a dozen enemy aircraft, and shot up rail rolling stock that got in their sights. Returning from this sortie, Lt. Mike Brezas had some bad moments when one of the main gears would not extend. He managed a highly skillful landing that caused minimal damage, saving his P-38 for another day.

On 19 October 2nd Lt. Carl Mellstrom (37th Squadron) was killed when he failed to pull up during a dive-bombing practice. He had only just joined the squadron on 2 October.

Lt. Jim Eddins shows the massive damage incurred from a German AA round that hit in the gun bay of his gondola. Exploding ammunition damaged the right engine over Yugoslavia. (USAF)

On 22 October a pair of 37th Squadron pilots, Lts. Warren Bates and Anthony Jerasonek, collided in mid-air at high altitude right over Triolo airfield. The two pilots both parachuted successfully. However, personnel on the ground who witnessed the incident were temporarily transfixed by the scene of the two disabled P-38s, which fell from the sky like maple leaves to land God only knew where. Buildings were evacuated, and base personnel were all spectators as one P-38 crashed harmlessly near Group Operations, and the other in a field beyond the bivouac area.

October losses were somewhat tempered by the return from the dead of several members: F/O Gerald Hanson, Capt. Robert Zimmerman, and 1st Lt. John Wakeman. Also, word was received of the release from captivity of Maj. Forrest Barker.

Again, a month had passed without any aerial contact with the *Luftwaffe*, or "the Flying Dutchmen," as the official history called them. This fostered rumors that the war in Europe was about to end, and the 14th Fighter Group would be transferred to the Pacific.

The wet, cold weather that had characterized October abated somewhat in November, and flight operations surged. There were 29 missions: 21 escort, one dive-bombing, two strafing, and three chaff dispersal. The later involved fighters preceding the heavy bombers and dispensing aluminum foil designed to frustrate enemy radar.

There was also a new bombing technique involving a socalled "Droop Snoot" equipped P-38. A Lightning's nose was modified to allow for a bombardier in a prone position. Thus equipped, the Droop Snoot would lead other P-38s for a high-level mass bombing. The 82nd Fighter Group owned the strange aircraft, and the 14th Fighter Group went along to salvo their bombs with the bombardier. The group conducted two of these level bombings.

On 1 November the group flew a long, dull escort to Vienna, then on the return the P-38s went down on the deck to hunt targets of opportunity. They accounted for nine locomotives and a string of 25 tank cars that would no longer haul fuel for the *Luftwaffe*. During the attack Lt. John Hurley (48th Squadron) had three feet of his right wingtip removed as he flew slightly above taxi level.

At the same time Lt. James Eddins was pounded by a 40mm AA gun that knocked out his right engine, and set off ammunition in the gun bay. The resulting explosion ripped off the skin of the gondola from the nose to the windscreen. A piece of the nose hit his left propeller, and still he managed to fly home some 500 miles through bad weather.

2nd Lt. Ray Trombley was last seen during the strafing attack, and was presumed killed, but he turned up a POW in Hungary.

The 14th Fighter Group escorted reconnaissance aircraft to Munich and Augsburg on 5 November and then, having been relieved of their shepherd duties, went back to low level strafing of the German rail system. By post mission accounts the group destroyed four locomotives and a variety of rolling stock for the loss to flak of Lt. Lawrence Bach of the 37th Squadron. As it turned out, he avoided capture and was returned by Yugoslav guerillas a few days later.

Bach was brought to the island of Vis, totally under the control of friendly Yugoslavians and British forces, and from which both air and sea rescues were conducted. During his brief stay he was

48th Squadron ground personnel pose for a "camp" picture at Triolo in October 1944 (L. to R.): Standing: John Hay, Ted Alsobrook, Ray Crawford, Robert Calhoun, Niles Miller, Harold Blazer, and Mike Suscreba. Kneeling: William Frazier, Al Bischoff, J. Moran, James Coleman, and Harry Slemmer. (Dickenson)

The 14th Fighter Group encountered their first German jet fighters on 22 November 1944 near Munich. This photo shows an example of the Messerschmitt 262.

The Fifteenth Air Force began using radar to bomb through clouds late n 1944. The near 97th Bomb Group B-17 has a radar unit in its belly in place of the two-gun ball turret. (Lambert)

The war was progressing well enough in late 1944 that both officers and enlisted men were granted short leaves for rest and recuperation. The scene here is an idyllic beach on the isle of Capri. (USAF)

made aware of the political split between the partisan forces of Tito and those of the Chetniks, which would involve the post war ascendancy of Marshal Tito's communists to power in Yugoslavia. Tito's people were requesting bombing attacks on the Chetniks even before the German occupiers were completely gone.

A test hop ended in a fatality on 12 November when the P-38 of 2nd Lt. John Hurley (48th) plummeted out of control from high altitude to crash some six miles southeast of Triolo airfield. There was no radio communication, and no explanation for the accident.

On 15 November the group escorted a photo reconnaissance aircraft to southern Germany. It was another milk run, until the P-38s went down to strafe targets of opportunity over northwest Yugoslavia. The light caliber flak, always dangerous at treetop level, reached out to claim a pair of 48th Squadron pilots: Maj. Wilbur Grumbles and 1st Lt. Dock Welch. Welch had been just one mission shy of his 50-mission quota.

The 14th Fighter Group joined with the 82nd in a pair of high-level bombing missions, with the man in the Droop Snoot P-38 doing the aiming, and everyone else salvoing their 500s with the lead bombardier. The first mission was aborted because of cloud cover, and the bombs were dumped in the Adriatic—no report on the fish score. The second, at a village crossroads in Yugoslavia, was intended to hamper German columns retreating north. The bombing was impressive, but made the fighter pilots feel more like dump truck drivers.

The main building at Triolo was named Triolo Tech, housing educational and other facilities for the benefit of 14th personnel. (USAF)

Veteran Capt. Harvey Honeycutt (37th) led several group missions. (Stitt)

One of the new guys, 2nd Lt. Sterling Brubaker, got to fly his first missions about this time, and recalls the experience vividly:

"It was an escort trip to Vienna, but with a kicker. We were assigned to go in before the bombers and drop chaff. It provided my first close-up view of those innocuous little black puffs that, as I believed, were never meant for me. The leader (Robert Groom) was an experienced pilot who maneuvered violently, having had more exposure to flak than I. All went well.

On the next flight, still flying as Red Two, I suddenly became group leader! The bomber commander complained that a strange plane had joined his formation, and asked us to cut him out. The group leader undertook that task, telling me to maintain course. There I was, sitting magnificently in front of 48 mighty P-38s, and hoping that nothing would happen.

The strange bomber proved stubborn, but my leader, like a quarter horse working cattle, finally managed to force him out. Now the bomber commander demanded that we take that stranger back, and see that it landed in Italy. Finally the stray came on the radio, and I was assigned to take him back. Now chastened, he requested my permission to bomb an alternative target enroute. 'Granted.'"

On 17 November, following an escort mission to Vienna, F/O Bill Karstetter was forced to parachute from his P-38 over Yugoslavia due to lack of fuel. He was circled as he dropped successfully, and Capt. William Teare reported that Karstetter was last seen talking to a young slender lady in a black dress—so the day wasn't a complete loss. Partisans assisted Karstetter in a long trek through the rugged country. He traveled by foot, horse, and captured Italian and German trucks, meeting other British, South African, and American prisoners along the way. The Allied contingent was eventually picked up along the Adriatic coast by a landing craft and returned to Bari, Italy, on 4 December 1944.

The Hunter brothers managed to stay together during their Army service. The 49th Fighter Squadron was fortunate to have the musical siblings. (L. to R.) Standing, twins Richard and Verner, and brother Gerald, kneeling.

An escort of B-24s to Munich on 22 November was noteworthy because the 14th Fighter Group encountered three enemy aircraft, sans propellers. While flying at 26,000 feet the group formation saw the strange craft (later identified as a pair of Messerschmitt 262 jets and a rocket-powered Me 163) diving from out of the sun toward the 49th Squadron. The group dropped belly tanks and turned into the attack. Never getting too close, the mysterious visitors thundered past, and did a 360-degree turn as if to institute a second attack. However, with the noses of three-dozen P-38s pointed their direction the German pilots settled for a half-hearted pass at the bomber stream and dove away. Lt. Gene De Martini, "tail-end Charlie" in the last flight of the 49th, was closest to the attacking jets. He saw their tracers going over his canopy, and figured since they had all the advantage he should have been dead. "Their gunnery was damn lousy," he observed.

As the group was making a 90-degree turn through heavy weather during this mission, the P-38 of 2nd Lt. Carl Ergott vanished from the 37th Squadron. He did not respond to radio calls, and was never heard from again. In fact, he had become a victim of a Me 262 of JG 7. (See *Me 262 Combat Diary* by Foreman & Harvey, pg. 97.)

The first dogfight for the 14th in three months occurred on 26 November, when the P-38s were assigned to attack Seregelyes A/D in Hungary. As they approached from low altitude, prepared to strafe, a variety of enemy aircraft were seen in the landing pattern. While the 37th Squadron provided top cover, the 48th and 49th went after the rare airborne targets, which consisted of Ju 87 Stukas and a Me 109 Gustav. Single kills were scored by the following pilots: Capt. William Teare, and Lts. Rene Therriault, Stanley Walters, Arthur Moenkhaus, Marvel Taylor, Victor Zuzeck, and Don Utermahlen. Lt. Charles Hughes had downed a small military transport enroute to the target, and 1st Lt. John McGowan destroyed an FW 190 along the departure route.

However, the low-level melee proved to be a field day for the flak batteries defending Seregelyes. They took out four P-38s of the 49th Squadron. The pilots were: Capt. William Edwards, and Lts. George Baird, Gene De Martini, and Lawrence Goffena. None survived.

One final disaster was averted when a 49th Squadron tent, occupied by four new pilots, caught fire in the middle of the night. Although losing some clothing and personal possessions, everyone survived this potential catastrophe.

The Thanksgiving dinner—the third overseas for the 14th Fighter Group—was turkey with all the trimmings; those earlier Thanksgiving meals on canned British mutton were a distant memory for the older vets.

Some of those old timers among the enlisted men were now being favored with 30-day furloughs back to the States. And leaves were being granted to Capri and Rome, a sure sign that World War II was in the home stretch.

The innovation of radar in the four-engined heavies of the Fifteenth Air Force banished mission aborts due to targets being obscured. Hence, in December 1944 the 14th flew 52 missions, and nearly 1,000 sorties. Forty-nine of the month's operations were of the escort variety, with strafing on the return at the discretion of group and squadron leaders. The strategic targets were primarily oil and transportation, and the region of operations was primarily over Germany, Austria, and Northern Italy. No more wide ranging flights to France or Greece, as the Allied armies were tightening the three-front noose, and squeezing the German armies toward the Fatherland. Russian troops, after crashing through Rumania, had forced the capitulation of Bulgaria, and Belgrade had fallen in late October.

On 2 December a small force of P-38s conducted an armed reconnaissance of the Zagreb area. They found little of interest, except for a lone Ju 88 bomber that wandered onto the scene. Lt. Col. Tom Whitehouse, leading the mission, chased the German aircraft and shot it down. He bore the evidence of its defensive fire on the nose of his P-38.

There was a brief encounter with the *Luftwaffe* over Czechoslovakia on 6 December, as the 14th Fighter Group escorted B-24 Liberators bombing marshalling yards. The Big Friends called that they were under attack, and as soon as the P-38s appeared a force of some fifteen Me 109s dove through cloud cover to escape. One laggard got in the sights of Lt. Oliver Bryant (49th Squadron) and was shot down.

There was another brief sighting of German jets on 9 December, as the group escorted a photo recon ship near Munich. The contrail of two Me 262s was seen at 23,000 feet, 3,000 above the P-38s. As the formation turned to meet the jets, the swift ships made an ineffective diving pass and disappeared into cloud cover. Shortly thereafter another pair of Me 262s made a brief appearance. Lt. Sylvon Vidrine, 37th Squadron, fired at them from beyond effective range. The jets then broke sharply to avoid the P-38s, and vanished in the overcast. The P-38 pilots were awed by the speed and maneuverability of the German jets, but were also amazed at their reluctance to engage.

Sometimes the weather was more formidable than the enemy. Such was the case on 10 December, when the group was assigned as escort to bombers destined for Brux, Germany. The group leader was Capt. Harvey Honeycutt, a veteran of 65 missions, back on his second tour of combat. He took off on instruments 30 minutes ahead of the rest to find a clear assembly area. After successfully gathering his 36 Lightnings below the overcast, he proceeded to climb through the soup toward rendezvous, breaking out on top at 29,000 feet. In the meantime, the bombers had been recalled because of the terrible weather conditions over Germany, but the escort failed to receive the message. Eventually the P-38s broke into separate flights for safety. Honeycutt dutifully marched on as ordered to the rendezvous and, finding no bombers, turned back.

Now leading just three others, he spotted a train through a hole in the clouds and went down to strafe it. With fuel supply almost exhausted he led the formation down the Adriatic, flying under 500 feet to land at Triolo. The round trip had been 1,200 miles, and had taken more than six hours. Colonel Campbell, 14th Group CO, later commented, "That mission separated the men from the boys."

On 17 December the 14th Fighter Group was dispatched on two 30-ship escort missions for separate bomb wings attacking oil refineries in southern Germany. One mission encountered no enemy aircraft, but lost a P-38 to heavy, radar-tracking AA. While flying at 21,000 feet near Blechhammer, Lt. George Johnson's 49th Squadron aircraft took a direct hit. His plane rolled over, and then began an uncontrolled spin toward the ground. A wing was seen to break off at about 6,000 feet, but no chute was seen. In fact, Johnson managed to bail out and was taken prisoner.

On the return route, 2nd Lt. Lorenz Weiglein (37th) suddenly had engine troubles, followed by fire, and was obliged to bail out

Christmas 1944 at Triolo, the third overseas for some veterans of the 14th Group, was shared with the children, priest, and nuns of a local Catholic orphanage. (USAF)

over the Adriatic. On his descent he spotted a ship, but thought it had ignored his plight. Sometime later, as he floated in his one-man rubber dingy, the vessel reappeared, approaching him cautiously. It seems that Weiglein had landed in a minefield. He was, however, rescued by the partisan crew, taken to Vis Island, and returned to Bari, Italy, within a few days.

The other wing of the 14th Group, led that same day by 1st Lt. Louis Swirczynski (48th Squadron), observed many FW 190s and Me 109s approaching the B-24 formation near Odertal Refinery. P-38s of the 48th and 49th Squadrons engaged the enemy with the following results:

1st Lt. Robert Groom, 48th	1/0/0
2nd Lt. Walter Stimler, 48th	1/0/0
2nd Lt. Arthur Moenkhaus, 48th	0/1/0
2nd Lt. John Michelsen, 49th	1/0/0
2nd Lt. Rivas Sirmon, 49th	1/0/0
1st Lt. Edwin Baquet, 49th	0/0/2
1st Lt. Robert Hauser, 49th	0/0/1
2nd Lt. George Hochstetler, 49th	0/0/1
1st Lt. Ernie Latham, 49th	0/0/1
Totals	4/1/5

The engagement resulted in the loss of two P-38s and their pilots. 2nd Lt. Ernest Roundtree was last seen attacking an enemy fighter, and it was believed he flew into the path of the fire from a P-51 also attempting to down the German. He was never seen again.

2nd Lt. David Miles called that he had an engine on fire, and was bailing out over Czechoslovakia. He parachuted successfully, and was made a prisoner.

Lt. Col. Tom Whitehouse had gotten a late start in joining the group that day, but was unable to locate them, and proceeded to chase the mission north. He spotted a pair of trains that deserved attention near the Austrian-Czech border and, after strafing one locomotive to a stop, he was engaged by a pair of 109s. In a brief maneuvering joust he managed to down one, and the second retreated.

The recent aerial engagements had led to the belief that the *Luftwaffe* was re-emerging. But the dogfights of the 17th proved to be the last enemy contacts for the month.

Veteran pilot Capt. George Wightman rejoined the 37th Squadron, volunteering for another tour of combat. He had previously served in the North Africa and Sicily campaigns.

Christmas and New Years parties—the third overseas for some enlisted men, the North African veterans—were elaborate affairs, celebrated with much gusto in the ever improving facilities at Triolo. There was always music for such occasions, particularly because of the three Hunter brothers of the 49th Squadron. Gerald, Richard, and Lowell Hunter had managed to get themselves into the same outfit after aviation mechanic school, and brought their love of music and their instruments with them: a guitar, violin, and even a bass fiddle.

The 48th Squadron boasted another accomplished musician, Lonnie King, who played Gershwin by the hour on the piano at the Officer's Club.

The men of the 14th did not forget the most needy among the civilian population, with parties and gifts for children from a nearby orphanage.

Any hopes for a German rout in Italy were dismissed, as German forces dug in near Bologna launched a brief counteroffensive. Divisions transferred to Southern France and Greece (a continuing goal of Winston Churchill) had depleted Allied forces, and although not strong enough to push the Germans back, they stemmed the brief Christmas offensive.

Sunny Italy in the winter of 1944. (Stitt)

10

Workin' on the Railroads

During 29 combat missions in the month of January 1945, the 14th Fighter Group did not record a single engagement with enemy fighters. Indeed, the entire Fifteenth Fighter Command did not record more than a dozen claims against German aircraft of all types, reflecting the ghastly casualties that had been inflicted on the *Luftwaffe* in prior years. Its fighter production had climbed steadily throughout the first half of 1944, but its experienced aircrews had been lost at an irredeemable rate. The German veterans got occasional leave, but lacked a certain mission quota. They served until they died. And the combined onslaught of the strategic air forces from England and Italy, plus the demands of the Russian front, had kept gnawing at German fighter strength. By 1945 the capability of surviving air defense forces had been seriously impaired.

Kesselring's German ground forces, although doggedly battling along the Po River Line, were also in jeopardy. The narrow front permitted Allied tactical squadrons to hammer the battlefield, and stifle road and rail supply. These ground support squadrons were in such abundance that several had been withdrawn from Italy to operate from Corsica and Southern France. While the ground situation was relatively static, Allied planners began to see their mission more as one to prevent Kesselring from retreating. The plan was to deny the use of his forces on either the Western Front, now approaching the Franco-German border, or the Eastern Front, where Russian troops drove relentlessly forward. Indeed, by January the Germans were beginning the process of selected withdrawal of divisions toward the Russian menace. The tactical air forces concentrated their efforts on rail and highway communications to prevent either the arrival of supplies, or the removal of German troops and armor.

Assisting in this effort, the Fifteenth Air Force focused its attention against the deeper lines of communication, particularly the rail and highway route over the Alps from Italy to Austria—the Brenner Pass.

Capt. George Whitman, a North African veteran, returned for a second tour of combat with the 37th. He was shot down and killed by large caliber AA fire on 4 January 1945. (Crocker)

This was more or less typical of late war tent-type housing at Triolo. Occupants were Tommie Thomas and Don Luttrell of the 49th. It had three rooms, a brick floor, and hot and cold running water. Note the use of an elevated drop tank as a liquid reservoir. (Luttrell)

Along with the standard escort missions to communications targets, the 14th participated on another level bombing mission with the bombardier of the 82nd Fighter Group doing the aiming from a Droop Snoot P-38. The target was a railroad bridge in northern Italy near Cismon, and fifty-five P-38s participated on 4 January. Bombing was from 15,000 feet. Post mission comments reflected the belief that bombing from such high altitude did little specific damage. However, flak batteries defended the area, and shortly after the bombs were salvoed a 88mm burst took the entire tail section and boom aft of the coolant radiators off one P-38. It was piloted by Capt. George Wightman, leading the 37th Squadron. The plane spun to the ground, and although a streaming parachute was seen, it never opened.

January harbored the normal number of casualties from flak, weather, and gremlins. On 11 January a pair of new 37th pilots were engaged in a training mission near Foggia when their P-38s caught fire within a few minutes of each other. Lt. Ingalls bailed out successfully, but Lt. James Logan was killed when his ship crashed. Sabotage was suspected, but the wreckage yielded no evidence as to the cause of the simultaneous failures.

On 20 January the group escorted B-24s to Linz, Austria, without difficulty, and some went down to strafe rail traffic near Villach, Austria. Near the same town, the P-38 of Lt. William Anderson was seen to catch fire for unknown reasons. Squadron mates witnessed the P-38 role over and crash to the ground, and assumed that Anderson had been killed. However, he had managed to bail out and was taken prisoner. By late afternoon, when the remaining P-38s had been accounted for (one at Ancona and another at Vis), there was yet another missing. Lt. Glen Cook had returned early because of mechanical problems. When he and an escort descended through overcast at 25,000 feet Cook did not emerge, and was never found. Both Anderson and Cook were 48th Squadron members.

Lt. Stanley Walters (48th) failed to return from a mission over Austria on 21 January, but turned up a POW.

Late in January, Lt. Paul Forster nearly became another victim of the excellent German AA gunnery. Crossing the Alps and heading down a valley between Spittal and Villach, Austria, the 49th Squadron went after some moving rail traffic, as Forster recalls:

"Just as I raised my wing to miss hitting a church steeple all hell broke loose. The bursts felt like a sledgehammer against the cockpit, and I figured I'd had it. Gas was gushing out of my left tank, and fire was blazing about five feet from the trailing edge of the wing. So I firewalled everything and got the hell out of there.

It was a miracle, because the fire went out, and I feathered the left propeller. Then I made a turn, headed my plane for base, and started praying. Due to the help I got from my call on the emergency homing channel I made it to a friendly, field but had to pump my wheels down to land. Did you ever pump landing gear down? With my knees still knocking, I got out of the cockpit, and found that all the gas I had left was ten gallons. I counted the flak damage to my ship. There were 58 holes of various sizes."

On the last day of January the 37th Squadron was strafing a rail siding over southern Austria. As the flight pulled up from the target Lt. John McGowan saw a puff of smoke behind him, and an aircraft burning on the ground. It turned out to be the P-38 of Lt. Ben Jackson, who was killed in the crash.

The 14th Fighter Group managed 47 missions and nearly 1,000 individual sorties in February, despite the fact that flight operations were rain shortened by five days. The targets for deep escort were the familiar industrial and communications centers of Regensburg, Munich, and Augsburg in Germany, and Linz and Vienna in Austria. There was just one dive-bombing mission, and three missions organized as strafing operations, but the group did freelance strafing on nine occasions after their escort duties were completed.

On 8 February, during a sweep near Vienna that followed bomber escort, the 37th Squadron was attacking rail targets when

Lt. Fred Branscombe of 14th Group Headquarters prepares for a mission. S/Sgt Gene Radkey (37th) assists with the parachute. Branscombe was killed in action on 9 February 1945 by AA fire while strafing over Austria. (Stitt)

Lt. Lawrence Bach spotted a flight of bogies in the distance. He gave chase and overtook some eight biplane trainers flying in tight formation. Bach dispatched two, probably destroyed a third, and damaged a fourth.

That same day, during strafing near Ybbs, Austria, Capt. Kyle Pinney and Lt. Fred Branscombe were victims of AA fire, and were both killed in action. Pinney had completed a tour of combat in B-24s, and had volunteered to return for some soldiering in fighters. He was on his fortieth mission when lost.

Again the same day, while escorting a photo recon aircraft, a five-ship formation from the 48th encountered German Me 262s. Lt. Robert Anderson (48th) was leading the escort near Munich when a pair of the German jet fighters made an ineffective attack from behind. A pair of P-38s pursued, but could not get within effective firing range. As they rejoined the escort formation another pair of 262s was seen attacking. As the swift jets fled a close encounter, the returning P-38 pilots fired on them without results. However, the Germans scored some hits on the aircraft of Lt. Richard Sherman, the Tail-end-Charlie. Although he was obliged to feather one engine, he managed to get back over the Alps and made a belly landing at Ancona, Italy.

New P-38L models were being ferried to Triolo on 15 February when one split-essed into the ground from 4,000 feet for no apparent reason. The wreck, with Lt. Nunzie Mineo inside, was found near Lesina landing ground. The young pilot had yet to fly a combat mission.

16 February was one of those escort missions where, after completing duty to the bombers, the 14th went after German railroads. The P-38s spiraled down from 22,000 feet to tree top level, and shot up rolling stock in the Regensburg area. During the descent, the aircraft of F/O Frederick Farrar was seen to burst into flame at 6,000 feet. He rolled over as if to bail out, but no chute was observed.

Successive rail attacks followed on the next three days, in which the group destroyed dozens of locomotives and scores of rail cars. Lt. Colonels Hugh Griffith (48th CO) and Charles Chitty (14th Operations Officer) led the rail scoring, as they entered a sort of loco-busting competition.

2nd Lt. Dan Wilson (37th) was lost on the strafing attack of 19 February, crashing to his death near Bruck, Austria.

Despite the absence of any aerial combat, losses continued to plague the 14th Fighter Group. Lt. Lyle Shrader (48th) was killed in a crash at Triolo on 20 February.

Before the month closed out Lt. Leon Stephen, 49th Squadron, was seen to crash land in Yugoslavia. He was immediately surrounded by a throng of locals—mostly women—who treated him like Prince Charming. He later explained:

"I thought it unwise to refuse any of the food, and after I started to eat what appeared to be fried sardines, I must admit I was glad, because I found the dish very tasty. The liquor was without a doubt the most potent alcoholic drink I have ever tasted, and the people insisted on constantly refilling my glass.... The most amusing thing was the treatment given me by the women. Contrary to custom in America, the female population eyed me from head to toe with a curious but pleasant look, my only regret being that I could not understand what they were saying."

Lt. Dan Wilson (37th) was shot down and killed while strafing over Austria on 19 February 1945. (Luttrell)

Stephens was "rescued" a few days later, and returned to Italy. By this time the partisans controlled much of the coast, and all the mountainous regions of Yugoslavia.

During February, veterans Capt. Jim Ribb and Beryl Boatman returned to the 49th Squadron for second tours of combat duty, and Capt. John Meidinger rejoined the 48th Squadron.

In March 1945 assignments for the 14th Fighter Group continued in the same vein: escort duty followed by railroad attacks. The dual strategy continued to be to starve German forces in Italy, and prevent their retreat to Germany. That meant maintaining steady pressure on the Brenner Pass corridor, and routes out of the Balkans to Austria. The group flew 48 missions of all types that involved 1,146 sorties, a record.

The mission of 1 March was more or less typical. The goal of the bombers was Moosbeirbaum, Austria. After the uneventful escort duty was complete, the P-38s, led by Lt. Col. Griffith, broke

Lt. Colonels Hugh Griffith of the 48th (left) and Charles Chitty (14th) congratulate each other on another victory over the German transportation system. (USAF)

into smaller units and, like marauding Huns, they pillaged rail lines on the return route. During one of these low-level strafing runs the Lightning of Lt. Fred Clifgard was seen to catch fire. An explosion occurred, and the plane rolled over and hit the ground, where it burned. The 48th Squadron pilot had eleven missions to his credit, and was just short of his 20th birthday.

Along with the group effort at escort missions, the 14th frequently put up smaller formations of P-38s to accompany supply drops into Yugoslavia, where the Germans were rapidly losing control of outlying territory and withdrawing north.

Missions followed to Linz, Weiner-Neustadt, and Maribor, Yugoslavia, with the same routine of escort, and then random strafing of every stretch of communications that seemed to bear any movement. The *Luftwaffe* had been long absent from this region, and now even flak was light, and only periodically encountered. However, on 10 March Lt. Herschel Sinclair had an engine fire from an unknown cause. He bailed out successfully over the Adriatic, but circling pilots lost sight of him.

Two days later fifty P-38s of the 14th Group were dispatched to dive-bomb and strafe rail targets in the Austrian panhandle. On this occasion the AA batteries were in place and functioning. Lt. Charles Pask of the 37th Squadron took a hit in his right engine while strafing an empty airdrome near Zeltweg. He immediately feathered the prop and turned into his good engine, but both engines caught fire, and the P-38 flew into a hill.

Colonel Campbell completed his tenure as commanding officer of the 14th and departed in mid-March, turning the group over to Lt. Col. Tom Whitehouse. The next day Whitehouse led a dive-bombing mission to the southern end of German controlled territory.

The fifty P-38s carried a mix of 500 and 1,000 pound bombs that destroyed bridge spans and cratered tracks. When the bombing had been completed, the pilots sought out locomotives and rolling stock for punishment from strafing. The aircraft of Lt. Clark Cornell crash-landed in Yugoslavia, and he was seen to walk away from the wreckage. Cornell was assisted by partisans, and returned to Italy a few days later.

On 16 March 1945 the 14th flew an escort mission of record length. The target for the heavy bombers was the Florisdorf oil refinery at Judenburg, Austria. There was no aerial opposition, and the group strafed targets of opportunity on the return flight. Some pilots logged six and one-half hours flying time, but everyone made it back.

Another dive-bombing mission was ordered for 18 March, this one against the previously visited railroad bridge at Varazdin, in northeastern Yugoslavia. As Capt. John Meidinger (37th) was pulling out of his dive on the target he was hit by flak at 1,500 feet. His P-38 crashed in flames, and he was lost. It was just the third sortie of the second tour of combat for this veteran.

After bombing the bridge, the group scattered to hit rail targets, and during these attacks Lt. Richard Small of the 49th Squadron was lost to small caliber fire while flying at low altitude.

Small had been flying on the wing of Capt. Temple Bowling. When an aircraft in the rear of the 49th formation saw Small's right engine erupt in flames he radioed a warning, mistakenly using Bowling's call sign. Bowling immediately released his canopy, and then took a hasty look at the engine prior to bailing out. Since he could see no fire, and his instruments showed no abnormality, he continued his bomb run. Bowling had a cold ride home without a canopy, and on landing announced: "Brother, lead me to a bottle of whiskey and let me go at it. I thought sure I'd had it, and didn't believe I'd be here to tell the tale."

The group racked up the usual score of locomotives and freight cars, including a flak car that accompanied one train.

The following day, 19 March 1945, involved another marathon flight. Escorting bombers to Landshut marshalling yard in Germany, some P-38s were airborne for seven hours, twenty-five minutes. Despite the depth of the incursion, a number of pilots strafed on the return route. Although several aircraft landed at advance fields with battle damage and low on gas, there were no losses.

That same day 2nd Lt. Arthur Tamamian, 49th Squadron, was on a test hop near Bari, Italy, when his P-38 fell from the sky for no known reason. Tamamian was found dead in the wreckage.

Vienna was the escort destination on the 20th, and it was back to Judenburg on 21 March. These were six and one-half hour sorties respectively with no losses. However, the Judenburg mission involved a strange encounter. Near the Yugoslav/Hungarian border, a flight of three 48th Squadron P-38s flying at 4,000 feet observed a pair of single-engine fighters that were immediately identified as Russian Yaks. The Russians were approaching them head-on. Flight leader Capt. Mike Brezas and the others immediately dipped their right wings several times to display aircraft profile and national insignia. One of the Yaks raised its nose and fired an ineffective burst at the P-38s, then dove to low level, zoomed back up, and fired a second errant burst. Both Yaks were then observed to dive toward the deck as if dive-bombing, only to zoom back to high altitude above and behind the P-38s, from which position they instigated another pass. Brezas departed the area at full throttle, according to the official mission report, but there are those who believe that he hosed some tracers in the direction of the undisciplined Russians.

The incident may have been a case of mistaken identity. However, P-38s from another group had inadvertently strafed a Russian motorized column in Yugoslavia in November, and any P-38 may have been suspect in the eyes of the Soviet airmen. (See *AAF in World War II*, Vol. 3, page 476.) Allied liaison officers had immediately worked with the Russian high command to establish an understanding of the fluid bomb line, but this could not prevent the air forces from occasionally intersecting, and the scope of the war made it almost certain that some individual aircrews would be uninformed.

On 22 March, while providing penetration escort to heavy bombers, the 14th Fighter Group flew its longest mission of the war. The target of the B-17s was the Ruhland Oil Refinery, some 60 miles south of Berlin. Fifty P-38s accompanied the 163 bombers, and then departed for lower altitude and targets of opportunity. Early in the return trip Lt. George Hochstetler (49th) encountered and downed a twin-engined transport.

Shortly after that a pair of FW 190s made an uncharacteristically aggressive head-on pass at a flight of 49th Squadron P-38s. Lt. John Burke returned fire, and one of the enemy aircraft was seen falling with smoke and flame evident, but it was not followed. The second Fw dove for the deck and the sanctuary of a German airdrome's flak batteries. Lt Malcolm Swimley followed and hit the German with two bursts, watching it crash to the ground. Despite the aerial combat and a grueling seven-hour plus mission, all P-38s returned.

As the group continued the daily routine of bomber escort followed by strafing operations on 24-26 March, they were menaced by a DeHaviland Mosquito in British markings one day, and then two days later were again approached by a flight of Russian fighters. After exchanging suitable recognition signals, the Yaks flew formation with the P-38s for a few minutes, then departed. A short time later, strange fighters bearing Yugoslav national markings were seen. The skies seemed to be full of everything but Germans. These sorties took place in the Austro/Yugoslav border region.

Three days of sour weather over Europe was followed by a 30 March fighter sweep of the Zagreb area by 16 Lightnings of the 14th Fighter Group. When a biplane (likely a Henschel or Gotha) with *Luftwaffe* markings was sighted, no less than eight P-38s entered the hunt. Diving to low altitude, the hapless German attempted to dodge his pursuers, but 1st Lt. Tom Collins of the 48th Squadron won the chase and downed the aircraft. It crash-landed, and was strafed to a fair-thee-well by others anxious to get a piece of the *Luftwaffe*.

On this mission pilots witnessed roads jammed with retreating military traffic and refugees. On orders from the Fifteenth Air Force they did not strafe, out of concern that civilians and possible POWs might be among the streams of humanity.

However, no mercy was shown to rail targets the following day. After escorting bombers to Linz, Austria, 47 Lightnings went down on the deck in smaller flights to hunt the railway system. Led by Lt. Col. Chitty, they shot up locomotives and other rolling stock, but found relatively few targets compared to previous missions of this type. The continuous battering of the transport system, along with track breaks, was having the desired effect. In eastern Austria Lt. Col. Hugh Griffith's P-38 took flak in the right engine and hydraulic system. With flaps and nose gear hanging down, he made an attempt at returning, but ran out of gas over Yugoslavia, and belly landed in a partisan controlled area. He returned to Italy a few days later.

Triolo in the spring was a lake, and then a sea of mud. (USAF)

11

The Grinding Finale

By April 1945, it was obvious to everyone but Adolph Hitler that the war was lost, and that the defenses of Germany were crumbling. The Allied armies in the west had crossed the Rhine, and were plunging into Germany's heartland. The Russian Army in the east was closing a vice on Berlin. In Italy, the German Army conducted a fighting retreat, but were trapped south of the Alps. The *Luftwaffe* was almost out of fuel, and was running out of fighter pilots.

The Fifteenth Air Force was also running out of strategic targets, and concentrated its efforts on the Brenner Pass, and assisting the ground campaign. They did so over Italy without the aid of fighter escort, because of the total decline of aerial opposition.

Relieved of escort duty to the heavies, the 14th Fighter Group continued shellacking German lines of transport and communication, while occasionally joining in the effort to support the ground campaign. The ebb and flow of battle in Italy was changing so fast that the fighter pilots had to constantly review intelligence on the location of the bomb line.

World War II in Europe was within weeks of being over, but people still kept falling from the sky. In April, pilots of the 14th flew sixty-seven missions totaling 1,241 individual sorties. In the process they lost fifteen P-38s and several pilots.

On 1 April fifty-one Lightnings bombed bridges in Austria, followed by strafing rail lines, racking up an array of victories over locomotives and oil and freight cars. East of Vienna, a flight of ten Russian Yaks was sighted lining up for what appeared to be a head-on pass at the P-38s. As the two formations closed, the Russians dropped into a dive that seemed to signify recognition. Then the

When the Eastern front advanced west, Russian tactical aircraft and Fifteenth Air Force units intersected in the same air space, often with unpleasant results. This is a line of Russian Yak 9 fighters at a Soviet base. (Lambert)

last Yak in the Russian formation pulled up as if to make a pass at a 48th Squadron P-38. The pilot lowered his nose and fired a warning burst. The history of the Lightning equipped 1st Fighter Group also comments on unfriendly encounters with the Soviet aircraft.

The following day the 14th Fighter Group sent two forces to the Vienna area. The first 36 Lightnings escorted heavy bombers on penetration and withdrawal. The second force of 34 Lightnings was assigned to sweep the area west of Vienna. The escort had no encounters, and returned to base. The second force was strafing rail lines when it encountered Russian aircraft (Migs and Ilyushin Stormoviks) that began firing at the P-38s. One of the Russians made a pass at Lt. Joe Onesty, who turned into the attacker. Recognition of the all too recognizable P-38s finally defused the encounter.

On that same day, Capt. Michael Brezas (48th Squadron, on his second tour of combat and 68th sortie) was strafing when he absorbed flak hits in his left engine and left rudder. With coolant streaming from the inoperative left engine, Brezas knew that he could not return to Italy. After radioing his situation to his wingman, Lt. Ken Scilley, Brezas elected to head for Rumania, then under Russian occupation. As it turned out, he might have been better off in a Stalag run by the *Luftwaffe*.

A month later, when Brezas returned to the 48th Squadron, he said that after his crash-landing he was first feasted and honored by Russian flyers. Then the Russian Army put him in a prison cell,

Capt. Mike Brezas boards his 48th Squadron P-38. (Dickenson)

where he was unable to stand or lie down, and was forced to sit in his own excrement for several days while under the constant observation of an armed guard. When finally repatriated and flown to Bari he was infected with lice, cooties, and fleas, all of which had caused open sores on his body. He had to be deloused before being returned to the squadron. It was hard for Brezas or any of the 14th Group to understand the suspicious paranoia of the Soviets that provoked such treatment toward their comrades in arms. It seems that the Cold War had already begun.

There was another encounter with German jet fighters on 4 April. A flight from the 49th Fighter Squadron was escorting an F-5 on a photo reconnaissance mission over Bavaria when a pair of Me 262s attacked from behind and below. The tail assembly of one P-38 was shot off, and the aircraft entered a flat spin. The other P-38s followed the jet in a diving turn, but could not keep up. They observed 2nd Lt. Bill Randle descending in his parachute, and he was taken prisoner.

From 5-10 April the 14th hit railroad targets in northern Italy and southern Austria without slackening. The only other activity of the group was an escort of C-47s on a supply drop to Yugoslav partisans. None of these missions incurred anything worse than an occasional hit from small arms fire.

On 11 April the luck ran out during low-level strafing of the rail corridor between Munich and Salzburg. Forty P-38s rampaged along the line in small units, destroying vast numbers of rolling stock. Flak was constant along the route, and inevitably found its mark. Capt. Harold Hoover, 37th Squadron, called that his aircraft was on fire, and said that he was bailing out. He climbed to 3,500 feet, and a minute later his P-38 was seen to go into a tight turn to the left, roll over on its back, and spin into the ground. Hoover did not exit.

About 30 minutes later a 37th flight led by 1st Lt. Robert Whitehead was just reforming from a strafing attack at 2,000 feet when a pair of FW 190s was spotted. As the P-38s attempted a turn toward the Germans, one of the 190s attacked Whitehead from behind and slightly to the rear. His P-38 burst into flames and dove into the ground. Whitehead's wingman, 1st Lt. Harry Morris, followed the German firing, got strikes, and saw the enemy pilot bail out. The other 190 escaped. It turned out to be the last aerial victory of the war for the 14th Fighter Group.

Meanwhile, the rest of the group went on with its strafing attacks. 1st Lt. Robert Therriault, leading a flight from the 48th Squadron, had just pulled up from a strafing run at a locomotive when AA hit his P-38 in the right engine. Feathering the right prop, he managed to climb to 2,000 feet and announced his intention to follow the Danube to Russian lines. With 2nd Lt. Harold Archer escorting him, Therriault gained some altitude and confidence that he could reach the Adriatic. He turned south, advising Archer that he would make for Zara, Yugoslavia. Archer went ahead, looking for a crash strip at Glina, and lost sight of the other P-38 in haze. Later he got a radio call from Therriault advising that oil pressure on the one good engine was low, and that he was steadily losing altitude, and would have to belly in somewhere. Archer did not hear further from Therriault, and it is unknown where he went down. The veteran of 52 missions was never found.

All three of the pilots lost on 11 April 1945 were apparently killed in action.

The work of interdicting the German lines of communication continued without respite. Dive-bombing bridges and rail lines in Austria and northern Italy was a seemingly endless task, because the enemy were masters at repairing broken track and severed bridges. But by April the rail cars that were being shot up were often stationary, and the stationary locomotives were cold, and not giving off steam when hit.

Five Me 262 jet fighters were observed on 17 April near Salzburg, Austria. But they only made half-hearted passes, breaking away at high speed as the P-38s turned into them. There were no casualties from that encounter, but flak batteries on rail cars caused damage to four P-38s. All pilots returned to base, but one crippled aircraft was a destroyed in a crash landing.

Photo recon missions with small flights of P-38s escorting F-5s were intermittent, and were undisturbed by either conventional or jet powered German fighters.

On 19 April fifty P-38s dive-bombed and strafed rail facilities at Weilheim, Germany. Pilots found only a single locomotive underway and strafed it. The marshalling yard contained 100/125 rail cars that looked as if they had been previously damaged.

The rail line between Innisbruck and Rosenheim, Austria, was the 14th Group's target on 20 April. As the heavily loaded P-38s were taking off from Triolo 2nd Lt. Lyle Shrader, 48th Squadron, was thought to have pulled his landing gear up prematurely. His aircraft skidded, rupturing a belly tank, then settled down on the 500-pound bombs, which exploded, blowing pilot and plane to pieces. The balance of the group carried on to "posthole" the rail line, observing no movement. Flak caused slight damage to three P-38s, but all returned.

The same section of railroad was the target of the 14th Fighter Group on the following day, 21 April. During dive-bombing, the P-38 of Capt. Robert Groom was hit by AA fire near Munich, and he was wounded. Feathering one engine, Groom was escorted by 48th Squadron Lts. Henry Duebar and James Stanhope. They proceeded west to an area known to be under Allied control, and landed safely at Wurzburg, Germany.

The 37th Squadron had just completed its bombing run through automatic weapons fire when the nose wheel doors of Lt. Richard

The rail marshalling yard at Weilheim, Germany, shows the results of a 19 April 1945 attack by the 14th Fighter Group. (Ethell)

Maj. Robert Hullsiek (left), a veteran back on his second tour of duty, and Lt. Milton Anderson, 37th Squadron, in 1945. (USAF)

Lambert's P-38 were seen to open, likely from flak damage. Before Lambert could gain altitude, Me 262s were seen approaching, and a member of his unit called for the P-38s to break left. Lambert's P-38 started to turn right, then reversed into a sharp left turn, rolled on its back, and plunged into the ground. The pilot had no opportunity to parachute.

Other P-38s of the group were alternately harassed or enticed by Me 262s. The German jet pilots seemed experienced, but their runs were not aggressive, more like feints. Some seemed to reduce speed, attempting to lure pursuers over areas of heavy flak concentrations. The Germans only got close enough on one firing pass to cause minor damage to a single P-38. The 14th pilots tried, but could never get within firing range of the jet fighters.

On 22 April the 14th Group was assigned to conduct armed reconnaissance over northeastern Italy from the Alps to the Adriatic. Forty-one P-38s participated, cratering rail lines and highways with 500-pounders, then strafing targets of opportunity. The pickings were pretty slim. There seemed to be no rail traffic moving, only scattered military movement on highways. Many German vehicles bore Red Cross markings that were suspect, but were respected.

Small arms fire was evident in many locations, and it caught the plane of Maj. Charles McIntire as he led the 37th Squadron at Ficarola. His P-38 was only about 300 feet above the town when it slid off to the left and crashed.

2nd Lt. Sterling Brubaker (48th Squadron) recalled the mission, and his views on the dangers of this low-level work:

"I was Tail-end Charlie, and my element leader was 1st Lt. Milo Gnewikow, who had served a previous tour, but was unfamiliar with our leader of the day, Lt. Col. Chitty. I hated to fly behind Chitty, especially in that position, because he flew low and slow, and seemed oblivious to what happened in his wake. I briefed "Genny" beforehand that if he wanted to survive the day, we should lose the rest of the formation as soon as possible.

Sure enough, Chitty led us over the German line in Italy as 48 sitting ducks for the German gunners, and to no purpose. I saw what was happening ahead of us and got on the radio with a simple, 'Now!' Genny saw the wisdom of my advice, and we dove out.

Armed with bombs, we started looking for targets of opportunity, and soon came on our own little railroad bridge. He dove and missed (bridges are hard to hit), and I followed, blowing up the tender's house at the end of the span.

As we pulled out I noticed a bomb hung on the other plane, and so informed him. He acknowledged, and swung around for another go. Too late I realized what he was doing. He tried to skip bomb the bridge with an impact-fused bomb. I shouted 'No!,' but too late. As he pulled up I called to tell him that his right engine was smoking. He acknowledged and feathered. A moment later I called to give him the same message about the other engine. He was losing power. After some palaver, I suggested that if he could make it to the water I would call air-sea rescue to pick him up. 'Roger.' However, he didn't quite make it—only to the beach.

I flew low and slow to observe the fate of my now preoccupied and silent partner. My hope was to see him clear of the plane so I could go in and strafe it, as we were instructed to do. Suddenly, the

Lt. Milo Gnewikow, 48th Squadron, returned from brief captivity and rescue by Italian partisans with this trophy flag. (Dickenson)

M/Sgt Chris Stanton, 37th Squadron, served in two World Wars. (USAF)

sky around me erupted with intense flak. I am especially proud of the speed and effectiveness with which I reacted. I knew instantly what I would do. I was at point-blank range and had no speed. I dove, turning left for open water [Adriatic]. But I knew the gunners would quickly follow the track, so I made an uncoordinated turn, carrying top rudder. They took the bait, firing ahead and above me, with shrapnel rattling off my canopy. By the time they could adjust from my apparent course to the true one, I was able to flatten out over the water. After gaining some altitude, I tried to stick my nose back in there to see what happened to Genny, but now they were all firing at me, and I realized it would not work.

He had gone down amid a veteran German flak battalion that believed they had shot him down, and he didn't disabuse them of that idea. They invited him to a celebratory dinner, at which they regretted their failure to get me. Subsequently, he was loaded onto a boat to Venice, removed by partisans, hidden in Venice until the Germans departed, and then went to German headquarters, where he appropriated a huge swastika flag and brought it back to our club."

The German army may have been in retreat, but their AA gunners were still fighting the war. On 23 April, during an armed reconnaissance of the Badia-Verona area, a flight from the 49th Fighter squadron let down from 7,000 feet to 300 in order to observe the cargo on some wagons. No one saw any flak batteries, but Lt. Anthony Sumares called out that he had been hit and was losing fuel. Lt. Col. Nance saw fire flare out on Sumares' right wing, and called to him to jump. Sumares pulled up to 2,000 feet and parachuted, landing without difficulty, and waving at the other P-38s. Sumares was captured by German troops and taken to an airfield, where Americans subsequently subjected him to a bombing. He was with retreating German troops when Allied forces overtook them. Sumares was returned to his parent unit on 4 May.

The following day, several small formations of the 14th spent the day over the Po River region on armed reconnaissance. They bombed any bridge that appeared even moderately intact, and strafed whatever looked like enemy troops, vehicles, or rail targets that seemed to get in the way. There were so many aircraft over the area on similar missions that many Spitfires were seen working the same territory, and one P-38 got into a gunnery pattern with some P-51s. There was little to show for the effort, other than a few trucks and a motorcycle with a sidecar. All the rail targets were stationary.

During low passes both British and American ground force vehicles were observed, the occupants waving furiously to avoid coming under fire from the marauding P-38s. There was small arms fire directed at the Lightnings from the German side, but no serious damage, and all aircraft returned having logged some 58 sorties.

In the closing days of April 1945, the 14th Fighter Group flew an escort to Linz, Austria, a photo recon escort to Innisbruck, escorts of supply drops, and armed reconnaissance over the Po River region. There were virtually no worthy targets and no losses.

The month of May 1945 was almost anti-climactic. Indeed, there was a group mission on 1 May escorting bombers to Salzburg, Austria, with Maj. Robert Hullsiek leading. A routine escort of photo-reconnaissance aircraft on 4 May was the finale. Both missions were without incident or loss.

And then, suddenly the shooting stopped. German army units still in Northern Italy, hemmed in by Allied armies to the south and the impassable Alps to the north, surrendered. The formal capitulation of all German air, ground, and naval forces by the acting German government took place on 8 May 1945.

Several pilots went on sightseeing tours. Tom Collins describes the scene when peace broke out:

"We were free to fly wherever we wanted. The aircraft were fully loaded and the guns were hot. We would fly up the Po valley, fly over to Yugoslavia, and then fly from Munich to Regensburg to look for some of the damage we may have inflicted.... The road up the Brenner Pass was clogged with devastation: wrecked vehicles, trucks, and railroad cars."

Sterling Brubaker had flown over a patch of Bavarian woods weeks earlier and drawn a barrage of flak. After hostilities ended he flew to the same location for another look. 'The woods were full of Messerschmitts that had been landed on the autobahn and concealed among the trees."

Several pilots who had been POWs returned to Triolo: Louis Benne, Moses Long, and Milo Gnewikow. Michael Brezas returned from "incarceration" by our Russian allies on 11 May. The war was over, but for the bitter Brezas there was one more unofficial mission to be flown. Tom Collins describes the incident:

"So one day, probably about 15 May, I was on the flight line waiting for an engineering flight—slow time on a new engine or something like that—when Mike walked up and said, 'Tom would you want to fly?,' and I said, 'Sure.' Mike got into his airplane and I got into one. I didn't believe he knew who I was. He was a hero, and I was one of the new guys in the squadron.

Finally heading home: Above: All worldly possessions in two duffel bags. Below: Ready to board the ship at Naples. (USAF)

We took off heading north over the Adriatic, and Mike came over the radio and said, 'Check your guns and leave them hot.' So I fired a few rounds, why not. We went straight for Vienna, and I guess we had climbed up to about 20,000 feet, and we started a gentle turn to the left around the city.

I'd seen it before, but really from afar during the war, escorting B-17s and B-24s, and mostly watching those huge orange blossoms develop in the sky as the big bombers were being blown to bits by flak. Now, as we were in the real clean, clear air of Vienna, Mike came over the radio with, 'Watch out for enemy aircraft!,' and I'm thinking of Germans, and I started looking. That is your mindset.

No sooner had Mike called the warning than I called him back and said, 'There are four aircraft at four o'clock coming in hard and starting to shoot. Break right!'

In less than 10 seconds—three seconds? 30 seconds? or four minutes? You know how time evaporates. We'll say in less than a minute, two of the Russian aircraft, and possibly a third [believed to be captured Japanese Jacks] were blasted out of the air, and there weren't any others in the sky but our two P-38s.

I had fired a few rounds, and don't know if I got lucky, or the other fellow got unlucky. We pointed our noses south down the Weiner-Neustadt corridor and returned to Triolo. After we landed I saw Mike take the gun camera film cartridge from my camera and from his, and that was the end of my Russian crusade with Mike Brezas.

I know of at least two other times that he tried to locate the Russian prisoner camp in Rumania where he had been held. I'm sure he had the intent to do harm to anyone he found there. I know that he flew back to Vienna looking for more Russians. One evening at the club I said, 'Mike, how are things going? You know, are you still flying?'

He looked up and said, 'Aw, it's no fun anymore. All you have to do is point your nose at the cowards and they scatter like pigeons.' I only flew that one mission with Mike. A day or two later he disappeared, and was unceremoniously sent home. And a day or two after that a pair of officious looking people, one English and an American, appeared at 48th Fighter Squadron to question Mike. They got no answers on the extra curricular post war activity of Captain Brezas."

Joy and relief were the common themes within the fellowship of the14th Fighter Group. Games and celebrations abounded after VE-Day. There were airplane rides for ground personnel, and trips to rest camps. There were promotions galore, and still a lot of replacements and new aircraft arriving. The supply pipeline had been full, and it took some time to shut the spigot. And while some new-timers worried about being redeployed to the Pacific, the old-timers, some of whom had been with the squadrons since formation, began packing their bags for home. A point system had been established by the Army to qualify men for rotation and discharge. It involved time in service, time overseas, and other factors. The magic number for discharge was 85. Some members of the 14th Fighter Group had accumulated 125 points.

Had there been an oldest old-timer award in the 14th, it would have been won hands down by M/Sgt. Chris Stanton, from the engineering section of the 37th Fighter Squadron. He had served in the First World War in the Signal Corps, and had been with the 37th since its formation.

By the end of May, 88 officers and 308 enlisted men had been transferred back to the United States. Those who had been with the group since its arrival in North Africa were entitled to wear twelve Battle Stars on their theatre campaign ribbon. Another throng of personnel got their tickets back home in June, and some of the newcomers were transferred to the 2nd and 97th Bomb Groups, both slated for occupation duty in Germany. By September 1945 the people drain had been completed, and the group was disbanded.

During World War II the 14th Fighter Group had conducted combat operations for two and one-half years. According to the official group summary they flew 1,032 missions totaling 19,687 individual sorties. During aerial combat, pilots destroyed 426 enemy aircraft in the air, probably destroyed 87, and damaged another 194. Ground attack operations cost the enemy another 96 aircraft destroyed, along with 473 locomotives, 118 freight cars, 302 tank cars, 2 passenger cars, and 508 motor vehicles of various types.

The statistics of combat operations define the remarkable achievements of the members of the 14th. However, the true scope of their sacrifice is revealed in their casualties (Exhibit A), a somber reflection of the 14th motto: To Fight To Death.

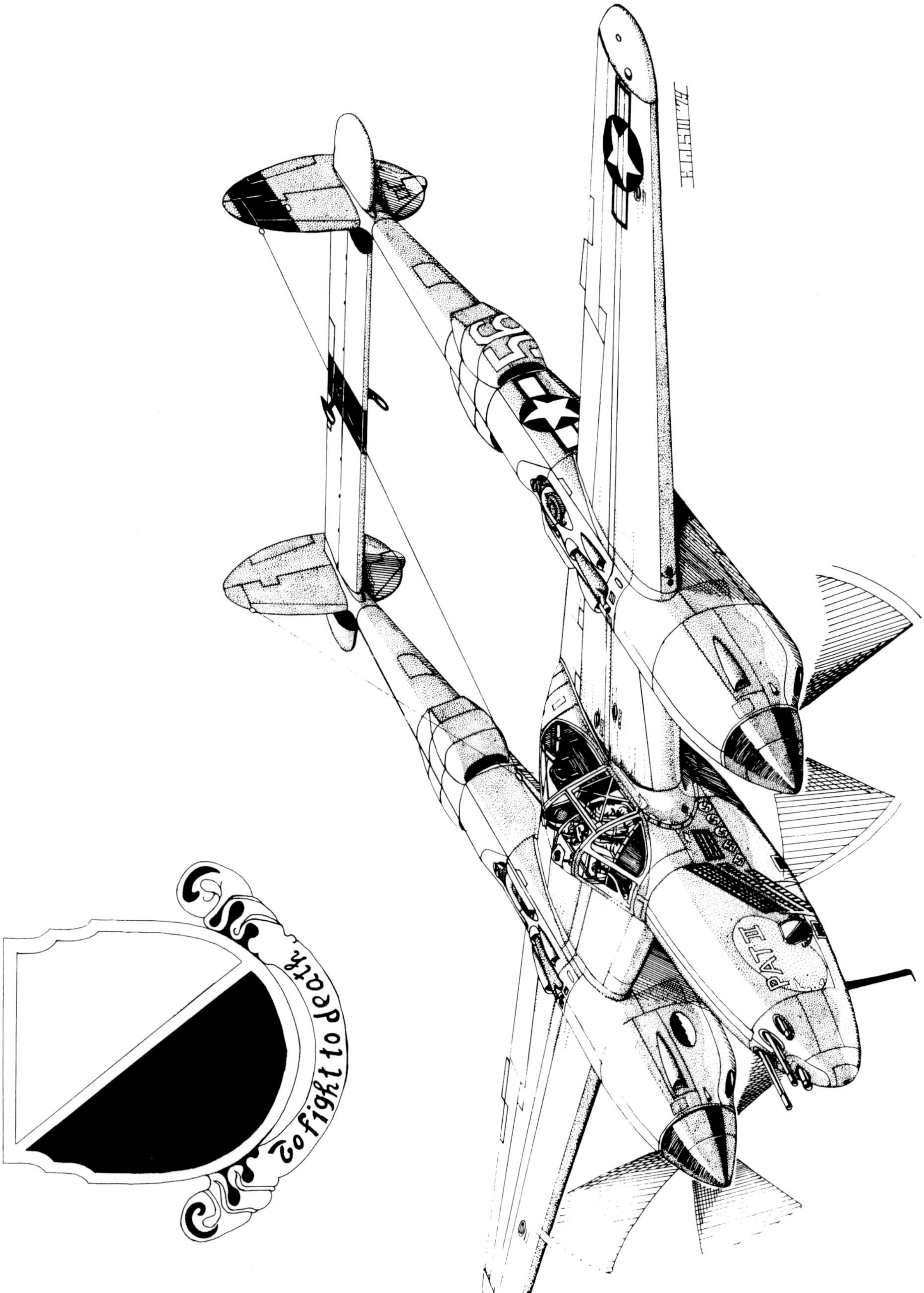

The P-38G of Col. Oliver B. Taylor, 14th Group CO, and the group shield. (By Earl W. Steininger III)

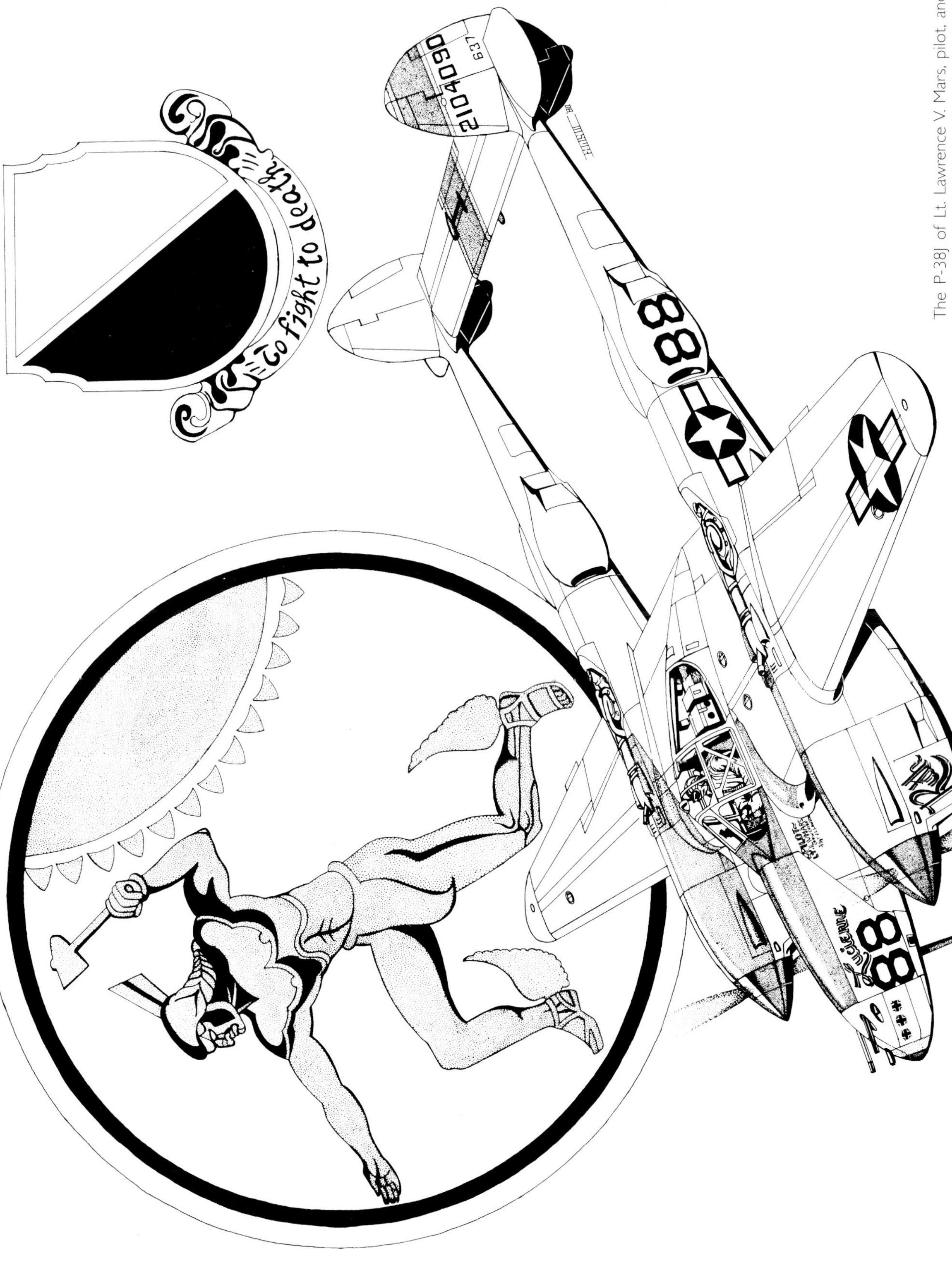

The P-38J of Lt. Lawrence V. Mars, pilot, and T/Sgt. Joseph L. Lawson, 37th Fighter Squadron, with squadron insignia and group shield. (By Earl W. Steininger III)

Maps

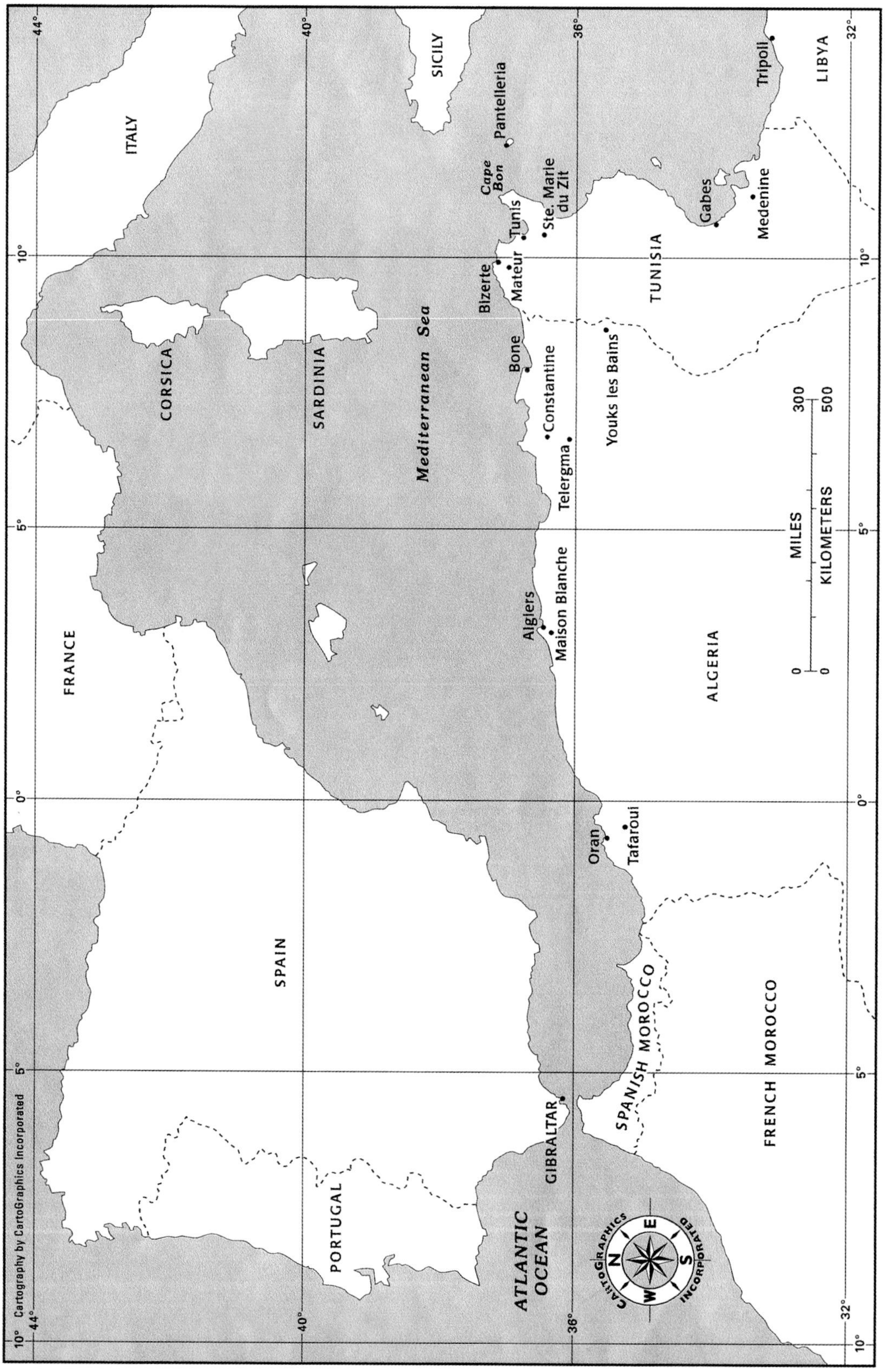

Cartography by CartoGraphics Incorporated
ITALY
SICILY
Pantelleria
Tripoli
LIBYA
Cape Bon
Tunis
Ste. Marie du Zit
Gabes
Medenine
TUNISIA
Bizerte
Mateur
Mediterranean Sea
CORSICA
SARDINIA
Bone
Constantine
Youks les Bains
Telergma
FRANCE
Algiers
Maison Blanche
ALGERIA
MILES
KILOMETERS
0
300
500
Oran
Tafaraoui
SPAIN
SPANISH MOROCCO
FRENCH MOROCCO
GIBRALTAR
PORTUGAL
ATLANTIC OCEAN
CARTOGRAPHICS INCORPORATED
N
E
S
W
44°
40°
36°
32°
10°
5°
0°

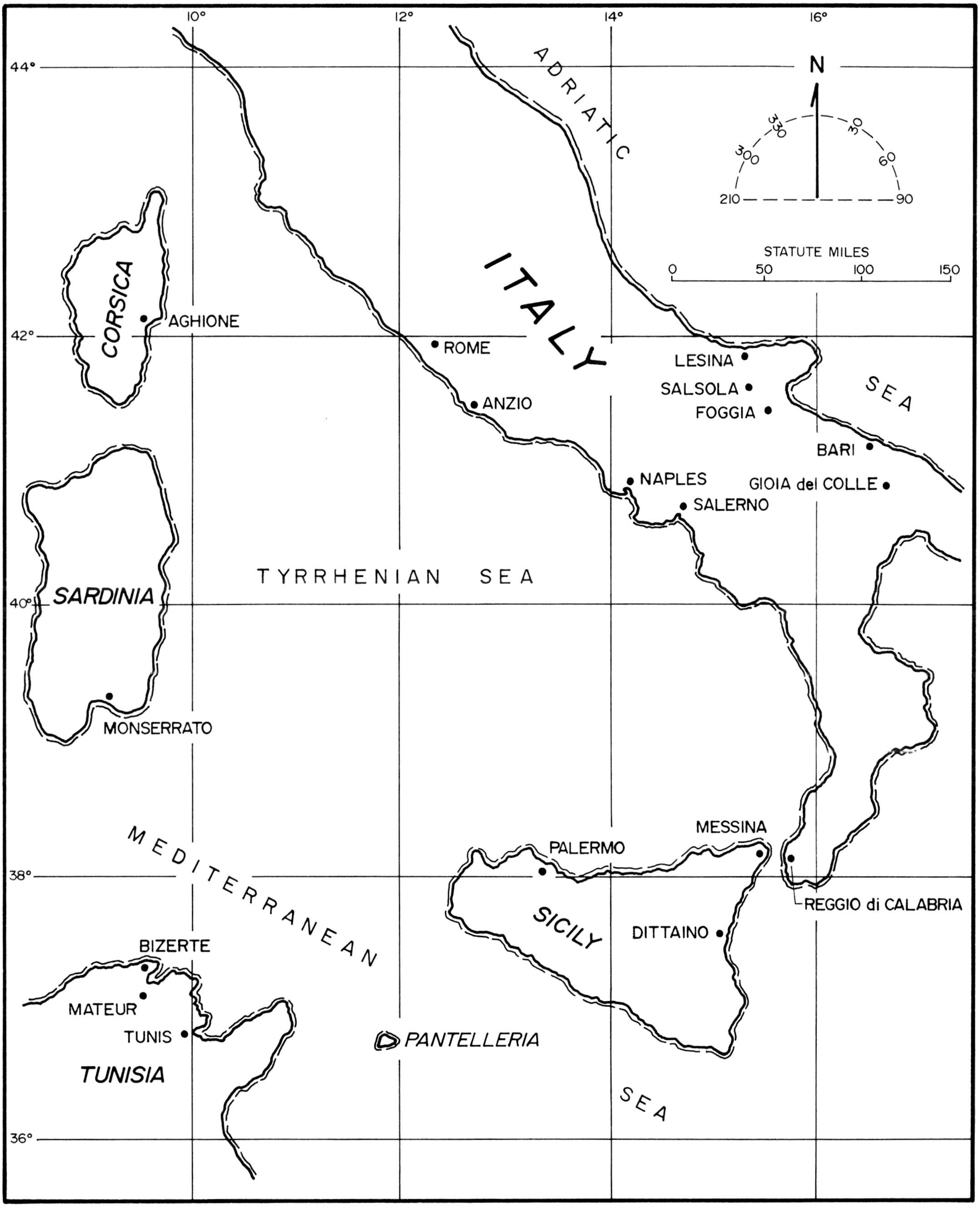
10°
12°
14°
16°
44°
42°
40°
38°
36°
N
330
30
300
60
210
90
STATUTE MILES
0
50
100
150
ADRIATIC
SEA
ITALY
CORSICA
AGHIONE
ROME
ANZIO
LESINA
SALSOLA
FOGGIA
BARI
NAPLES
GIOIA del COLLE
SALERNO
TYRRHENIAN SEA
SARDINIA
MONSERRATO
MEDITERRANEAN
SEA
MESSINA
PALERMO
REGGIO di CALABRIA
SICILY
DITTAINO
BIZERTE
MATEUR
TUNIS
TUNISIA
PANTELLERIA

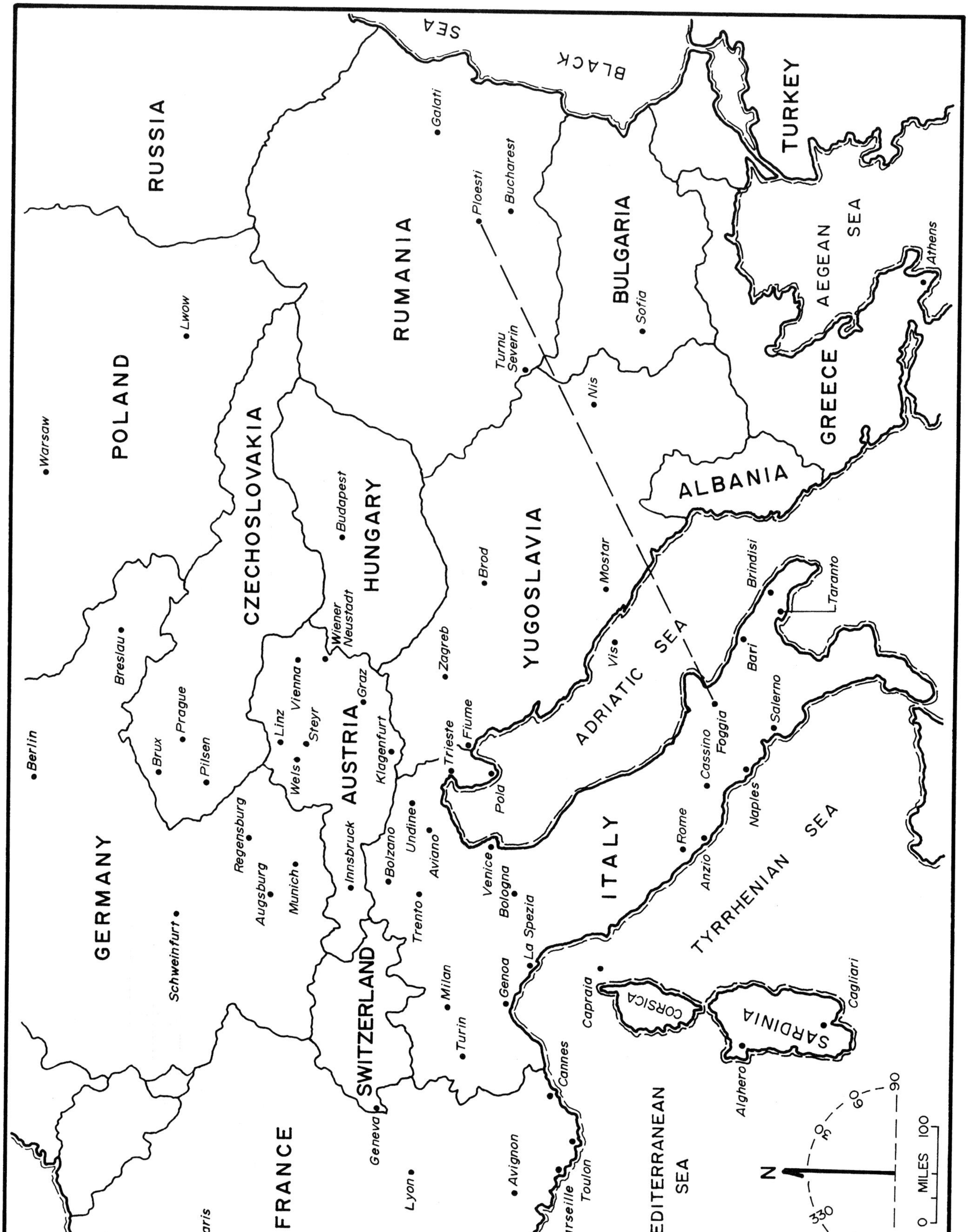
RUSSIA
POLAND
CZECHOSLOVAKIA
GERMANY
FRANCE
SWITZERLAND
AUSTRIA
HUNGARY
RUMANIA
BULGARIA
YUGOSLAVIA
ALBANIA
GREECE
TURKEY
ITALY
CORSICA
SARDINIA
BLACK SEA
AEGEAN SEA
ADRIATIC SEA
TYRRHENIAN SEA
MEDITERRANEAN SEA
Galati
Ploesti
Bucharest
Sofia
Turnu Severin
Nis
Athens
Lwow
Warsaw
Budapest
Wiener Neustadt
Vienna
Linz
Steyr
Wels
Graz
Klagenfurt
Innsbruck
Breslau
Prague
Pilsen
Brux
Berlin
Regensburg
Augsburg
Munich
Schweinfurt
Paris
Lyon
Geneva
Avignon
Marseille
Toulon
Cannes
Zagreb
Brod
Mostar
Vis
Fiume
Trieste
Pola
Bolzano
Undine
Aviano
Trento
Venice
Bologna
La Spezia
Genoa
Milan
Turin
Capraia
Cagliari
Alghero
Rome
Anzio
Naples
Salerno
Cassino
Foggia
Bari
Brindisi
Taranto
N
0
30
60
90
330
300
210
0 MILES 100

Color Gallery

A 49th Fighter Squadron P-38 taxis toward the runway at Triolo. (Stitt)

Wheels up, a fully loaded P-38 takes off on a mission. (Stitt)

Above: The mission returns, as Lightnings peel up and around for landing. (Stitt) Below: A 48th Fighter Squadron P-38 settles in for a landing. (Stitt)

The four .50 cal. machine guns and the 20mm cannon of a 14th P-38. (Stitt)

As the sun sets over Italy, ground crews labor to prepare their mounts for the next day. (Stitt)

An engine change in the open air hangar at Triolo. (Stitt)

Harold Bassett (left) and Fred Colton work on a tire change. It's still done much the same way six decades later. (Stitt)

Above: "Muchacho" with engines turning. (Stitt) Below: "Sleepy Time Gal" graced bombers and fighters on all battle fronts. (Stitt)

Above: A distant view of the town of Cassino and the overlooking Abbey. (Stitt) Below: The complete destruction of Cassino is evident in a closer view. (Stitt)

Above: Dining out in Corsica, August 1944: nearest the camera is Marlin Richardson, and next to him is Willie Sheehan. (Stitt) Below: 37th Fighter Squadron ground crewmen (L. to R.): Hoyle Stuart, Conine Sparlin, Robert Gibson, and Harry Fink. (Stitt)

Lt. Boone Haddock (37th) organizes his flight gear. (Stitt)

Maj. Richard A. Campbell, an ace from the 1943 campaigns, returns to Italy for a visit with the 37th Squadron and his old crew chief (right), M/Sgt. John Wiley. (Stitt)

Above: Volleyball at Triolo: Col. Dan Campbell squats as teammate, M/Sgt. Hoyle Stuart, keeps his eye on the ball. (Stuart) Below: The hot water at the shower is ready when the flag goes up. (Stitt)

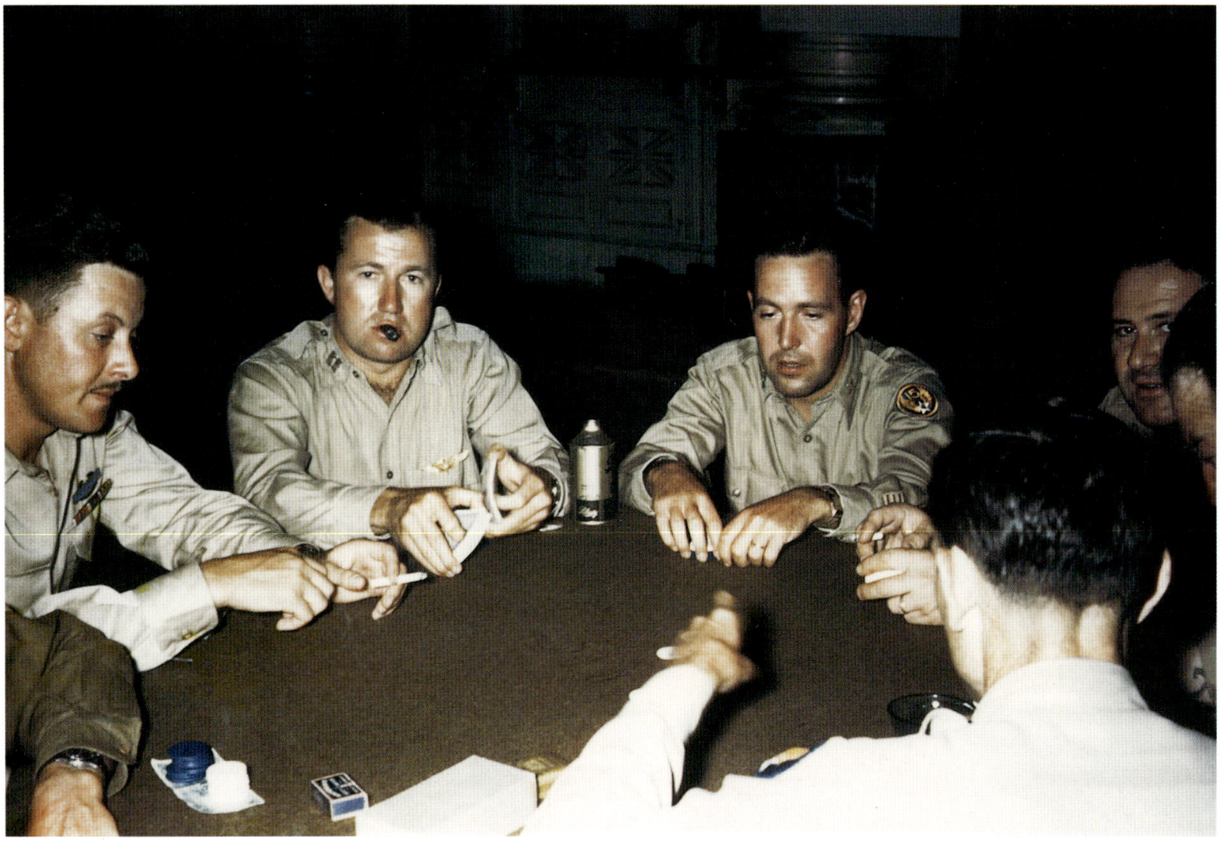

Above: Payday poker among officers of the 14th and some visiting firemen. (Stitt) Below: Lt. Frank Cupo (49th) entertains (L. to R.) M/Sgts. Leeper and Crooks, and Bill Shaper, Allison Tech Rep. Bill had previously been in China with the Flying Tigers. (Stitt)

Above: (L. to R.) Doc Curtiss, flight surgeon, and Bill Shaper. (Stitt) Below: Lt. Col. Tom Whitehouse, the last wartime commander of the 14th Fighter Group. (Stitt)

You have to be young to fly fighters (L. to R.): Pilots Frank Krug and Milt Anderson. (Stitt)

The base chapel at Triolo, Italy. (Stitt)

Above: The idyllic isle of Capri, off the coast of Italy in the blue Aegean, was a popular rest and recuperation location for men for the 14th Fighter Group. (Stitt) Below: Old soldiers meet to reminisce some 20 years after the war (L. to R.): Harry Crim, Jim Stitt, and Bill Leverette. (Stitt)

Appendix A: 14th Fighter Group Casualties

Name	Unit	Date	Circumstances
2nd Lt. George H. Bennett	48th	19 Mar 42	KPC, Calif.
2nd Lt. Richard D. Moore	48th	18 Apr 42	KPC, Mid-air collision, Calif.
1st Lt. John E. Dixon	48th	18 Apr 42	KPC, Mid-air collision, Calif.
2nd Lt. Whymans	48th	27 May 42	KPC, Calif.
Lt. Herbert A. Goodrich	50th	July 42	Missing Enroute Iceland
T/Sgt. John Akers	49th	22 Aug 42	Killed C-47 crash, England
T/Sgt. Robert E. Anderson	49th	22 Aug 42	Killed C-47 crash, England
T/Sgt. Israel Gross	49th	22 Aug 42	Killed C-47 crash, England
T/Sgt. Raymond S. Nash	49th	22 Aug 42	Killed C-47 crash, England
T/Sgt. Jesse L. Patterson	49th	22 Aug 42	Killed C-47 crash, England
2nd Lt. Lyle L. Williams	49th	11 Sept 42	KPC, England
T/Sgt. Robert J. Hayes	48th	20 Nov 42	WIA, Youks les Bains
1st Lt. James E. Butler	49th	28 Nov 42	KIA, Tunisia
1st Lt. Carl F. Skinner	48th	28 Nov 42	KIA, Tunisia
2nd Lt. Arthur V. Cole	48th	30 Nov 42	POW near Tunis.
2nd Lt. Carl T. Williams	48th	3 Dec 42	KIA near Tunis
Capt. Harold Lewis	49th	5 Dec 42	KIA near Sidi Nsir
2nd Lt. John P. Steif	49th	5 Dec 42	KIA near Sidi Nsir
2nd Lt. Robert F. Elliott	49th	5 Dec 42	KIA near Sidi Nsir
Pvt. Tom S. Maxwell	49th	10 Dec 42	WIA Youks les Bains
2nd Lt. James Tollen	48th	11 Dec 42	KIA near Tunis
2nd Lt. Livie F. Mullinax Jr.	49th	28 Dec 42	POW near Tripoli, EV *
Capt. Thomas Morris	49th	30 Dec 42	KIA off Libya
1st Lt. Virgil Smith	48th	30 Dec 42	KIA near Gafsa
2nd Lt. Richard J. Carroll	48th	30 Dec 42	POW near Gabes, later died. **
2nd Lt. Clark W. Smith	48th	30 Dec 42	POW near Gabes
Capt. Paulett Spivey	14th	2 Jan 43	WIA Youks les Bains
Cpl. Alan D. Cohrs	49th	5 Jan 43	WIA Berteaux
Cpl. Loren E. Bolen, Jr.	49th	5 Jan 43	WIA Berteaux
Pvt. Albert D. Fillmore	49th	5 Jan 43	WIA Berteaux
1st Lt. Robert H. Woodward	48th	8 Jan 43	KIA near Kairouan
2nd Lt. Robert P. Kirschke	48th	8 Jan 43	KIA near Kairouan
2nd Lt. Robert J. Moffatt	49th	8 Jan 43	WIA over Tunisia
1st Lt. Albert C. Wolfmueller	49th	8 Jan 43	WIA over Tunisia
1st Lt. William J. Hoelle	49th	8 Jan 43	WIA over Tunisia
Capt. William J. Fulmer	14th	15 Jan 43	KIA off Cape Bon
2nd Lt. Lawrence E. Driver	49th	15 Jan 43	KIA off Cape Bon
2nd Lt. Elmer M. Warren, Jr.	48th	18 Jan 43	POW near Enfidaville
1st Lt. William Schottelkorb	48th	23 Jan 43	KIA in So. Tunisia
2nd Lt. Guy E. Stuteville	48th	23 Jan 43	KIA in So. Tunisia
2nd Lt. Kenneth W. Harley	48th	23 Jan 43	KIA in So. Tunisia
2nd Lt. Richard H. Soliday	48th	23 Jan 43	KIA in So. Tunisia
2nd Lt. Leo M. Yates	48th	23 Jan 43	KIA in So. Tunisia
Capt. Charles L. Earnhart	49th	28 Jan 43	POW near Sfax
1st Lt. Carl Hahn	48th	27 Apr 43	Killed in auto accident en route Telergma
2nd Lt. Robert T. Thayer	37th	6 May 43	MIA Straits of Sicily
2nd Lt. Gail E. Moore	49th	6 May 43	MIA Straits of Sicily

2nd Lt. Dewey F. Varndell	37th	10 May 43	MIA over Sicily
2nd Lt. Wayne M. Chaves	49th	11 May 43	MIA over Sicily
2nd Lt. John F. Burton	49th	13 May 43	MIA near Sardinia
2nd Lt. Edward G. Terwilliger	37th	14 May 43	KIA Sicily
Maj. Clarence L. Tinker, Jr.	14th	18 May 43	MIA near Sicily
2nd Lt. Robert B. Benton	48th	18 May 43	MIA near Sicily
1st Lt. James H. Goff	37th	18 May 43	POW near Sicily
2nd Lt. James J. Toth	37th	18 May 43	MIA near Sicily
1st Lt. Frank C. Howk, Jr.	49th	19 May 43	MIA near Trapani, Sicily
1st Lt. John L. Wolford	49th	19 May 43	MIA near Trapani, Sicily
1st Lt. Albert Little	49th	21 May 43	MIA near Sicily
2nd Lt. Burton J. Snyder	49th	21 May 43	MIA near Sicily, POW
2nd Lt. John C. Henry, Jr.	37th	22 May 43	MIA near Sicily
1st Lt. William M. Collins	37th	25 May 43	MIA near Sardinia
2nd Lt. Albert G. Barber	48th	25 May 43	WIA Tunisia
2nd Lt. Fred M. Sanders, Jr.	48th	26 May 43	MIA near Sicily
2nd Lt. Harry E. Simmons	48th	28 May 43	MIA near Pantelleria
1st Lt. John H. Green	49th	4 Jun 43	KIA off Sicily
2nd Lt. William A. Bergersen	49th	4 Jun 43	KIA off Sicily
1st Lt. Iner W. Anderson	37th	11 Jun 43	Killed in auto accident
2nd Lt. Thomas E. Kearns	37th	12 Jun 43	Died of injuries in auto accident
Capt. Donald Anderson	48th	15 Jun 43	KIA over Sicily
2nd Lt. Fred Browne	48th	15 Jun 43	KIA over Sicily
1st Lt. Bruce L. Campbell	49th	18 Jun 43	POW after parachuting near Sicily
2nd Lt. George B. Church	49th	18 Jun 43	KIA off Sicily
2nd Lt. Harold R. Alexander	37th	24 Jun 43	KIA over Sardinia
1st Lt. William D. Neely III	49th	26 Jun 43	KIA when his P-38 failed over Sicily
2nd Lt. Wallace Kennedy	48th	7 Jul 43	KPC Tunis
2nd Lt. Sidney R. Booth	49th	10 Jul 43	KIA Ramacca, Sicily
1st Lt. Wallace G. Bland	49th	10 Jul 43	KIA Palagonia, Sicily
2nd Lt. Allen W. Knepper	49th	10 Jul 43	KIA Palagonia, Sicily
Capt. Forrest H. Barker	37th	10 Jul 43	WIA from flak over Sicily
2nd Lt. Robert H. Hermann	48th	12 Jul 43	MIA off Sicily
2nd Lt. Jerry S. Stidham	48th	13 Jul 43	MIA over Sicily
2nd Lt. Donald J. Lister	48th	13 Jul 43	MIA over Sicily
2nd Lt. Herbert J. Walker	37th	13 Jul 43	WIA over Sicily
1st Lt. Mark C. Hegney	49th	16 Jul 43	KPC El Bathan, Algeria
2nd Lt. Robert C. Thompkins	48th	17 Jul 43	MIA over Tyrrhenian Sea
2nd Lt. Lloyd O. Hendrix	37th	4 Aug 43	MIA over Mediterranean Sea
2nd Lt. Jack L. Tarr	48th	17 Aug 43	MIA near Cape Spartivento, Italy
2nd Lt. Harold I. Texter	48th	17 Aug 43	MIA near Cape Spartivento, Italy
2nd Lt. Jack L. Moak	49th	19 Aug 43	POW after parachuting Foggia, Italy
2nd Lt. Walter L. Hoke	49th	20 Aug 43	KPC St. Marie du Zit, Tunisia
2nd Lt. Russell K. Moomaw	37th	23 Aug 43	MIA Tyrrhenian Sea
1st Lt. William K. Hester	49th	25 Aug 43	KIA Foggia, Italy
S/Sgt. Eldon F. Heistand	37th	27 Aug 43	WIA by land mine, St. Marie du Zit
F/O Earl J. Dion	37th	28 Aug 43	KIA over Italy
F/O John D. McCoy	49th	29 Aug 43	POW when downed near Rome
Maj. John G. Bright	14th	30 Aug 43	POW after parachuting near Viterbo
1st Lt. Louis D. Ogle	49th	15 Sep 43	KIA Fisciano, Italy
1st Lt. Martin Faust	49th	18 Sep 43	KIA Foggia, Italy
2nd Lt. Homer L. Sprinkle	37th	18 Oct 43	KPC St. Marie du Zit, Tunisia
Sgt. Julius T. Friend	37th	18 Oct 43	KPC St. Marie du Zit, Tunisia
2nd Lt. William H. Green	49th	9 Nov 43	MIA near Sardinia
2nd Lt. Eugene N. Pitre, Jr.	37th	16 Dec 43	MIA over Italy

1st Lt. Harrison H. Hannah	48th	30 Dec 43	MIA near Padua, Italy, POW
2nd Lt. Chester D. Erwin, Jr.	48th	30 Dec 43	MIA near Padua
2nd Lt. David C. Fritz	49th	3 Jan 44	KIA No. Italy
2nd Lt. L.D. Wells	48th	3 Jan 44	MIA over Italy
Capt. George E. Richards	48th	10 Jan 44	MIA near Sofia, Bulgaria
2nd Lt. Ralph W. Sebring	48th	13 Jan 44	KIA over Rome
2nd Lt. R.F. Williams	48th	16 Jan 44	MIA over Austria
2nd Lt. Kenneth L. Stahl	37th	16 Jan 44	KIA over Austria ??
2nd Lt. Elmer LaRue	37th	16 Jan 44	MIA over Austria ??
2nd Lt. Frank O. Rooks	37th	18 Jan 44	KIA near Roseta Valfortare, Italy
2nd Lt. Arthur V. Duff	49th	20 Jan 44	MIA over Tyrrhenian Sea
2nd Lt. Paul J. Wingert	49th	22 Jan 44	MIA near Anzio, EV
2nd Lt. Glen J. Viertel	48th	23 Jan 44	MIA near Rieti, Italy, EV
2nd Lt. Melvia T. Waldrop	48th	23 Jan 44	MIA near Rieti, Italy
2nd Lt. Harry R. Greenup	49th	27 Jan 44	MIA over So. France
2nd Lt. James G. Riley, Jr.	49th	27 Jan 44	KIA over So. France
2nd Lt. John B. Grant	49th	27 Jan 44	WIA over So. France
2nd Lt. Richard D. Dalrymple	48th	10 Feb 44	MIA near Vicovaro, Italy
2nd Lt. D.W. Darnold	48th	10 Feb 44	POW near Vicovaro, Italy
F/O Robert W. Bowerman	48th	10 Feb 44	KIA near Vicovaro, Italy
1st Lt. Nathaniel G. Raley	48th	10 Feb 44	MIA No. Italy, POW .
1st Lt. Donald R. McMahon	37th	14 Feb 44	MIA near Verona, Italy
2nd Lt. George F. Wood	48th	14 Mar 44	KPC at Triolo, Italy
2nd Lt. Robert L. Hames	48th	14 Mar 44	KPC at Triolo, Italy
1st Lt. Roy C. Lyles	49th	17 Mar 44	MIA parachuted over Yugoslavia
2nd Lt. William B.Tucker	48th	29 Mar 44	MIA parachuted near Venice
1st Lt. Charles C.Townsend	37th	30 Mar 44	MIA over Yugoslavia or Adriatic
2nd Lt. John W. Lindstrom	48th	5 Apr 44	MIA over Yugoslavia, EV
2nd Lt. Wesley B. Crow, Jr.	49th	7 Apr 44	MIA over Northern Italy
2nd Lt. Richard Zimmerman	48th	7 Apr 44	MIA over Adriatic
Col. Oliver E. Ford	14th	15 Apr 44	KIA over Rumania
1st Lt. Robert G. Zimmerman	37th	15 Apr 44	MIA over Rumania, POW
2nd Lt. John C. Ingram	37th	15 Apr 44	MIA over Rumania
2nd Lt. Joseph H. Garrity	37th	15 Apr 44	MIA over Rumania
1st Lt. Richard D. Wilhelm	37th	21 Apr 44	KIA over Rumania
Maj. Forrest H. Barker	37th	30 Apr 44	MIA near Milan, Italy, POW
2nd Lt. Robert N. Griffith	48th	5 May 44	MIA Yugo. POW
2nd Lt. Earvie T. Cloyd	37th	7 May 44	MIA over Rumania, POW
2nd Lt. John A. Jones	37th	10 May 44	Parachuted Yugo. EV
2nd Lt. Herbert L. Aldrich	48th	12 May 44	MIA near Bologna, Italy
1st Lt. Paul G. Winston	48th	12 May 44	MIA near Bologna, Italy
1st Lt. Robert K. Siedman	49th	14 May 44	KIA near Udine, Italy
2nd Lt. William A. Lavery	48th	14 May 44	KIA over Adriatic
2nd Lt. Paul J. Wingert	49th	18 May 44	KIA over Bulgaria
1st Lt. Andrew S. Sziich	37th	22 May 44	KPC at Triolo A/D, Italy
2nd Lt. Quentin A. Teige	49th	24 May 44	MIA near Weiner Neustadt, Austria
2nd Lt. John H. Penning	49th	24 May 44	MIA near Weiner Neustadt, Austria
2nd Lt. Richard L. Fowler, Jr.	49th	25 May 44	POW near Po River, Italy
2nd Lt. Edward Hemmerlein	49th	26 May 44	Died from injuries on Corsica
1st Lt. James F. Martin	14th	29 May 44	KIA over Yugoslavia
1st Lt. Louis Benne	49th	14 Jun 44	MIA over Hungary, POW
2nd Lt. Clyde L. Jones, Jr.	49th	14 Jun 44	MIA over Hungary, POW
2nd Lt. Bill D. Williams	49th	14 Jun 44	MIA over Hungary, POW
2nd Lt. John L. McLaughlin	49th	14 Jun 44	MIA near Budapest, Hungary
2nd Lt. Wesley L. Jule	49th	14 Jun 44	MIA near Budapest, Hungary

2nd Lt. William L. McClain	37th	15 Jun 44	MIA over Southern France, EV
2nd Lt. Robert Powers, Jr.	37th	15 Jun 44	MIA near Orange, France
2nd Lt. Warren E. Semple	49th	15 Jun 44	MIA near Orange, France
2nd Lt. Swanson T. Shortt	49th	20 Jun 44	KPC at Triolo, Italy
2nd Lt. John S. Wakeman	48th	22 Jun 44	MIA near Bologna, Italy, EV
2nd Lt. Billy T. Turner	49th	3 Jul 44	MIA near Sarajevo, Yugo. POW
F/O Bernard Martin	48th	8 Jul 44	MIA near Vienna, Austria
2nd Lt. Henry D. Mitchell	48th	8 Jul 44	MIA near Vienna, Austria
Capt. John G. Schill, Jr.	49th	14 Jul 44	KIA, mid-air over Hungary
2nd Lt. Clyde E. Durbin	49th	14 Jul 44	MIA, mid-air over Hungary
2nd Lt. Frank M. Higdon	48th	14 Jul 44	MIA near Budapest, Hungary
2nd Lt. Ward L. McCombs	48th	14 Jul 44	MIA near Budapest, Hungary
2nd Lt. Gustav E. Strom	48th	14 Jul 44	MIA near Budapest, Hungary
2nd Lt. Leon E. Neubuck	37th	17 Jul 44	KPC during night training flight
2nd Lt. Aurelian L. Jekot	37th	19 Jul 44	MIA, mid-air, Munich, Ger., POW
2nd Lt. David L. Watson	37th	19 Jul 44	MIA, mid-air, Munich, Ger., POW
2nd Lt. Richard R.Thompson	49th	19 Jul 44	KIA mid-air near San Giorgio, Italy
2nd Lt. Cody D. Stout	48th	19 Jul 44	KIA mid-air near San Girogio, Italy
2nd Lt. Donald J. Van Gilder	48th	19 Jul 44	MIA near Munich, Germany
1st Lt. George J. O'Connor	48th	22 Jul 44	MIA over Rumania, POW
2nd Lt. Donald V. West	48th	22 Jul 44	MIA over Rumania
Capt. James C. Smyth	37th	26 Jul 44	MIA over Austria, POW
2nd Lt. David W. Reid, Jr.	49th	28 Jul 44	MIA near Niksic, Yugoslavia
2nd Lt. Frederick W. Ribie	48th	28 Jul 44	KPC near Campobossa, Italy
2nd Lt. Robert D. Simpson	48th	6 Aug 44	KIA Valence A/D, France
2nd Lt. Roy R. Sielert	48th	7 Aug 44	KIA near Blechhammer, Germany
1st Lt. Leroy C. Strader	37th	10 Aug 44	Lost during ferry flight from England
2nd Lt. Donald A. Tracy	49th	13 Aug 44	KIA at Orange, France
2nd Lt. Elmer Torgeson	37th	13 Aug 44	MIA over southern France
2nd Lt. Clarence R.Thompson	37th	13 Aug 44	KIA over southern France
2nd Lt. Moses J. Long	49th	14 Aug 44	MIA at Montfrin, France, POW
2nd Lt. Walter C. McConnell	49th	14 Aug 44	MIA at Montfrin, France
2nd Lt. William J. Tippett	48th	14 Aug 44	KIA southern France
2nd Lt. Wayne R. Woody	49th	16 Aug 44	KPC off Corsica
Maj. Franklin L. Robinson	48th	16 Aug 44	KIA off southern France
1st Lt. William T. Starbuck	48th	16 Aug 44	KPC at Aghione, Corsica
2nd Lt. Duane J. Kurtz	14th	16 Aug 44	KPC at Aghione, Corsica
T/Sgt. Edward L. Duncan	37th	16 Aug 44	KPC at Aghione, Corsica
Cpl. Benjamin H. Franklin	14th	16 Aug 44	KPC at Aghione, Corsica
Capt. Richard F. Halford	48th	16 Aug 44	KPC at Aghione, Corsica
Sgt. James F. Brennan	37th	16 Aug 44	Died of crash injuries at Aghione
Cpl. William J. Lammey	48th	16 Aug 44	KPC at Aghione, Corsica
T/Sgt Edward R. Segelken	49th	16 Aug 44	KPC at Aghione, Corsica
Sgt. Francis M. Purtell	49th	16 Aug 44	KPC at Aghione, Corsica
Cpl. Richard Schrodt	49th	16 Aug 44	KPC at Aghione, Corsica
Cpl. John Herrion	49th	16 Aug 44	KPC at Aghione, Corsica
T/Sgt. Walter E. Jones	49th	16 Aug 44	KPC at Aghione, Corsica
Pvt. Donald E. Brehm	37th	16 Aug 44	KPC at Aghione, Corsica
2nd Lt. Daniel M. Haley	49th	17 Aug 44	MIA near Balgnac, France
2nd Lt. Stephen P. Lannan	37th	18 Aug 44	MIA near Arlis, France, EV
2nd Lt. Darrell K. Stoyke	37th	19 Aug 44	MIA near Aix, France
2nd Lt. Mitchell S. Cwiek	37th	22 Aug 44	MIA over Austria, POW
1st Lt. William T. Church	48th	2 Sep 44	MIA over Yugoslavia
2nd Lt. Neal Maloney	37th	2 Sep 44	MIA over Yugoslavia
2nd Lt. Allan H. Mohr	37th	2 Sep 44	KIA near Cuprija, Yugoslavia

2nd Lt. William F. Hopman	48th	2 Sep 44	MIA over Yugoslavia, EV
2nd Lt. George V. Reiman	48th	17 Sep 44	KPC near Triolo, Italy
F/O Gerald W. Hanson	37th	21 Sep 44	Parachuted over Yugo. POW, EV
1st Lt. John A. Jones, Jr.	37th	6 Oct 44	MIA near Salonika, Greece, POW
2nd Lt. William Milton	37th	6 Oct 44	KIA near Salonika, Greece
1st Lt. Richard A. Schmidt	48th	6 Oct 44	KIA near Salonika, Greece
1st Lt. Lloyd A. Bro	49th	6 Oct 44	MIA near Salonika, Greece, POW
2nd Lt. David W. MacArthur	49th	6 Oct 44	KIA near Salonkia, Greece
1st Lt. Joseph F.Weber	49th	8 Oct 44	Injured in plane crash, Italy
1st Lt. Paul J. Ragusa	49th	13 Oct 44	Injured in plane crash, Italy
2nd Lt Robert C. Groom	48th	13 Oct 44	MIA over Hungary, EV
1st Lt. Leo Alston	37th	14 Oct 44	MIA near Lake Balaton, Hungary
F/O John M. Wilke	49th	14 Oct 44	MIA Yugo, EV
2nd Lt. Carl F. Mellstrom	37th	19 Oct 44	KPC over Italy
2nd Lt. Raymond Trombley	48th	1 Nov 44	MIA over Hungary, POW
1st Lt. Lawrence V. Bach, Jr.	37th	5 Nov 44	MIA over Yugoslavia, EV
2nd Lt. John M. Hurley	48th	12 Nov 44	KPC near Triolo, Italy
1st Lt. Dock A. Welch	48th	15 Nov 44	KIA over Yugoslavia
Maj. Wilbur J. Grumbles	48th	15 Nov 44	KIA over Yugoslavia
F/O William B. Karstetter	48th	17 Nov 44	MIA over Yugoslavia, EV
2nd Lt. Carl E. Ergott	37th	22 Nov 44	MIA over Germany
Capt. William H. Edwards	49th	26 Nov 44	MIA near Seregelyes, Hungary
1st Lt. George W. Baird, Jr.	49th	26 Nov 44	MIA near Seregelyes, Hungary
1st Lt. Eugene P. De Martini	49th	26 Nov 44	MIA near Seregelyes, Hungary
1st Lt. Lawrence Goffena	49th	26 Nov 44	MIA near Seregelyes, Hungary
2nd Lt. Ernest V. Roundtree	37th	17 Dec 44	MIA near Blechhammer, Germany
1st Lt. George T. Johnson	49th	17 Dec 44	KIA near Gyor, Hungary
2nd Lt. David R. Miles	48th	17 Dec 44	MIA over Czechoslovakia
2nd Lt. Merle D. Rowland	37th	17 Dec 44	Injured in crash near Foggia
1st Lt. George T. Johnson	49th	17 Dec 44	KIA over So. Germany
2nd Lt. Archie H. McMillan	37th	20 Dec 44	KPC near Foggia
1st Lt. Thomas J. Maroney	37th	20 Dec 44	Injured in crash No. Italy
2nd Lt. Merle D. Rowland	37th	27 Dec 44	Injured in crash at Foggia
Capt. George D. Wightman	37th	4 Jan 45	KIA near Bassano, Italy
2nd Lt. James A. Logan	37th	11 Jan 45	KPC over Italy
2nd Lt. Glen A. Cook	48th	20 Jan 45	KIA over Austria
1st Lt. William F. Anderson	48th	20 Jan 45	MIA over Austria, POW
1st Lt. Stanley W. Walters	48th	21 Jan 45	MIA near Vienna, POW
1st Lt. Ben R. Jackson	37th	31 Jan 45	KIA over Austria
Capt. Kyle J. Pinney	48th	8 Feb 45	KIA near Ybbs, Austria
1st Lt. Fred R. Branscombe	14th	9 Feb 45	KIA near Ybbs, Austria
2nd Lt. Nunzie J. Mineo	48th	15 Feb 45	KPC near Lesina, Italy
F/O Frederick G. Farrar	37th	16 Feb 45	KIA near Regensburg, Germany
2nd Lt. Daniel S. Wilson	37th	19 Feb 45	KIA near Bruck, Austria
2nd Lt. William Schultz	48th	22 Feb 45	MIA over Yugoslavia, EV
2nd Lt. Leon B. Stephens	49th	24 Feb 45	MIA in Yugoslavia, EV
2nd Lt. Fred C. Clifgard	48th	1 Mar 45	KIA over Austria
2nd Lt. Herschel T. Sinclair	49th	10 Mar 45	KIA when parachuted to Adriatic
2nd Lt. Charles E. Pask	37th	12 Mar 45	KIA near Zeltweg, Austria
2nd Lt. Clark Cornell	48th	14 Mar 45	MIA over Yugoslavia, EV
2nd Lt. Richard E. Small	49th	18 Mar 45	KIA near Strasz, Austria
Capt. John Meidinger	48th	18 Mar 45	KIA near Varazdin, Yugoslavia
2nd Lt. Arthur Tamamian	49th	20 Mar 45	KPC near Nico, Italy
Lt. Col. Hugh Griffith	48th	31 Mar 45	Crash-landed in Yugoslavia, EV
Capt. Michael Brezas	48th	2 Apr 45	MIA over Rumania ***

2nd Lt. Bill Randle	49th	4 Apr 45	MIA over Bavaria, Ger. POW
1st Lt. Robert W. Whitehead	37th	11 Apr 45	KIA near Munich, Germany
Capt. Harold D. Hoover	37th	11 Apr 45	KIA near Munich, Germany
1st Lt. Rene A. Therriault	48th	11 Apr 45	MIA over Yugoslavia
2nd Lt. Lyle E. Shrader	48th	20 Apr 45	KPC at Triolo, Italy
1st Lt. Richard K. Lambert	37th	21 Apr 45	KIA near Munich, Germany
Capt. Robert C. Groom	48th	21 Apr 45	Landed at Wurzburg, Ger. WIA
Maj. Charles R. McIntire	37th	22 Apr 45	KIA near Ficaralo, Italy
1st Lt. Milo E. Gnewikow	48th	22 Apr 45	MIA near Venice, POW ****
2nd Lt. Anthony Sumares	49th	23 Apr 45	MIA near Verona, Italy, POW

* Mullinax escaped after the Italian surrender and returned to duty 10 Jun 44.
** Carroll was taken prisoner and placed on an Italian submarine for transfer to Italy. Shortly after departing Tripoli, the sub was sunk by RAF. Carroll was one of those lost.
***Brezas landed in Russian occupied territory and was eventually repatriated
****Gnewikow was captured briefly by Germans but released by Italian partisans.

Author's note: The 22 August 1942 crash of a C-47 in England that cost the lives of five 49th Squadron enlisted men also took the lives of five 48th Squadron members on the same airplane. The names of those 49th ground crews were listed in its casualty records. No such data has been found in the surviving records of the 48th, and I regret that my search of various archives has failed to surface any names for those five individuals.

Glossary of casualty terms:

EV	Evaded or later escaped
KIA	Killed in action
KPC	Killed in plane crash
MIA	Missing in action
POW	Prisoner of war
WIA	Wounded in action

Glossary of other terms:

A/D	Airdrome
ASR	Air Sea Rescue, ships or aircraft
CO	Commanding Officer
E/A	Enemy aircraft
F/O	Rank of flight officer
IP	Initial Point: Start point of the bomb run
Lufbery Circle	Defensive maneuver named for WW I ace Maj. Raoul Lufbery

Appendix B: Original Pilots Completing Combat Tours, Feb '43

Col. Thayer S. Olds	14th
Maj. Wade C. Walles	48th
Capt. Herbert E. Johnson	49th
Capt. Mark J. Mourne	14th
Capt. Ralph J. Watson	48th
Capt. Ralph L. Knapp	49th
Capt William J. Hoelle	49th
Capt. Andrew J. Bing	48th
1st Lt. Ervin C. Ethell	48th
1st Lt. Wallace A. Sorrenson	48th
1st Lt. Oscar G. Blueher	49th
1st Lt. Redmond E. Evans	49th
1st Lt. William P. Moore	49th
1st Lt. Albert C. Wolfmueller	49th
1st Lt. Robert H. Eubank	48th
1st Lt. John W. Singleton	48th
1st Lt. John A. Stege	48th
1st Lt. Robert N. Carleton	49th
1st Lt. Virgil W. Lusk	49th
1st Lt. James E. Ribb	48th
1st Lt. William H.Working	49th
2nd Lt. Henry D. Ayers	48th
2nd Lt. Walter E. Bestgen	48th
2nd Lt. William J. Miles	49th
2nd Lt Paul A. Ziegler	48th
2nd Lt. Lewis H. Gregory	49th
2nd Lt. Robert J. Moffatt	49th
2nd Lt. Arthur O. Beimdick	48th
2nd Lt. John A. Goebel	48th
2nd Lt. A.G. Seagraves	48th
2nd Lt. Jerome M. Adler	49th
2nd Lt. Russell F.Gustke	49th
2nd Lt. Emil A. Kielbasa	49th
2nd Lt. John B. Grant	49th
2nd Lt. Philip O. Works	49th
2nd Lt. George C. Hand	49th

Appendix C:
1st Fighter Group Pilots Reactivating the 14th Fighter Group, Mar 1943

	Enemy Aircraft	Claims
Maj. Joel Owens	3 w/27	2 w/14
Capt. Roger Stemen	3 w1	
Capt. Bernard Muldoon	1 w/48	
Capt. Vern Schoenfeldt	2 w/71	1 w/48
1st Lt. John Wolford	5 w/27	1 damage w/49
1st Lt. Robert McCord	3 w/48	
1st Lt. Robert Riley	2 probable w/27	
1st Lt. William Newman	2 w/49	
1st Lt. Vincent Rethman	1 probable w/71	
1st Lt. Joe Smith	5 w/71	

Note: All survived their extended tours of combat duty with the 14th Fighter Group except John Wolford, who was killed in action 19 May '43.

Appendix D: Claims for the Destruction or Damage of Enemy Aircraft in Aerial Combat

DESTROYED/PROBABLE/DAMAGED

14TH GROUP HEADQUARTERS

Col. Daniel S. Campbell	1/0/0	
Lt. Col. Troy Keith	2/0/3	
Col. Thayer S. Olds	1/0/0	
Maj. Joel A. Owens, Jr.	2/0/0	3/1/1 with 27th Sq, 1st FG
Capt. Paulette Spivey	1/0/0	
Col. Oliver B. Taylor	5/2/2	
Lt. Col. Thomas B. Whitehouse	4/0/2	
2nd Lt. Richard D. Wilhelm	1/0/0	

37TH FIGHTER SQUADRON

2nd Lt. Richard G. Atckison	1/1/0	
1st Lt. Lawrence V. Bach, Jr.	2/1/1	
Maj. Forrest H. Barker	1/0/1	
1st Lt. Hubert M. Blair	2/0/0	
2nd Lt. Wayne L. Blue	1/0/1	
2nd Lt. Robert F. Boettger	0/0/1	
2nd Lt. Fredrick R. Branscombe	0/0/3	
Maj. John. G. Bright	2/0/0	3/0/0 in CBI
2nd Lt. Walter Brower	0/0/1	
1st Lt. Richard A. Campbell	6/1/2	
2nd Lt. Donald L. Clark	2/0/0	
Capt. Charles J. Crocker	1/0/1	
1st Lt. Marvin R. Elston	1/0/0	
2nd Lt. John S. Garbett	2/0/0	
1st Lt. Robert F. Gardner	2/0/2	
2nd Lt. Joseph A. Garrity	0/1/0	
Maj. Kenneth A. Gaskin	3/0/0	
F/O Albert V. Ginder	0/1/1	
1st Lt. Wesley C. Hancock	1/1/0	
1st Lt. Harry T. Hanna	5/0/1	
1st Lt. Jack R. Harrow	1/1/1	
2nd Lt. Lloyd O. Hendrix	4/0/0	
F/O Herbert C. Hickman	2/0/0	
2nd Lt. Robert L. Highsmith	1/0/1	
1st Lt. James M. Hollingsworth	3/0/2	
1st Lt. Robert E. Hullsiek	3/0/0	
2nd Lt. John C. Ingram, Jr.	1/0/0	
2nd Lt. Regis Jeffries	0/0/1	
2nd Lt. John A. Jones	0/0/1	
2nd Lt. John D. Joyce	1/0/2	
2nd Lt. Elmer H. LaRue	0/1/0	
2nd Lt. Milford R. Lee	0/0/1	
1st Lt. Enoch P. Lemon	3/2/2	

2nd Lt. Charles S. Leonard	1/1/1	
Lt. Col. William L. Leverette	11/0/2	
2nd Lt. Marcus C. Linn	0/1/1	1/0/3 with 27th Sq, 1st FG
1st Lt. Robert L. Margison	3/0/0	
1st Lt. Lawrence V. Mars	3/0/0	
1st Lt. Morgan H. Mathews	2/1/1	
1st Lt. Porter H. McClaine	2/0/0	
2nd Lt. Robert A. Miller	0/0/1	
2nd Lt. James W. Mitchell	1/1/0	
2nd Lt. Russell K. Moomaw	1/0/0	
1st Lt. Harry R. Morris, Jr.	1/0/0	
1st Lt. Robert B. Nourie	1/0/0	
Capt. Sam L. Palmer	0/1/0	
1st Lt. Frank V. Phillips	4/0/0	Later 4 vic. CBI, 449th Sq., 51st FG
Maj. Carl F. Rudder	4/0/4	
F/O Harvey Scott	0/0/2	Later 0/0/2 with 82nd FG
1st Lt. Thomas W. Smith	1/0/1	
2nd Lt. Homer L. Sprinkle	3/1/0	
2nd Lt. Kenneth L. Stahl	1/0/0	
2nd Lt. Sylvester P. Steffes	1/0/0	
2nd Lt. Darrel Stoyke	0/1/0	
2nd Lt. Kenneth C. Sullivan	1/1/0	
1st Lt. Cleveland J. Tatum	3/2/1	
2nd Lt. Ed A. Tindell	0/1/0	
1st Lt. Charles C. Townsend	1/0/0	
2nd Lt. Dale W. Tyler	0/0/1	
1st Lt. David A. Vann	1/0/1	
2nd Lt. Kenneth L. Waldron	0/1/0	
2nd Lt. William O. White	1/0/0	
1st Lt. George D. Wightman	1/1/0	
2nd Lt. Paul H. Wilkins	5/1/1	
Capt. Robert H. Wilson	1/1/1	
1st Lt. Robert G. Zimmerman	0/1/0	

48TH FIGHTER SQUADRON

Maj. Nathan M. Abbott	4/0/0	Includes 1 victory with 49th Sq.
2nd Lt. Daniel D. Africa	1/0/1	
1st Lt. Ronald E. Ashmead	1/0/0	
2nd Lt. Earl N. Baker	0/1/0	
2nd Lt. Albert G. Barber	2/0/1	
2nd Lt. George Barcak	0/0/2	
2nd Lt. Arthur O. Beimdiek, Jr.	0/0/1	
Capt. Andrew J. Bing	.5/0/0	
2nd Lt. William A. Blocker	0/1/0	
Capt. Michael Brezas	12/0/4	
1st Lt. William T. Church	3/1/1	
1st Lt. Thomas G. Collins	1/0/0	
2nd Lt. Robert P. Cowie	3/1/0	
2nd Lt. Arnold H. Dickenson	2/1/0	
1st Lt. Ervin C. Ethell	4/1/0	
1st Lt. Robert H. Eubank	2/0/1	
2nd Lt. John A. Goebel	.5/0/0	
1st Lt. Robert H. Griffith	1/0/0	
1st Lt. Robert C. Groom	2/0/1	

Capt. William E. Hanes	3/0/0	
1st Lt. Harrison H. Hannah, Jr.	3/0/1	
F/O Fred J. Haupt. III	2/0/0	
2nd Lt. Vaughn M. Herdell	0/0/1	
F/O Jack Homan	4/0/0	
1st Lt. Nello L. Infanti	2/0/3	
2nd Lt. Charles H. Ingram	1/0/1	
2nd Lt. Richard H. Jennings, Jr.	1/0/0	
2nd Lt. Clarence J. Jones	2/0/0	
2nd Lt. Wallace R. Kennedy	0/0/1	
1st Lt. W. Boyce Langley	2/0/1	
2nd Lt. William A. Lavery	0/0/2	
1st Lt. Donald M. Leighton	3/0/0	
2nd Lt. John W. Lindstrom	3/0/0	
1st Lt. James F. Martin	1/0/4	
Capt. Robert R. McCord	3/0/0	
1st Lt. John W. McGuyrt, Jr.	5/2/0	
1st Lt. John C. Meidinger	2/1/0	
1st Lt. Joseph E. Miller, Jr.	4/0/1	Later 1 vic. ETO, 429th Sq., 474thFG
2nd Lt. Arthur E. Moenkhaus	1/1/0	
Capt. Bernard R. Muldoon	0/0/1	.5 vic. with 71st Sq, 1st FG
2nd Lt. Edward J. Lynn	0/1/0	
2nd Lt. George J. O'Connor	1/1/2	
2nd Lt. George G. Partin	1/0/0	
2nd Lt. Richard A. Pitner	2/1/2	
2nd Lt. Nathaniel G. Raley	1/0/0	
Capt. George E. Richards	0/1/0	
2nd Lt. William A. Robertson	0/0/2	
Maj. Franklin L. Robinson	3/0/1	
Maj. Herbert E. Ross	7/1/1	
1st Lt. John E. Saum	1/0/0	
2nd Lt. William A. Schleich	0/1/0	
Capt. Verl B. Schoenfeldt	1/0/0	1.5 vic. w/71st Sq., 1st FG
1st Lt. William F. Schottelkorb	1/0/0	
2nd Lt. Alfonso G. Seagraves	0/0/1	
2nd Lt. Ralph W. Sebring	1/1/0	
1st Lt. William E. Shannon	1/0/0	
1st Lt. Mark K. Shipman	2/0/0	Later 1.5 vic. ETO, 38th Sq., 55th FG
1st Lt. John M. Singleton	2/0/0	
1st Lt. Orson T. Smith	1/0/1	
1st Lt. Virgil H. Smith	6/0/0	
1st Lt. Wallace A. Sorenson	2.5/0/0	
2nd Lt. Donald O. Starbuck	1/0/1	
2nd Lt. Jerry S. Stidham	1/0/0	
2nd Lt. Walter J. Stimler	1/0/0	
2nd Lt. Cody D. Stout	1/0/0	
2nd Lt. Marvel M. Taylor	1/0/0	
Capt. William K. Teare	1/0/0	
1st Lt. Rene A. Therriault	1/0/0	
2nd Lt. Myrvill F. Thornberry	1/0/2	
2nd Lt. Harold R. Thysell	1/1/0	
2nd Lt. Selmer O. Underdal	0/.5/0	
2nd Lt. Henry G. Van Horn	1/1/0	
1st Lt. Michael L. Wagner	4/2/5	
Capt. Wade C. Walles, Jr.	2.5/1/0	

1st Lt. Stanley W. Walters	1/0/0	
2nd Lt. Elmer M. Warren, Jr.	1/0/0	
Capt. Ralph J. Watson	3/1/2	Later 2/0/1 MTO, 2nd Sq., 52nd FG
Capt. Sidney W. Weatherford	5/0/0	
2nd Lt. Dock A. Welch	3/1/1	
2nd Lt. Robert J. Welsh	0/0/1	
1st Lt. Walter A. White	4/0/1	
2nd Lt. Carl T. Williams, Jr.	1/0/0	
1st Lt. Donald E. Wimmer	3/1/4	
2nd Lt. Paul G. Winston	1/.5/1	
2nd Lt. George F. Wood	0/1/0	
Capt. Max G. Wright	5/1/0	
2nd Lt. Edgar L. Yarberry	1/0/1	
2nd Lt. Thomas M. Yarwood	1/1/0	
2nd Lt. Victor Zuzeck	1/0/0	

49TH FIGHTER SQUADRON

2nd Lt. Soren E. Anton	0/1/1	Later 1 vic. MTO, 96th Sq., 82nd FG
1st Lt. Edwin C. Baquet	0/0/2	
1st Lt. William W. Becker	1/1/1	
1st Lt. Louis Benne	5/0/1	
2nd Lt. Albert L. Bess	0/0/1	
2nd Lt. Fred Bitter	0/1/1	
1st Lt. Wallace G. Bland	0/1/1	
1st Lt. Oscar G. Blueher	1/0/0	
Capt. Beryl L. Boatman	2/3/2	
F/O Orse Brewer	0/1/0	
2nd Lt. William T. Brewer	0/0/1	
1st Lt. Oliver Bryant	1/0/0	
2nd Lt. John Burke	0/1/0	
1st Lt. James E. Butler	4/0/0	
1st Lt. Robert N. Carlton	2/0/0	
2nd Lt. Eugene Churchill	0/0/2	
2nd Lt. Paul R. Cochran	1/0/0	Later 4 vics. MTO, 96th Sq, 82nd FG
1st Lt. John Cullen	1/0/1	
Capt. Richard E. Decker	1/0/0	
Capt. Lloyd K. DeMoss	4/0/0	
2nd Lt. Aldo E. Deru	0/1/1	
1st Lt. Charles L. Earnhart	1/2/2	
1st Lt. Lothrop F. Ellis	2/0/0	
2nd Lt. George J. Ensslen, Jr.	0/1/0	
1st Lt. Anthony Evans	4/0/0	
1st Lt. Redmond E. Evans	1/0/0	
2nd Lt. Richard L. Fowler	1/0/2	
2nd Lt. Philip M. Goldstein	3/0/2	
2nd Lt. John B. Grant	1/0/0	
2nd Lt. Lewis H. Gregory	1/0/0	
1st Lt. William J. Gregory	0/1/0	
2nd Lt. Russell F. Gustke	1/0/0	Later 2 vics. ETO, 77th Sq., 20th FG,
1st Lt. Mark C. Hegney	1/0/0	
2nd Lt. Edgar G. Hammerlein	0/0/1	
1st Lt. Harold T. Harper	2/0/0	
2nd Lt. John M. Harris	1/1/1	

1st Lt. Robert Hauser	0/0/1	
1st Lt. George E. Hochstetler	1/0/1	
1st Lt. William J. Hoelle	2/1/0	
1st Lt. Robert E. Hoke	2/.5/1	
2nd Lt. Walter L. Hoke	2/0/1	
1st Lt. Charles A. Hughes	1/0/0	
Capt. Norman W. Jackson	2/0/1	
2nd Lt. George T. Johnson	1/0/1	
Capt. Herbert L. Johnson	0/0/1	
2nd Lt. Clyde L. Jones, Jr.	4/0/0	
2nd Lt. Warren L. Jones	5/0/2	
2nd Lt. Wesley L. Jule	1/0/0	
1st Lt. Arthur W. King, Jr.	1/0/1	
2nd Lt. Robert P. Kirschke	1/0/0	
Capt. Ralph L. Knapp	1/0/1	
1st Lt. Carroll S. Knott	5/0/0	
2nd Lt. Herman Kocour	0/0/1	
Capt. Raymond J. Kopecky	0/1/3	
1st Lt. Ernie Latham	0/0/1	
1st Lt. Marlow J. Leikness	5/0/0	
2nd Lt. Donald Leiter	0/1/0	
2nd Lt. Jack Lenox, Jr.	5/1/3	
1st Lt. John D. Lewis	1/1/1	
2nd Lt. Roy C. Liles	1/0/1	
2nd Lt. Moses J. Long	1/0/0	
1st Lt. Virgil W. Lusk	5/0/1	
2nd Lt. Donald A. Luttrell	2/0/1	
2nd Lt. Wayne M. Manlove	4/0/2	
Maj. Burton E. McKenzie	1/0/.5	
2nd Lt. John E. Michelsen	1/0/0	
2nd Lt. Robert J. Moffatt	1/0/0	
2nd Lt. George Monnier	0/0/2	
1st Lt. William P. Moore	3/0/1	
1st Lt. Thomas J. Morris, Jr.	1/0/1	
2nd Lt. Livie F. Mullinax, Jr.	1/0/0	
1st Lt. Houston C. Musgrove, Jr.	1/1/1	
1st Lt. William G. Newman	2/0/0	0/0/1 with 71st Sq, 1st FG
Capt. William H. Oldhouser	3/1/0	
2nd Lt. Lawrence A. O'Toole	1/0/1	
Capt. William R. Palmer	2/0/2	
2nd Lt. John H. Penning	1/0/1	
1st Lt. Thomas L. Purdy	4/0/3	
1st Lt. James E. Ribb	0/0/1	
F/O Charles W. Richard	2/0/0	
2nd Lt. James G. Riley	0/0/1	
Capt. John D. Sandifer, Jr.	3/0/1	
2nd Lt. Jackson R. Schetler	0/0/2	
1st Lt. John G. Schill, Jr.	1/0/0	
2nd Lt. Herbert C. Schoener	1/.5/2	
1st Lt. Robert K. Seidman	5/0/1	
2nd Lt. Warren E. Semple	2/0/1	
2nd Lt. Swanson T. Shortt	3/0/2	
1st Lt. Harold Simmons	2/0/1	
2nd Lt. Revis G. Sirmon	1/0/0	
2nd Lt. Rupert T. Sparks	0/0/1	

1st Lt. Malcom B. Swimley	1/0/0	
2nd Lt. Quentin A. Teige	1/0/0	
2nd Lt. John B. Thomas	1/0/0	
2nd Lt. Gunvald B. Thorson	0/0/1	
1st Lt. James W. Tipton	0/1/0	
1st Lt. Donald C. Untermahlen	1/0/0	
2nd Lt. Wilbur E. Vardel	1/0/1	
1st Lt. Harry Vogelsong	0/2/.5	
2nd Lt. Paul J. Wingert	0/0/1	
2nd Lt. Robert H. Woodward	1/0/1	
1st Lt. John L. Wolford	0/0/1	5/0/1 with 27th Sq., 1st FG
1st Lt. William H. Working	1/0/1	

Individual claims for enemy aircraft destroyed / probably destroyed / or damaged in aerial combat are reflected in this appendix. Source for the information comes from unit records; the additional post war search of Col. Oliver B. Taylor; and the extensive research of historian Frank B. Olynyk. The latter spent years delving through archival records of the USAF and the National Archives to publish several volumes on air-to-air credits for World War II. The Office of Air Force History commissioned its own Study #85, published in 1978, but it contains errors and omissions. The Olynyk research is far more complete as he worked with copies of mission reports. Although these were sometimes cryptic, and often only used last names, the basic information was timely. Thanks to Harry Crim's rosters we were able to attach first names in all cases.

Claims for victories, probables or damaged enemy aircraft before and following service with the 14th Fighter Group are shown after the unit claims.

Appendix E:
14th Fighter Group Aircraft Markings

Early:

48th Squadron	ES
49th Squadron	QU

Mid-1943:

37th Squadron	1-30
48th Squadron	31-60
49th Squadron	61-90

After 1944, with more than 30 a/c per squadron the third digit was applied: 100

Bibliography

Bekker, Cajus, *The Luftwaffe War Diaries*, 1966, Macdonald House, London, England

Craven, Wesley F. and James L. Cate, *The Army Air Forces in World War II, Vol. 2, Europe: Torch to Pointblank,* 1958, University of Chicago Press, Chicago, IL

---, *The Army Air Forces in World War II, Vol. 3, Europe: Argument to VE-Day,* 1965,University of Chicago Press, Chicago, IL

Foreman, John and S.E. Harvey, *The Me. 262 Combat Diary,* 1996, Air Research Publications, Walton-on-Thames, England

Hammel, Eric, *Aces Against Germany, Vol II, The American Aces Speak Series,* 1993, Pacifica Air Military History, Pacifica, CA

Morison, Samuel Eliot, *History of United States Naval Operations in World War II, Volume IX, Sicily-Salerno-Anzio,* 1975, Little, Brown and Co., Boston, MA

---, *History of United States Naval Operations in World War II, Volume XI, The Invasion of France and Germany,* 1975, Little, Brown and Co., Boston, MA

Mullins, John D., *An Escort of P-38s, The 1st Fighter Group in World War II*, 1995, Phalanx Publishing Co., St. Paul, MN

Olynyk, Frank J. *USAAF (Mediterranean Theatre) Credits for the Destruction of Enemy Aircraft in Air- to- Air Combat in World War II.* 1987, Frank Olynyk, Aurora, Ohio

Punka, Gyorgy, *Hungarian Aces of World War 2,* 2002, Osprey Publishing, Oxford, U.K.

Rust, Kenn C. *Twelfth Air Force Story*, 1975, Historic Aviation Album, Temple City, CA

---, *Fifteenth Air Force Story,* 1976, Historic Aviation Album, Temple City, CA

Shores, Christopher, Hans Ring and William N. Hess, *Fighters Over Tunisia,* 1975, Neville Spearman Limited, London, England

Steinhoff, Johannes, *Messerschmitts Over Sicily,* 1969, Nautical & Aviation Publishing Co., Baltimore, MD

The Long Campaign
The History of the 15th Fighter Group in World War II
John W. Lambert

The 8th Air Force: Victory and Sacrifice
A World War II Photo History
John W. Lambert

in World War II. Japan would come later. The destruction of Germany's vast military-industrial base was the mission assigned to the RAF and the U.S. Eighth Air Force. Starting from scratch in July 1942 and operating from bases in England, the Eighth Air Force assumed the task of daylight precision bombing of Occupied Europe. In a three-year struggle against fortifiable German air defenses and the legions of the Luftwaffe, the Eighth paid a terrible price. It suffered 55,000 casualties (killed, wounded and Prisoners of war), more than any other numbered U.S. military unit. This volume seeks to provide an historical perspective of the air campaign over Western Europe, utilizing 270 representative photos and detailed captions to depict the deadly nature of that aerial combat some six decades ago.

ISBN: 0764325345 Size: 8 1/2" x 11" Illustrations: over 270 b/w and color photographs, maps 160 pp
hard cover $39.95